VEDANTA VIGNETTES

VEDANTA VIGNETTES

Dhruv S Kaji

(with forewords from Swami Tadatmananda Saraswati and Swami Paramarthananda Saraswati)

MLBD PUBLICATIONS

Motilal Banarsidass Publications

MOTILAL BANARSIDASS
PUBLICATIONS
4741/23, Ansari Road, Daryaganj, New Delhi - 110002 (India)
Email: *mlbd@mlbd.com* | *sales@mlbd.com* | *exports@mlbd.com*
Website: *www.mlbd.com*

Vedanta Vignettes
by
Dhruv S Kaji

First Edition Published in 2022

Published in India by Motilal Banarsidass Publications

ISBN : 978-93-91759-25-4 (HB)

Printed and bound in India

The greatest good
you can do for another
is not just
to share your riches
but
to reveal to him his own

—Benjamin Disraeli

There are two ways of
spreading light:
To be the candle
or
the mirror that reflects

—Edith Wharton

CONTENTS

arsha bodha center

for the Spiritual Teachings of Ancient India

Swami Tadatmananda, resident teacher

Foreword by Swami Tadatmananda Saraswati

I am delighted by the publication of this new book written by my good friend, Dhruv Kaji. He is an unusually passionate seeker of spiritual wisdom, as I saw again and again in our many long, intense dialogues over the years. In those discussions, he constantly pushed the boundaries of his understanding, diving deep into the most profound realms of spiritual practice and realisation.

Dhruv has studied extensively with some of the world's finest teachers of Advaita Vedanta, including the renowned Swami Dayananda Saraswati. He has thoroughly grasped the extraordinary insights discovered by the sages of ancient India and later systematically explained by the great scholar and saint, Shankaracharya. I am amazed at how Dhruv somehow manages to express all this in simple, engaging language that he delivers with a wry sense of humour. In this book, he first introduces the central principles of Vedanta, not in a dry, academic manner, but by appealing to the basic human desire for inner peace and lasting contentment. Then in later chapters, he explores a number of issues that are crucial for proper understanding of Vedantic teachings. Along the way, he skillfully dismisses a number of common misconceptions that stand like roadblocks on the path of understanding. He concludes with appendices that provide a foundation for all this.

According to a common metaphor, the teachings of Vedanta are like a vast ocean. But the ocean is not only vast, it is salty as well, and that salinity makes its water hard to drink. So too, the teachings of Vedanta are not only vast, but are also exceedingly complex, and that complexity makes them hard to understand and assimilate. When rain clouds absorb water from the ocean, they extract pure water alone, and leave all the saltiness behind. Then they drench the land with life-giving rain. In a similar way, Dhruv seems to absorb wisdom from the vast ocean of Vedanta, extracting only its essence, and leaving all the complexity behind. Then he shares this distilled wisdom through books like this one.

Dhruv is to be congratulated for his fine work. Many are sure to be benefitted by it.

Swami Tadatmananda
Somerset, N.J.
June 10, 2022

Foreword by Swami Paramarthananda Saraswati

Scriptures declare that self-knowledge is the means for liberation. Naturally, the seeker of liberation will be interested in the pursuit of self-knowledge. But there is a hitch. All our sense organs, with or without their perception-augmenting instruments, are extroverted in nature.They can only explore and know external objects. But the self is not one of those objects. It is the conscious being behind the knowing instruments. So, the question is how do we know the knower?

Scriptures themselves give a solution. Just as we use a mirror to look at our face, we have to use a relevant mirror to know the knower. And that mirror is a spiritual guru. The guru uses a methodology of communication suggested by the scriptures. Such communication, by properly employed words, serves as a verbal mirror that will help the spiritual seeker to know the self. Thus, traditional teaching based on the scriptures is indispensable for a spiritual seeker.

Dhruv Kaji has been fortunate to receive these teachings from several traditional masters over a period of time. In this book, he is sharing certain aspects of Advaita Vedanta based on the teachings of these masters. I congratulate Dhruv for bringing out such a book and hope that the readers will be inspired to explore more.

Swami Paramarthananda
Chennai, T.N.
5th June, 2022

BEFORE WE BEGIN

This book contains a selection from my notes, articles and discussion papers on Vedanta, written over a period of time.

The contents here are centred on advaita Vedanta championed by Adi Shankaracharya. It is not a structured work designed to set out all the issues that advaita Vedanta covers but a collection of snapshots which deals with some specific aspects. Unlike my earlier books, this book includes discussion on several issues which surface only when one progresses on Vedanta's journey. But for those who want a quick recap of a few basics, an outline of Vedanta's overall scheme is provided in an appendix; appendices also contain a brief overview of Indian philosophical systems as well as a glossary of Sanskrit terms.

The core vision of Vedanta is quite simple in its essentials and not particularly difficult to understand. The real challenge is in its full assimilation. Our pre-conditioned reactions and our die-hard commitment to our own individualities create formidable hurdles against internalising and owning up to the new understanding that Vedanta brings in. The result is the non-availability of the real benefits of Vedanta. This is not surprising because Vedanta's basic teaching is that everything we experience is only a temporary and insubstantial projection based on a single reality. Such a radical view is not supported by our usual experiences. One way to overcome this problem is by repeatedly going over the teachings of Vedanta to assist in the assimilation of their counter-intuitive truths. In keeping with this, you will find repetition of key ideas over several places. Also, because this book is likely to be more useful if it is not skimmed through at one go, some repetition has been used to make each piece self-contained.

As you read this book some of you may feel that I am hard-selling Vedanta and implying that nothing else is a worthwhile pursuit. In this context I am reminded of an exceptional teacher, Swami Dayananda, who used to say that if you go to a carpenter, all his suggestions are likely to be centred on a hammer and nails! Similarly, I write about advaita Vedanta because I happen to be steeped into it. But I also write about it because I have found it to be the most coherent, the most complete and the most satisfying source of answers to questions which have vexed me for a long time. My intention here is to share some of what I have learnt and exhort others to explore this extraordinary wisdom. This is with the hope that they will derive from it the same joy and benefits which I have been blessed with.

The world in which we live is constantly telling us that the path to fulfilment is more and more. Be smarter, faster, richer, more popular, more admired, more envied and do more, make more, own more, be more. This constant prodding by our consumer culture and the goading of *hey-look-my-life-is-cooler-than-yours* message of social media drives us to ever-increasing levels of activity and consumption. But, unfortunately, this approach actually drives us away from peace, joy and contentment which are the very things we ultimately need. Advaita Vedanta can play a crucial role in restoring balance in our lives and help us to get off this ever accelerating treadmill of *more* which does not really get us anywhere.

However, my personal conviction about Vedanta's value does not mean that I don't recognise that others may have a different take. Some see no problems with their lives as they are; they are, therefore, not driven by the need to re-look at their lives from a different perspective. For some others, the pursuit of wisdom from other cultures is the answer. And even for those who turn to Indic traditions, there is a large variety of viewpoints (often completely contradictory) based on different foundations such as devotion, mysticism and knowledge. Advaita Vedanta, though a vital and probably the most rigorously developed of the knowledge-based streams in India, is yet only one viewpoint amongst many. Therefore, while what I write focuses on advaita Vedanta, this is not to suggest that others may not find what they are looking for by taking other paths.

It should also be noted that the core insight on which Vedanta is based is not Vedanta's monopoly. Elements of other cultures, such as Taoism from China, Sufism from Islam and the mystical stream within Christianity, all speak of the same, undivided oneness which Vedanta talks about. The difference lies in the depth and detail which Vedanta provides and in the unbroken teaching tradition which Vedanta has developed and preserved over millennia. This unique teaching methodology renders comprehensible that which would otherwise seem mystical or recondite and permits its effective transfer to any eligible seeker.

One other thing must be said here and this applies to all books on Vedanta. Books on this subject provide insights and inspiration, both of which are very valuable. But even though a good writer can create a temporary sense of identity between himself and the reader, the words of a book continue to belong to the writer, not the reader. Ultimately, the reader must make a personal journey, not a vicarious one through someone else's mind. This personal journey includes self-inquiry, contemplation and mindfulness. It also requires consistent effort to reorient life so that it begins to reflect the wisdom of Vedanta in thoughts, words and actions. Without this personal commitment and effort towards making internal change, one may become even a scholar of Vedanta and yet never obtain its real benefits. This needs to be kept in mind while reading even the most venerated of books on this subject.

No study of Vedanta can be fruitful without a proper teacher. As always, I would like to again acknowledge with deep gratitude all the wisdom given to me, freely and lovingly, by many wonderful teachers who have blessed my efforts. My principal teachers, in the order in which I met them, have been:

Professor S. A. Upadhyaya
Mr. Ramesh Balsekar
Swami Dayananda Saraswati
Swami Tadatmananda Saraswati
Swami Tattvavidananda Saraswati
Swami Paramarthananda Saraswati

I offer my special and heartfelt thank you to Swami Tadatmananda and Swami Paramarthananda who have both been so very kind in providing their forewords to this book.

I must also acknowledge some great insights I have obtained by listening to online talks of Swami Sarvapriyananda of the Ramakrishna order; I hope I have the good fortune of meeting this amazing teacher someday.

Apart from teachers, I would like to thank:

R. Raghuraman, an old friend and a senior fellow-student of Vedanta, whose companionship and counsel have been a constant and invaluable support from the very beginning.

Several newcomers to Vedanta who have added to my own understanding as I shared aspects of what I have been taught with them. Amongst this group, Prakash Mody, a successful business person and a keen recent student of Vedanta, needs special mention for his dedication to learning.

Dr Harsha V Dehejia, a renowned scholar in many fields, who despite his contrarian views on Shankaracharya's teachings, encouraged me to get this collection published.

Kersi Khambatta, an accomplished author with many other talents, who helped in improving the readability of my writing.

Paulomi Shah who has done an excellent job of designing this book.

Pranav Jain of Motilal Banarasidass who has published this book.

Finally, whatever may be the view of life we take and whatever be the tradition we may choose to follow, these should never stop us from wishing well for all. In the words of an ancient prayer from the Vedas:

Sarve bhavantu sukhinaha
Sarve santu niramaya
Sarve bhadrani pashyantu
Ma kashchid dukkha bhaga bhavet
Om shanti shanti shanti

May all be happy
May all be without any afflictions
May all come across only the good and auspicious
May sorrow not be anyone's lot
May peace prevail in all aspects of life.

Dhruv S Kaji
Mumbai, 15th July 2022

A quick look at a few preliminaries
and
the importance of constructive discussion.

TO BEGIN WITH

Vedanta is a view of the nature of ultimate reality and its relationship with us, coming from sages of ancient India. But it is more than just a view, it is really a method to deal with unnecessary suffering. Its purpose is to help us at the personal and most fundamental level of our lives by helping us discover peace and contentment which it says are already integral to us but hidden because of ignorance. Obtaining real benefit from the insights of Vedanta is a subtle process. It truly works only for an adequately prepared student who is exposed to the scriptures of Vedanta, under the guidance of a competent teacher, for an adequate period of time.

The word *Vedanta* is a combination of two words: *veda* (the name of ancient Hindu scriptures) and *antah* (end). Vedanta thus refers to the small portions mainly at the end of the Vedas. Apart from this positional meaning, *end* also conveys that these portions are the culmination and final goal of the Vedas. These same portions of the Vedas are also known by another name: *upanishads*. Vedanta or the upanishads have a different flavour and purpose when compared to the much more voluminous earlier sections of the Vedas. The earlier sections of the Vedas focus on making our individual lives better by promoting religiosity, ethics and supportive attitudes. Vedanta, on the other hand, concentrates on making us understand the enormity of our permanent and real nature which goes beyond our bodies and minds. Thus, Vedanta is more a proper view of life rather than a way of life.

The term *Vedanta* is also used in a broader sense to refer to views originating in the upanishads but organised and detailed further in later scriptures like the Brahma Sutras and the Bhagavad Gita. In this broader sense, Vedanta also includes the works of a series of thinkers and teachers such as Adi Shankaracharya.

Vedanta's objective is to address our need for total and abiding happiness which is fundamental and universal. Why should our quest for happiness be looked upon as a problem which needs to be addressed? Is it not natural and useful? Does it not lead to progress and prosperity? Let us pause here to take a look at what our hunt for happiness makes us do.

In very basic terms, all our lives consist of us, the individuals, handling the rest of the world in order to experience personal fulfilment. It is important to recognise the universal validity of this simple sounding statement. We must be able to see that the need to find personal fulfilment is always the driving force behind all our activities. It is this need which is behind the loving mother bringing up a child with care and behind the saint working to alleviate the suffering of others; it is this same need to find fulfilment which is behind the unscrupulous business person misleading someone for quick profit and behind the psychopath carrying out his sadistic inclinations. (As an upanishad puts it in Sanskrit, *atmanastu kaamaaya sarvam priyam bhavati*: everything is dear only because it leads to the experience of a pleased self.)

There are obvious and important ethical differences involved in these instances but the commonality is that all these activities are carried out in an attempt to experience personal fulfilment. Even when we deny ourselves happiness for the sake of another person or for an impersonal cause (such as a soldier willingly sacrificing his life for the sake of his country), we do so because it is ultimately expected to give us a higher level of satisfaction.

The fact that everything we do is for obtaining happiness is based on two important assumptions:

- We know ourselves as lacking in happiness, and
- Happiness that we want is contained in the world of other people, objects and situations outside of us.

Vedanta asks us to consider some fundamental questions here: do we really know the true nature of our own selves as well as the true nature of the world which we interact with in our attempt to experience happiness?

These questions may seem irrelevant or with an obvious *yes* answer. After all, we do experience happiness or fulfilment when we obtain what we want or manage to keep away what we dislike in the world. However, Vedanta asks us to pause before readily going along with such an obvious and facile conclusion. This is because if our entire lives are going to consist of us manipulating the world to experience happiness, it is important that we properly understand:

- exactly who we ourselves are,
- what is the real nature of the world we manipulate, and
- whether our happiness is actually derived from the people and objects which constitute the world.

Unless we are clear and right in our understanding here, our entire lives will have been lived on the basis of a defective foundation.

In a different vein, Vedanta also asks us whether all our attempts so far for obtaining fulfilment, based on our current conclusions about ourselves and the world, have produced results which have been abiding. After decades of single-minded pursuit of happiness, if we are yet thirsting for more happiness, how and when are we ever going to reach our goal? Vedanta therefore suggests that we explore a completely different approach where we direct our attention inwards rather than outwards, to the experiencer rather than to experiences.

The teachings of Vedanta unfold a very different vision of the nature of ourselves, the external world we confront and the creator of ourselves and of the world; they also shed a completely different light on the source of our happiness. This vision of Vedanta, when properly imbibed, not only changes our understanding in these matters but also removes unnecessary suffering and resolves our unending search for happiness.

Vedanta's wisdom needs a different style of teaching compared to the teaching of more conventional subjects like history or physics. This is due to many reasons. To begin with, many of us are not very interested in what Vedanta has to offer so Vedanta has to first create some deeper interest in what it wants to tell us. Even amongst the interested few, there is a lack of personal qualities required to benefit from this wisdom. So, Vedanta also has to help us in acquiring essential qualities such as discrimination, dispassion, physical & mental discipline and a strong urge to seek what Vedanta has to offer.

Further, Vedanta's teachings guide an inquiry into our own true nature; as an inquiry into ourselves can only be done by ourselves, this poses the same difficulty which our eyes would face if they attempted to see themselves. To overcome this significant problem, Vedanta has to bring in methods which are not required in other areas of knowledge.

Finally, the teachings of Vedanta remain ineffective if they are transferred to a student as superficial information, without full personal internalisation and integration. This requires a further process which is not always required in conventional learning.

For these reasons Vedanta has to be studied with a proper teacher for an adequate length of time, usually along with a group of fellow students. Live teaching and interactions involve discussions in one form or the other, so it is useful to be clear about different types of discussions. In Sanskrit, there are different terms for four different types of discussions:

Samvada

One important type of discussion is called *samvada* which is a discussion between a teacher and student. Here, the primary role is the teacher's but the student occasionally asks questions and makes comments. These are neither to challenge the teacher nor to show how clever the student is but to resolve doubts or to re-confirm his understanding. An example of this is the well-known dialogue between Krishna and Arjuna in the Bhagavad Gita.

Vada

Vada is the name given to a discussion between equals, such as two students. The attitude of the participants here is expected to be non-dogmatic, open to both learning and correction. The classic example of this type of discussion is the one which is reported to have occurred between Mandana Mishra and Adi Shankaracharya (8th century CE) where both started with opposing views but, finally, Mandana Mishra accepted the validity of Shankaracharya's thesis. (Not only did Mandana Mishra accept that his views had been erroneous; after this encounter, he himself became an ardent exponent of his new master's teachings.)

Jalpa

Jalpa is a dialogue where the people involved are completely fixated on their own conclusions and are not at all open to the possibility that their views could be mistaken; here, the driving force is to prove that any contrary view is wrong and there is no room for learning or correction on one's own part.

Vitanda

The last type of dialogue, often seen in politics, is called *vitanda* where there is no concern with the veracity or merit of an opponent's argument; the objective here is to trash the other side's views not because they are wrong but only because these views belong to the other side for whom there is great animosity. This type of futile discussion also occurs in personal dialogues where there is a lot of hurt, anger or bitterness between the individuals concerned.

In the study of Vedanta, our discussions should be open-minded and participative, where we learn from the teacher as well as from the knowledge and experience of fellow-students. This ongoing openness and willingness to learn are necessary for a student of Vedanta because whatever we do throughout our lives, even outside of class, will help us imbibe Vedanta's very unusual insights only if we remain perpetual students with the right attitude.

Without understanding the precise nature of any problem,
a suitable solution cannot be found.
Behind all our problems, there is a fundamental problem which
Vedanta is meant to resolve and
which we need to recognise clearly.

THE FUNDAMENTAL PROBLEM

Vedanta is often looked at either out of intellectual curiosity or because of the need to know something about a subject held in high esteem in our culture. However, Vedanta is neither a sterile philosophical enquiry and nor is it just an interesting cultural artefact. Its real function is to operate as a remedy for a disease—a remedy which is still potent for a disease which is yet prevalent.

But what is this disease that Vedanta is trying to cure? It is the disease which manifests itself in the form of our need to perpetuate our existence, in our drive to know more and ever more and, finally, in our continuous yearning for something more satisfying, more enduring and more meaningful, irrespective of what and how much we have. These three basic hungers (to remain alive, to overcome ignorance and to experience unbroken fulfilment) are termed in Sanskrit as *jijivisha*, *jignasa* and *bubhuksha*. It is this constant need to be more than what we are now, this existential dissatisfaction, which is the universal and fundamental human problem.

We of course make full efforts to satisfy these three hungers. To preserve our existence we try to be health-conscious and take recourse to medical remedies.

We seek to extend our personal imprint beyond our own life-times by having children, writing books and creating institutions & monuments which will survive us (one author termed these our 'immortality projects'!). However, nothing can fully address our need to continue living.

What about our accomplishments, wealth and pleasures to deal with our need to know more and to experience fulfilment? We work very hard at obtaining these. Are they not enough to satisfy us? The upanishads say 'no' by bringing out the limitations of all these usual solutions through different characters in their stories.

In the Chandogya Upanishad, the learned sage Narada, after reciting a long list of his accomplishments (which included mastery over the Vedas, grammar, mathematics, logic, ethics, warfare, physical sciences, astrology and fine arts), confesses to his teacher that he is yet in inexplicable sorrow which he does not know how to overcome.

In the Brihadaranyaka Upanishad, Yajnavalkya's wife, Maitreyi, turns down a settlement of wealth because, as she says, no amount of wealth brings immortality; instead, she asks for the gift of knowledge which would lead her to immortality.

In the Katha Upanishad, the young boy Nachiketas is offered a long life filled with all imaginable pleasures. He refuses this gift because, as he observes, even a long life is ultimately finite and pleasures are not only temporary but they also sap energy and never lead to full contentment even while they last. Instead, he requests knowledge of fundamental truths.

These stories make the point that our usual pursuits of secular knowledge, possessions and pleasures do not cater to our deeper needs. Incidentally, the characters in these stories also indicate to us that our disenchantment with these common goals is not dependent upon gender or age—dispassion with regard to them can arise within anyone and at any time.

However, the real emphasis of Vedantic scriptures is not so much on the denial of these pursuits but more on pointing out their limitations as well as showing their disconnect with what we really need.

Vedantic teachings do not condemn secular knowledge (termed *apara vidya*) but point out, as in the case of Narada, that no amount of information about our world and the universe will satisfy our need for a deeper meaning to our existence; it will also not liberate us from anxiety and the fear of death or satisfy our urge for more. And we all know this for ourselves. We can see that huge leaps in our knowledge of science, technology and humanities have led to increases in comforts and life-spans but have done nothing for long-term human happiness.

Similarly, our traditions have never been against wealth earned by legitimate means or held out involuntary poverty as a laudable achievement. What they point out is that wealth used as a source of self-worth becomes a problem. When wealth is wrongly viewed, it gets judged in relation to the material worth of others around us. Wealth now becomes a continuously changing reference point which causes us anxiety & insecurity. It leads to hostility towards others who threaten our wealth-based notions of self-worth and reduces human beings to economic numbers. All this applies equally well to fame and power. And we know this. Many of us have started life on a low economic rung but over time, with hard work and luck, we have gathered money, power and fame beyond our own expectations. Despite this, peace, contentment and fulfilment remain as distant as ever. As someone once said, "*Not everything that counts can be counted and not everything that is counted truly counts*". And there are reports from care-givers to the terminally-ill which show that the final regrets of patients on their death-beds were not about having made less money but about having neglected avenues of inner fulfilment.

Coming to pleasures, they are one of the four human goals listed in our scriptures. In fact, in the Bhagavad Gita, Krishna says that pleasures which are not opposed to *dharma* are one of his forms. But scriptures also talk about our desire for pleasures as a problem. This should not be seen as a blanket ban on all desires. Such statements are like someone talking about blood pressure as a problem. Blood pressure within acceptable limits is normal; it is abnormal pressure which is problematic. Similarly, normal desires are not a problem for most of us; they become problems only when they transgress good values or when they are unbalanced in any one direction or when they lead to significant negative emotions like anger or jealousy. A great contemporary teacher of Vedanta, Swami Paramarthananda, uses the term 'ABC of desires' to help us remember that our desires need to be Appropriate (not transgressing dharma), Balanced (not only focused on selfish and material gains) and Clean (not generating polluting emotions).

However, even our legitimate desires create issues. Fulfilling them requires a fit body and mind, the availability of the object of pleasure and a conducive environment. These matters are often out of our control. Then, repetition of the same pleasure leaves us bored and comparisons with others make our pleasures seem less pleasurable. Finally, for someone looking for inner growth and maturity, too much preoccupation with even appropriate desires can be a major hindrance. So, Krishna says that pleasures come and go and a wise person is not content in them.

What about ethics and religion? Would not a righteous life accompanied by compassion for others and devotion to god fulfil our needs? Our scriptures put such qualities (of *dharma*) on a high pedestal and say that our pursuits of pleasures and security (*kama* and *artha*) must not transgress dharma. And scriptures go on to tell us that dharma generates merit *(punya)* which gives us a life of physical and mental comfort. Modern psychology also says that our happiness increases when we move upwards from passive pleasures to activities which engage our abilities in something constructive and then to things which give us meaning by involving us in matters larger than our individual selves (such as working for the welfare of others or finding a connection with god).

But righteousness and religion neither fully and permanently address our limitations nor provide convincing answers to questions about the nature and purpose of creation and the real goal of our individual lives. Even the noblest and most devout person remains small and insignificant when faced with an overwhelming, mysterious and uncontrollable universe. Ultimately, no objective attainment or experience (including doing good to others or relating to god) brings an end to the continuous cycle of lack, seeking and temporary fulfilment.

The limitations of our regular pursuits are not apparent to everyone. Even after long and eventful lives many of us continue to hold on to the assumption that further wealth, power, fame, possessions, relationships, pleasurable experiences and dharma will bring fulfilment. In this hunt for fulfilment we relentlessly seek objects, activities, relationships and states of mind which will make us happy and, equally relentlessly, resist whatever or whomever is perceived to jeopardise our happiness. Such seeking and resistance undoubtedly brings fulfilment but that is always limited and temporary because our seeking and resistance are only symptomatic of the underlying sense of lack or suffering which continues despite all our efforts. Only a few of us realise the futility of our standard game-plan for life and look for a solution which is out of the ordinary.

What do the scriptures advise a person who suffers from sorrow, from continuous want and from lack of meaning despite conventional success and is seeking a permanent solution? The Mundaka Upanishad gives categorical advice here:

A wise person, after examining worldly gains obtained by action, understands that the infinite cannot be created through finite efforts and becomes detached. To know the infinite he should go with proper attitude to a teacher who knows the Vedas and who is himself established in the knowledge of brahman.

Such a guru addresses a student of discrimination who has understood the limitations of ordinary goals and who has discerned that at the heart of every desire is a search for the limitless; this is why anything limited and finite never fully satisfies us. To such a seeker, a proper teacher imparts the wisdom of Vedanta which provides radically new answers which solve our fundamental problem at the fundamental level.

Shakespeare once wrote,
'This above all: to thine own self be true...'
This advice carries the implication that we already know ourselves because one can only try to be true to something one knows. In fact, we generally believe that we know nothing as well as we know our own selves. Vedanta throws a different light on this conclusion.

WHO AM I?

What is our reality? Are we not the body and mind combination that we usually take ourselves to be? Vedanta undermines this conventional notion of ours by reminding us of a fundamental fact which is based upon our own experiences: the knower is *always* different from the known. While this fact is quite obvious, it needs to be emphasised because it is the foundation for our discussion about who or what we are. We should recognise that any act of knowing invariably involves two distinctly different entities: the subject and an object or the knower and the known. When we point and say, "*fragrant red rose*", we say it because we are aware of that flower and its qualities. And we do not personally take ourselves as being red or fragrant because the rose has those qualities. We recognise that, as knowers of this rose, we are distinct from the rose which is known to us. This discrimination between the knower and the known is termed *drik drishya viveka* in Sanskrit.

But when it comes to our own bodies, such discrimination deserts us and we consistently take ourselves to be of the size, shape, colour, gender and age of our bodies. When we describe ourselves as being young, tall and good looking, we somehow forget that these are the characteristics of the body which are known to us. Here too, the rule that the knower is never the known should apply. And similarly with the state of our minds; here, again, we take ourselves to be happy, angry or sad despite the fact that these are mental conditions which we are aware of and we can never be that which we are aware of.

If this is so then why does everyone take the characteristics of his or her body and mind to be his or her own characteristics? Vedanta explains that this error primarily occurs because we do not know our own truth and we then, naturally, assume our personal and intimate adjuncts to be our reality. On the physical plane, our experiences come from our sense organs. Our largest sensory organ is the skin. Because our sense of touch stops at the boundary of our skins, this outermost covering of our bodies is taken to be the boundary between 'me' and 'not-me'. It is because of this assumption that a plateful of food which is 'not me' seems to become 'me' once it is eaten and is temporarily integrated with our physicality. On the mental plane, the contents of our minds are known only to us. Our sensations, thoughts and emotions are not available to anyone else. Because these are entirely personal, we identify with them. It is because of this special and intimate relationship with experiences derived from our individual bodies and minds that we falsely conclude that we *are* those bodies and minds.

But we know that our knees are painful, that our eye-sight is sharp and our skin is itchy. We know that our thinking is dull without the morning coffee, that our ego becomes more yielding in the presence of someone we look up to and that the mere mention of a particular person produces anger in our minds. All these things are known to us, the knowers, who are always different from whatever is known. We cannot be the bodies and minds whose conditions we know.

That the body-mind combination is not our reality is supported by our own statements when we say *my body* or *my mind*—what is *mine* can never be *me*. It is again supported when we see that the sense of self or 'I-ness' in a person is not diminished even when his body is reduced (for instance, by losing weight or by the amputation of a limb).

Our false identification with things close to us is not always restricted to our bodies and minds; this error also occurs in other areas. We see instances of this when a large loss of money leads some people to consider suicide—a strong sense of identity between their wealth and their own selves leads them to the conclusion that if their wealth is lost, they too are entirely lost.

If the body and mind are not really us but only objects known to us then who or what are we? Vedanta tells us that our essential nature is consciousness because of which we know both the body and mind as well as the rest of the world. This consciousness is our unchanging and always-present reality which makes us aware of our perceptions, deeds, thoughts and feelings. As the knower of our bodies and minds, it is different from them.

There are, of course, many objections to Vedanta's view that our deepest truth is consciousness and that we are not the body-mind combination that we usually take ourselves to be. People who describe themselves as rationalists say that the drik drishya viveka (the difference between the knower and the known) put out by Vedanta is faulty. In their thinking, discarding the body and mind as being 'not me' is like removing peel after peel of an onion and then asking "*Where is the onion?*". According to them, just as the combination of peels *is* the onion, the combination of body and mind *is* the real me. But what is missed out in their argument is consciousness. The onion does not know it is getting smaller with the removal of each peel but I do know I am getting thinner with every kilogram worked off. I am also aware of the changing states of my mind. I am not the layers of my body and mind; I am the consciousness because of which both my body and mind are known.

Because consciousness can never be denied, the materialists for whom the physical world is the only reality bring out another explanation. In their explanation, consciousness is a by-product of our body-minds, produced by the chemical and electrical activity in our brains. In other words, our bodies and minds are real and consciousness is only an epiphenomenon. But this model cannot explain the special nature of the first person experience we all have in any act of knowing. Using our power of sight as an example, when we see something it is not just seeing which happens. Our seeing is not like a camera recording a scene; our seeing is accompanied by a very personal '*I see*'. This unique first person experience cannot be generated by any electrical or chemical activity. However, despite the lack of any supporting evidence, many remain convinced that consciousness is somehow derived from matter.

There are many other views which have widely different conclusions about consciousness. In the Sankhya interpretation, consciousness and the material world (*purusha* and *prakriti*) are two parallel and independent realities.Then there are theists who hold that there is a supreme conscious being, the god of religions, who produces a real world using his mysterious powers and for reasons which are beyond human comprehension. A section of Buddhists proclaim that neither the physical world nor consciousness have any fundamental reality and the ultimate truth is a void or *shunyata*.

Vedanta has strong arguments against each of these contrary views. While we cannot get into a discussion on these arguments here, a proper study of Vedanta does convincingly establish that our reality is consciousness. But even after we agree with Vedanta that consciousness is our deepest truth, we may yet feel that our consciousness is personal; we may continue to believe that there is a pocket of individual consciousness within us which is unique to us. This is because in our usual understanding, consciousness is contained in the mind and the mind is contained in the body—a sort of nested Russian dolls arrangement! This conclusion seems justified because while we are all conscious beings, we individually know different things, have different thoughts, feelings & memories and act differently. But the conclusion that consciousness is individual is wrong. Vedanta goes on to tell us that this consciousness, which seems to be a part or property or product of our bodies, is really an independent and all-pervasive entity; it is neither restricted to our bodies nor affected by the presence, absence or condition of our bodies. The differences in thoughts, feelings and memories arise because our minds are different but the consciousness behind all minds is one and the same.

Actually, the consciousness which we personally lay claim to is just a reflection of universal consciousness in our minds. Vedanta tells us that our minds are like mirrors and have the unique ability to reflect universal consciousness. It is because of this reflected consciousness (*chidabhasa* in Sanskrit) that our bodies and minds become sentient. Our lives as knowers, thinkers, experiencers, performers or as the ones who desire are possible because our bodies and minds are enlivened by reflected consciousness. In a way, our personal consciousness can be compared with moonlight. Just as the moon has no light of its own, our minds are themselves inert; just as the moon appears to light up the earth on a moon-lit night by reflecting the sun's light, our minds light up the objects we know by reflecting universal consciousness. It is this reflected consciousness or chidabhasa which apart from giving us the ability to think, know, desire and act, also gives us our all-important sense of individuality.

Operating through individual bodies and minds, chidabhasa supports different thoughts and actions at the level of each individual. This is like light creating different images, depending upon sizes, shapes and conditions of different mirrors. Just as original light itself remains unaffected by its reflections, original consciousness remains unaffected by the doings of individual bodies and minds. When our minds lose their ability to reflect consciousness (like a mirror turning opaque or breaking), all functions stop. The result is death and a return of the body to the inertness of its constituting elements.

It is only with the knowledge of Vedanta that we can get over our false and limited identity which is based on our bodies and minds; we need Vedanta to understand our reality not only as consciousness but as universal consciousness. However, universal consciousness (termed *atma* in Sanskrit) can never be experienced by us as a separate object. It is the reflection of universal consciousness in our minds which makes any experience possible. If universal consciousness itself is to be experienced, who or what would make that experience possible? The very basis of experiencing cannot itself become an object of experience. Therefore, drik drishya viveka (the seer-seen discrimination), which is based on a subject being separate from perceived objects, has no place here. Atma is not something to be experienced or to be known as a separate object but something to be understood as the invariable presence in all our experiences.

The closest we can come to the experience of original consciousness is in its undistorted reflection in a prepared mind. The initial steps of Vedanta are geared towards removing disturbing mental effects which are caused by our over-powering desires and the resulting frenzy of activities. Strong desires and negative emotions cause so much turbulence that the reflection of consciousness in such an afflicted mind gets distorted and does not remain true to the original. It is only a prepared mind that can realise its own truth as the pure subject or witnessing consciousness (*sakshi chaitanya* in Sanskrit).

Vedanta does not stop here; it goes on to tell us that original consciousness or atma is *ekam advitiyam* (single, non-dual) and *sat chit ananda* (unchanging consciousness, without any limitations). Why should we take atma to be single, unchanging and limitless? Let us see if we can use our own experiences to help us here. What is the nature of consciousness which makes our bodies and minds sentient? The first thing we have to note is that consciousness has no attributes or characteristics of its own. It is because of consciousness that we become aware of the different attributes of other things: a yellow rose, a large mountain, a thin body, a calm mind. Now, if consciousness had its own attributes, it would have imparted those attributes commonly to everything we know, just as jaundiced eyes would make our whole world look yellow. It is because consciousness itself has no attributes that we are able to know different things by their dissimilar attributes.

The fact that consciousness has no attributes also makes it impossible for us to distinguish one consciousness from another consciousness. Having no attributes makes consciousness undefinable and we can never find any boundaries or limitations for something which has no attributes. As in the case of space, we cannot find characteristics or defining qualities in respect of consciousness and so it has to be boundless or unlimited. And the limitlessness of consciousness is further reaffirmed by the fact that everything – from the smallest to biggest and from the nearest to farthest – is within our consciousness. Because consciousness is limitless, we can include both an infinitesimal virus and a massive galaxy in our awareness.

Further, consciousness without boundaries has to be single because, by definition, it is not possible for two boundless entities to exist simultaneously —the presence of any second thing would limit and form the boundary of the first thing. Here again, the analogy from our experience is that of space; there is only one boundless, attributeless space.

Consciousness also cannot undergo any change because all change is with respect to some attribute of an object (such as fat becoming thin or distant becoming near or young becoming old); without any attributes, the very basis for change does not exist for consciousness.

Thus, our own experiences and logic support the Vedantic vision of a single, unchanging and limitless consciousness which is our innermost truth, atma. Vedanta then turns to an examination of the world which we individuals confront. In this context, Vedanta now tells us about *brahman*. Just as clay is the basis for the entire world of clay objects, Vedanta says that brahman is the basis for everything in the world. Just as atma is the reality behind 'I' (the individual), brahman is the common reality behind the 'Not I' (the entire world perceived by an individual). Vedanta then goes on to say (based on good but detailed reasoning which we cannot get into here) that brahman is changeless, conscious and boundless (*satyam jnanam anantam*). And, as we have just seen, our own truth (atma) is also consciousness which exists without change or boundaries.

Superficially, this may lead one to believe that there is one truth behind the world (brahman) and another truth behind every individual (atma). However, multiple boundless or unlimited things are not logically tenable and Vedanta tells us that there is only one conscious, boundless and unchanging reality which lends its existence to the temporary appearance of the objects of the world as well as to its numerous individuals; it is the common truth behind both the knower and the known.

That there is only one consciousness which appears both as the knower and the known is also supported by another fact drawn from our own experience: whatever we see, touch, hear, smell, taste or think about is invariably associated with consciousness. Without consciousness, no knowing is possible. If every known object can never be separated from consciousness, how can we say that objects and consciousness are two separate things? Things like a pot and a shirt can be seen separately because they are different from each other. But we can never separate the pot from clay because the pot is clay. Similarly, as no object can be separated from consciousness because of which the object is known, objects are not other than consciousness. Thus, the truth behind both the knower and the known is consciousness.

Brahman and atma are just two different names given to the same conscious reality, depending on whether one is looking at it as the truth behind the world of objects or as the truth behind us, the individuals. The perceived multiplicity of objects and individuals is only a temporary appearance based on their common truth, much as the people and things in our dreams are only a projection of our thought. This *aikyam* or oneness of brahman and atma is the crux of the upanishads and has great personal significance for us, the individuals. Our need to continuously seek fulfilment is rooted in our conclusion that we are small and mortal beings; our entire life then becomes a constant struggle to overcome these limitations. These limitations actually belong to our body and mind which always remain limited because that is their very nature. However, if Vedanta's insights are fully understood and imbibed by us then we get the liberating realisation that our bodies and minds are just temporary and insubstantial superimpositions on our reality, atma.

As atma is unchanging, I do not fear time and death which can only affect temporary and changeable things like my body and mind. As atma is boundless, there is nothing outside to be obtained. As atma is consciousness itself, the presence or absence of a specific piece of knowledge in any individual mind has no effect on me, the very basis of all knowing. The appearance of the entire world is based on universal consciousness which is also the truth behind me, the individual; as universal consciousness, I remain utterly unaffected by the events in the world. The world is only an appearance and while it affects bodies and minds which are also appearances, it can never touch my reality, the unchanging, boundless substratum of all.

Once we realise that atma or brahman is the only reality, our unfulfilled desires lose their force, the pressure to be hyper-active in order to finish agendas is removed, our dependencies & fears vanish, our fundamental doubts get resolved and we experience the peace and fulfilment which are the innate nature of pure consciousness.

What happens to the body and mind that we happen to be associated with at present, once the knowledge of Vedanta is assimilated by us? After we understand that our reality is unchanging and boundless consciousness, we still continue to participate in the ups and downs of our physical and mental attributes. But now our participation is not taken as being viscerally serious and it will no longer give rise to large upsurges of elation or despair. We now become like actors in a play or persons playing a game—we play our part but with the knowledge that whatever happens at the body-mind level is temporary and has no effect on our reality.

The realisation of this grand vision of Vedanta is not easy to grasp and to come to terms with.This vision is not needed by our reality, atma, but only by our minds which unnecessarily suffer by not realising the enormity of our truth and by falsely identifying with limited appearances, such as an individual body. And it is not enough that this vision is just understood. It has to be fully imbibed and integrated with our minds so that it is available to us spontaneously, without any delay or conscious effort. Only then can our minds go through life, free of driving desires & fears, full of peace & fulfilment.

This beautiful journey of realisation is the ultimate purpose of our lives and once some blessing puts us on its track, with the help of our own commitment, the guidance of a proper teacher, the companionship of fellow students, and the passage of time, we will undoubtedly reach our goal.

Understanding what is truly real is critical to our being able to understand and appreciate the teachings of Vedanta. Our usual ideas of reality are not what Vedanta sees as real.

WHAT IS REAL?

Our idea of reality is based on common experience—we take what we experience to be real. But then some of our experiences themselves contradict this definition of reality. We experience a sunset but the sun never really sets. We see the blue ocean but there is nothing blue in a handful of water from the same ocean. We jump in fright from the sight of a snake but it turns out to be a coil of rope. Because our experiences can be misleading, they cannot be the sole basis for determining what is real.

The second aspect is the role of our senses and of our minds in determining the nature of objects we see as real. If our eyes had the capacity to see upto the minute level of subatomic particles, what we perceive as solid objects would then appear as almost empty space. This is because matter is largely empty. An atom, the basic building block of matter, is like a miniature solar system with a tight nucleus playing the role of a sun orbited by planet-like electrons. But the nucleus is tiny compared with the orbits of its electrons. One estimate says that if an atom were to be compared with a large football field, the nucleus which contains 99.9% of an atom's mass would be the size of a pea in the field's centre.

And, on a different plane, we cannot even imagine what we would 'see' if, like bats, we were designed to use not light but reflected sound waves to form impressions of objects.

And it is not only our senses which come into play in creating a sensation, it is also our minds. Thus, if we are immersed in deep thought, we may not hear someone calling out our name even if the caller's voice is audible and our ears are functioning normally, because our mind is temporarily unavailable.

The point of saying all this is to note that there is subjectivity in the way in which we perceive objects and sensations. Qualities which seem so real to us are not absolute. A solid block of iron weighing 100 kilograms will weigh only 16.5 kilograms on the moon and 250 kilograms on Jupiter. Sub-atomic particles can whiz through this apparently solid iron because, for them, the iron's atoms are large distances apart. And this block of iron sitting motionlessly before us would be seen zipping around at 1,600 kilometres per hour for someone looking at it from space because that is the speed of the earth's rotation. In fact, we can never be sure that all we experience or know is absolutely true and not simply a reflection of the limitations of our senses and minds.

Vedanta goes further than just the subjectivity in our perceptions; it goes on to say that our usual notion that things in the world have an objective, independent existence is fundamentally flawed. It points out that everything that we see and know is both impermanent and dependent on something else; therefore, it does not pass the tests of reality. A foundational statement in Vedanta begins with *brahma satyam jagat mithya*. This asserts that the world we experience lacks absolute reality. This, of course, goes against all our conditioning and beliefs. It is, therefore, necessary to understand what Vedanta means when it says that the world lacks reality. To obtain clarity here we can turn to definitions of reality from Vedantic texts as well as to an analysis of our own experiences. Vedanta defines reality as that which has continuous existence in all the three periods of time: the past, the present and the future. To use Sanskrit terms, *satyam* has to be *trikala abadhit*. By this definition, to justify being classified as real, a thing has to be eternal – existing outside the bounds of past, present or future. However, we know nothing which is eternal – even our universe was not in existence once upon a time (it came into being some 14 billion years ago according to science) and so, while it is very very old, it cannot be called eternal.

In a small way, this test of permanence can be seen in relation to our own day-to-day experiences. If we have a cup of freshly brewed coffee, we would say that the coffee is hot. But is the coffee really hot? If we let that cup stand for a while, the coffee will lose its heat. If, on the other hand, we light a fire, there will be heat as long as there is fire—we never experience a cold fire. Heat is a permanent and intrinsic aspect of fire, it is a real quality which is always present. But, in the case of coffee, heat is only a borrowed and temporary quality. Because coffee is never really hot (the way fire is), we can have cold coffee. We therefore have to accept that the permanent heat of fire is 'more real' than the temporary heat of coffee. Similarly, if someone says "*I love you*" today and then stops demonstrating that love tomorrow then we say that such fickle love is not real. If it was real, we would expect it to be constant.

So, these examples from our own experiences tie in with Vedanta's assertion that unbroken and unchanging existence is the hallmark of reality. And, as we saw earlier, nothing in this world exists changelessly and eternally; therefore, in Vedanta's strict sense nothing that we know can be called absolutely real.

Another aspect which is required, if an entity is to be called real for Vedanta, is independent existence. If something is just a name given to a form (*nama rupa*) of another substance then that cannot be termed real. So 'bangle' is just a name given to a form of gold. It has no independent existence away from the gold from which it is formed – we cannot take away the gold and keep the bangle. Vedanta would therefore not call the bangle real. At the same time the bangle cannot be dismissed as being unreal – it is seen, felt and enjoyed. So such objects, which are merely names given to forms of other substances, are termed as *mithya*—things which are experienced but lacking independent existence.

Another example of mithya is an object like a book. A book has a front cover, a back cover and several pages. Let us now rip out the front cover (only in our imagination!) and see it separately. Is the front cover a book? Clearly not. Now let us rip out one page of the book at a time and examine each page. Is any one page a book? Of course not. The same with the back cover which also is not a book. So, by putting together a collection of non-book items (the front cover, individual pages and the back cover) we seem to have created a new entity called a book. But is it really a new entity? Does it have its own existence or is it just a name given to a certain arrangement of covers and pages?

Further, we recognise a book as a book only because the idea of a book has been planted in our minds from childhood by people around us. A member of a primitive tribe isolated in a forest would not see the book as a book because he has never had the idea of a book. So, is there a real book out there or is the book only in our minds? Is the constellation of Orion out there or is it only visible to a person with some knowledge of astronomy? In fact, the existence of all things is not only dependent on something more fundamental but also dependent on the mind of the knower. So, once again, everything in the world fails this second test of absolute reality—the test of independent existence.

But how does all this matter? Who cares if the universe is technically not eternal because it did not exist 14 billion years ago? And I still want that gold bangle even if it is only a name given to a form of gold. In day-to-day life this does not matter and it is perfectly all right for us to enjoy a sunset or to buy a book even though the sun does not actually set and a book is only a name given to an assemblage of covers and pages.

But what if we wanted to send a craft into space? Here, we cannot be indifferent to finding out whether it is the sun moving or it is the earth rotating. Similarly, if we are not satisfied with the usual goals and struggles of life, if we want to know the truth of things, if we want to find release from our compulsive & endless manipulation of the world, then proper understanding of the reality of things becomes vital. And it is vital because if we discover that the things we have been fretting over are not absolutely real, such knowledge can change the quality of our efforts in the world as well as show us a new avenue of finding fulfilment.

This is where Vedanta comes in. By showing us that the world we take so seriously lacks reality, it releases us from our endless struggle to extract happiness from the world; it also frees us from roller-coaster rides of elation and dejection which depend on whether our attempts to mould the world to our liking have been successful or not.

Vedanta does not stop at establishing that objects in the world lack absolute reality. Just as the imagined snake which frightened us at twilight needs a rope to support its appearance, objects which we experience in the world also need a real substratum. Vedanta terms this reality *brahman* or *atma* and shows us how only that meets the test of absolute reality. It further shows us that brahman or atma happens to be the truth of ourselves.

These insights of Vedanta do not appeal to everyone and many are content to continue taking the world and its objects as being absolutely real. But, interestingly, even those who take to Vedanta also operate in the world as if it is real.

Vedanta never denies the experience of the world—the world is tangible and needs to be dealt with appropriately at the practical level. When Vedanta says that the world is mithya, that does not mean that the world is non-existent or illusory—mithya is only an in-between category to cover things which are neither completely real (with permanent & independent existence) nor completely unreal (such as a square circle). Mithya merely refers to names given to temporary forms which do not exist independent of a more fundamental ground.

The change which the understanding of Vedanta's vision of reality brings is not outward or at the practical level. The change is inward, in understanding. The consequence of this change is not in stopping interactions with the world or in refusing to acknowledge the enjoyment which the world can provide or in walking away from the responsibilities of the roles which each one of us have in this life. The consequences are in a certain peace and equanimity irrespective of the success or failure of our efforts, in the disappearance of a compulsive force behind our likes & dislikes and in seeing life as more of a game rather than a life & death struggle.

Vedanta is unique in its classification of reality under four categories and in bringing in the concept of mithya *to cover things which are neither absolutely real nor completely unreal.*

DIFFERENT LEVELS OF REALITY

Seeing Your Own Eyes

Vedanta wants us to know our own real nature which it says is pure consciousness. But because anything we know becomes known only because of consciousness, what can we use to know consciousness itself? The problem here is similar to our eyes wanting to see themselves or to someone trying to lift himself up by himself! In the case of eyes, the problem is solved by using a mirror. In the case of self-knowledge, the problem is solved by the words of the upanishads which operate like a mirror for us in this field.

Words Become Critical

A good mirror has to be free of distortions and opacity. The mirror of Vedantic teachings is constructed with words so it is critical that proper words are chosen and used precisely. Use of proper words is, of course, important for anything to be conveyed but becomes all the more critical in the case of Vedanta. Therefore, where words in common parlance are not adequate, Vedanta has to create unusual words and classifications. One area where this happens is in respect of the concept of reality because proper understanding of what Vedanta means by *'real'* is so critical to its whole structure.

Categories of Reality

We generally place things we know into two categories: real and unreal. However, Vedanta uses four different terms to classify all things:

Asat (unreal)
Pratibhasika (subjective reality)
Vyavaharika (objective reality)
Paramarthika (absolute reality)

The Unreal

Let us first look at what Vedanta labels as unreal. In our normal usage, 'unreal' may include things like a snake mistakenly seen in place of a rope or objects in our dreams or figures on a cinema screen. We consider these to be unreal even though they are experienced. However, Vedanta has a much stricter definition of unreality which only covers things that never exist, that are absolutely unreal and that are never experienced by anyone. Examples of such truly unreal things are an elephant's egg or a square circle and the Sanskrit term used for them is asat (or *tuccham*).

Subjective and Objective Realities

But what about things which we do experience? The terms used by Vedanta here are *pratibhasika* (referring to subjective experiences) and *vyavaharika* (referring to objective experiences).

Subjective experiences are purely personal and examples here are our own dreams or mistakes like seeing a snake in the place of a rope or looking upon another individual as a personal enemy. These are subjective matters and are not shared by others. On the other hand, objective experiences are those commonly shared by all and include things such as mountains, rivers, the colour red or the heat of a fire; they form our consensus reality.

Subjective experiences are part of *jiva srishti* (an individual's personal creation) and are called pratibhasika which means existing only in appearance or looking like something which they are not. Objective experiences, on the other hand, are part of *Ishwara srishti* (god's impersonal creation) and they are what we normally consider real. Vedanta terms them as vyavaharika which means that can be transacted with by all. So, an imagined snake seen in place of a rope is pratibhasika (it only frightens one individual) and the rope itself is vyavaharika (it can be used by all).

The Provisionally Real

Vedanta then goes on to show that all things which are experienced, whether subjectively or objectively, fail the test of absolute reality. Vedanta defines absolute reality as *trikala abadhit*: something which exists in all three periods of time (past, present and future). Nothing that we know has such eternal existence. All things come into existence at a point in time, exist for a while and then go out of existence at another point in time.

In fact, not only are all things time-bound but they all also lack substance of their own. For instance, when we examine a shirt which we consider to be a real object, it is not only temporary but we also find that actually a shirt is not a substantial object in itself. Just as a pot is only a name given to a form of clay, shirt is only a name given to a form of fabric which, in turn, is only a name given to an arrangement of yarns and so on.

Vedanta says that all objects which are known, lack permanence as well as independent existence (because everything is based on another substance). Therefore, they cannot be called absolutely real. However, we cannot deny the experience of such objects and, further, they also have utility for us so they cannot be dismissed as being completely unreal. Vedanta, therefore, coins a new term, *mithya*, to cover things which are neither totally unreal nor absolutely real. Mithya covers everything we know or experience, whether it is in our dreams or in our waking state or as the result of an error (our famous rope-snake).

All these things are not absolutely real but Vedanta grants them relative or provisional reality only because we experience them, deal with them and utilise them. So, contrary to popular notions, mithya does not mean unreal or illusory. All it means is things which are not permanent and which do not have an independent substance of their own. And this, of course, covers every single thing, including our own bodies and minds.

One wrong idea that some have when they hear the term *mithya* is that Vedanta holds that the world is only a projection of our minds. This is what is termed as subjective idealism in Western philosophy but it has no place in Vedanta. If you tumble off your bed while fast asleep, you will still painfully hit the hard floor which continues to exist even when your mind is absent and you are not aware of anything including the floor. The vyavaharika world or Ishwara srishti, though mithya, is not our personal projection and it is not dependent upon the functioning of our individual minds.

The Really Real

The entire universe of mithya objects cannot exist without some basis or substratum—our snake needs the rope to support its appearance. And when we say that the shirt is based on fabric which, in turn, is based on yarn and so on, we cannot go down this chain indefinitely because that would lead to infinite regression which is logically untenable. The chain of dependencies of all objects must come to an end somewhere and that ultimate substratum is what Vedanta terms as *brahman*. This is the real reality, the final reality, the reality which is the basis for all mithya. It is brahman which is this paramarthika reality. (The terms *pratibhasika*, *vyavaharika* and *paramarthika* are worth remembering after being clearly understood because they are important and used often in the study of Vedanta.)

And a deeper study of Vedanta leads us further to see that brahman, in fact, is the only reality and that it is consciousness which is boundless, timeless, attributeless and unchanging. Vedanta finally shows us that brahman is also our own reality and the body-mind with which we identify ourselves is no more than just one other name and form superimposed on the reality of brahman.

The Point of All This

So now we know that Vedanta has its own views on what is unreal, what is mithya and what is absolutely real. But what good does all this do to us except provide, at best, an interesting philosophical discussion? The answer to this is that it does the same good that shedding more light on the rope-snake does. Once the snake is seen to be the mistake that it is, upon the recognition of its substratum (the rope), all our confusion and fear in respect of the snake vanish.

In our individual lives, all our fears and insecurity are centred around our body-mind and the world it confronts. If, instead of seeing these things as being absolutely real, we are able to see them as temporary and insubstantial superimpositions on brahman and also see brahman as our own truth, then our misplaced fears vanish.

An understanding of different levels of reality also makes another vital point clear: for things to affect each other, they have to be at the same level of reality. A snake falsely seen in place of a rope cannot actually bite us because the snake is pratibhasika while our body is at the vyavaharika level. It causes fear in our minds only because we wrongly understand this snake to be vyavaharika. In a similar vein, the vyavaharika world can affect only our body-mind but never our reality of consciousness because consciousness is paramarthika.

With the understanding that our truth as consciousness remains unaffected by everything, we are able to treat life as a game which we may play as well as we can but not take it so seriously that it causes us fear, insecurity, anger, guilt or regrets.

Of course, to enjoy this promise of Vedanta is not an easy or quick matter. Just having information about different levels of reality is unlikely to make an iota of difference to our personal lives. Vedanta requires a certain amount of initial preparation followed by a proper exposure to its insights under the guidance of a teacher. And, most important of all, it requires a further process for integrating its new knowledge into us so fully that it is able to override our habitual reactions and emotions. All this requires considerable effort, commitment and guidance which we should work for assiduously as well as pray for fervently.

Vedanta Only for Vyavaharika Problems

It must be remembered that Vedanta is for solving our problems at the vyavaharika level which arise from our false conclusion that we are small, mortal and lacking in knowledge. Further, Vedanta will not be of much help if we suffer from extraordinary pratibhasika problems (such as an abnormal mind caused by dementia or uncontrollable emotions). As Swami Dayananda used to say, Vedanta is for *normally abnormal* people, not for the *abnormally abnormal*! The preparatory stages of Vedanta are meant to reduce problems at the subjective or pratibhasika level of our lives and make us more objective so that Vedanta can do its job. However, if our pratibhasika issues are very deep and strong, we first need to use help from medicine or psychiatry to reach a state where Vedanta can become useful.

In this context we should also keep in mind that all of Vedanta (the scriptures, the guru and the teaching itself) is at the vyavaharika level. Like everything in the world, Vedanta too is in and of the mithya jagat. Vedanta is of no relevance to our real nature which is always limitless, unchanging and unaffected. Vedanta is only for the false 'I' which sees itself defined by a body, a mind and their possessions & relationships. Without Vedanta this false 'I' suffers unnecessarily. But from the standpoint of the ultimate truth Vedanta is a series of very useful but yet white lies. However, unlike the other things we transact with at the mithya level, Vedanta is special because it has the ability to awaken us to the realisation of our paramarthika reality. In this, Vedanta can be likened to the tiger in our dreams who, by pouncing on us, can startle us into wakefulness even though it is only a dream figment.

Our Fertile Minds

When Vedanta talks of levels of reality, it should be clear that we cannot pick an aspect from one level and apply it to another. The glass of water on your bedside table cannot be used to quench your dream thirst because the thirst is at the pratibhasika level while the glass of water is at the vyavaharika level. But our fertile minds can still come up with questions like, "*If the world is mithya then why does my toe hurt when it stubs a mithya table?*". The point which is missed here is that both the table and the toe are mithya; they are both at the vyavaharika level and at that common level both will affect each other much as the dream fire will singe the dream you.

The most damaging manifestation of such a mix-up is imposing aspects of absolute reality on our day-to-day lives in order to avoid the effort and discipline required to improve ourselves. Often, a person thinks that because he has learnt that the world is not absolutely real, the rules that govern its apparent reality no longer apply to him; he then goes on to conclude that he can do anything he wants, in the name of the world not being real. This is what is called imposing satyam on mithya.

It is true that brahman, which is at the paramarthika level, remains unaffected by the doings of our mithya level body-mind. But, as we have a body-mind, our lives are necessarily lived at the mithya level. If we don't take reasonable care of our bodies and if we don't work on reducing negative qualities in our minds, there will be consequences. Instead of the knowledge of reality helping us to get away from needless pain and suffering, by trying to use clever short-cuts to avoid doing what we need to do at the worldly level, we will end up with the opposite result. Vedanta used improperly can, at times, be more dangerous than no Vedanta at all.

Vedanta at its core is very different from theistic religion. However, it does use many valuable practices from the Vedic religion. In this context, it is important to debunk the notion that all religions lead to the same end. If different religions and their spiritual destinations are different, we cannot afford to be indifferent to the choice we make.

DO ALL RELIGIONS TEACH THE SAME THING?

It has become quite in vogue for some people (including religious leaders) to state that all religions ultimately say the same thing; another common statement made in a similar vein is that all spiritual paths finally lead to the same goal.

While these ideas sound very liberal because of the freedom they imply, we need to examine them properly to see if they stand up to scrutiny. After all, while it is good to be open-minded, as someone had once pointed out, we should not become so open-minded that we let our brains fall out!

Let us begin by looking at the main elements of religions. All major religions have cultural forms like rituals, liturgy and language. They all have ethical norms by which lives should be lived. And they have their own vision of god as the highest and most absolute presence.

Cultural forms obviously vary greatly between religions—we just have to attend a Christian mass, a Hindu *yagna* and a Muslim *namaaz* or compare the architecture of a cathedral, a mosque and a *mandir* to see these differences for ourselves.

Coming to ethics, while some norms are undoubtedly common (such as speaking the truth), there are many others which are at great variance. For instance, one religious tradition uses wine in its rituals while another finds this sacrilegious; one considers the killing and eating the flesh of a living creature to be sinful while another tradition encourages this; one has a record of accepting people of another faith in their midst with friendship while another has a history of persecuting those from a different religion.

And, of course, the idea of god is so very different for different religions. There is very little in common between Jesus, Allah and Krishna. In fact, in the Hindu tradition the concept of god is very unique as we will see a little later.

So, just because of some shared values such as the injunctions to be truthful and compassionate or the encouragement to pray, it is not at all correct to conclude that all religions say the same thing.

And nor do all spiritual paths lead to the same goal. The usual imagery used here is that of several paths on a mountain, all leading to the same peak. But the problem in this case is that the mountains themselves are different for different religions. The Christian goal of eternal life in Heaven in the presence of God on his throne with Jesus seated beside him is different from the much sought after-life in an Islamic Paradise, with its promise of material delights such as beautiful maidens, precious stones, delicious foods and constantly flowing water. A major Buddhist tradition, on the other hand, has the goal of *nirvana* ('blowing out'); in this view, an individual has to recognise himself as an insubstantial flicker and understand ultimate reality as nothingness *(shunyata)*. Jains aspire for *kevala* and for achieving this each person, by great effort and penance, has to rid himself of accumulated *karmas* and regain his original status of an omnipotent, omniscient individual.

And Hindu traditions, which differ even within themselves, have disparate goals ranging from wanting to be of service to a personified god in heaven, to the goal of recognising yourself as a microcosm of god (a tiny spark of a big fire) or to the startling-sounding goal of realising that an individual's reality is the only thing which truly exists and which is the basis of everything, including god himself.

How can we then say that all religions say the same thing or that all paths lead to the same goal? And while this false open-mindedness is wrong in general, it is particularly damaging to the Hindu religion.

When we hold out the notion that all religions lead to the same end, we are effectively saying that there is nothing special about any religion. This may not be very damaging if everyone genuinely believed and practised this 'live and let live' approach in religious matters. But this is not so. Historically, Hindu culture has been much more accommodating of other religious traditions than many other cultures. Such tolerance largely continues even now, despite the presence of a fringe minority which attempts to radicalise Hinduism. The openness of Hindu culture is evidenced by instances such as the welcome given to the foreign flows of Jews and Zoroastrians centuries ago or by the current peaceful co-existence of home-grown Jains, Buddhists and Sikhs in a predominantly Hindu society. This is in contrast to the attitude of many in the Abrahamic faiths who see conversion of others to their fold as a holy duty.

Further, a *laissez-faire* attitude would be more acceptable if the Vedic religion actually had nothing unique to offer. But the fact is that it does and that too at multiple levels.

We have already mentioned that the concept of god in the Hindu tradition is unique. The earliest Vedas present divinity as the known forces of nature such as fire and wind. Later, we are given anthropomorphic ideas of god: a person with human-like will, preferences and even emotions but with extraordinary powers. And such a god is presented in the form of several different personalities such as Shiva, Rama, Krishna, Laxmi, Saraswati, Durga and more, in endless variety. Here, Hindu tradition brings in the concept of *ishta devata* and gives us the freedom to personally choose a form of divinity to relate to, from a large pantheon of available deities. This humanising of divinity helps in evoking more intimate emotions such as *sakhya bhava* (friendship), *vatsalya bhava* (parental love for the chosen deity in its childhood form) and *madhurya bhava* (love for the beloved). Such emotions replace awe and fear which usual ideas of god can generate and make it easier for people with different mental make-ups to find an altar that suits their own personalities.

Divinity is also assigned to animals and plants (such as the *tulsi* plant and the cow). This, combined with the sacredness ascribed to aspects of nature (such as rivers, fire and wind), brought in environmental concerns into everyday lives well before these became the burning issues which they have today.

These initially appealing ideas of god are then overlaid by the more subtle concept of *Ishwara* who is held out to be both the material and the intelligent cause of the universe (*nimitta upadana karanam*). This conception absorbs the multiplicity of Hindu deities within the fold of a single divinity. Further, because Ishwara is seen to be the single and common cause behind every thing which exists, it follows that everything is nothing but Ishwara just as all pottery objects are nothing but clay. Thus, contrary to popular notions, Hindus don't actually have many gods. In fact, they don't even have one god—they have only god, nothing but god! And this idea of sacredness pervading every single thing (including our own bodies) is steeped into this culture in a way in which no other culture has emulated. When we come to Ishwara, instead of divinity being humanised as is done for one's ishta devata, everything in creation is imbued with divinity. This humanising of divinity and the divinising of the earthly is indeed an unique feature of Hinduism.

And some of the most evolved traditions within Hinduism don't even stop with Ishwara. So, advaita Vedanta has the unique vision of a single reality, termed *brahman* or *atma*, which is the only truth which exists independently and timelessly. This reality is the substratum on which the entire universe and its maker appear as temporary and insubstantial projections. The consequences of this understanding are of immense personal relevance and benefit to us —it holds out the promise of release from the most fundamental problems of any human being. This release is promised here and now, not in some unknown hereinafter. Further, this release is based on our understanding of underlying oneness, not dependent upon the benediction of a god in heaven or his messengers. The only requirement is that we put in the required time and effort to prepare and study with the help of a proper teacher. There is no other major religion in which such a view of reality and our salvation is incorporated in its main stream.

Another unique thing about advaita Vedanta is how it reconciles differing concepts of divinity which we get from different religions. So, in an Abhrahamic religion like Christianity, god is the perfect being who is 'up there'; such a transcendent god is other than us and is referred to as 'that' (*tat* in Sanskrit). In other religions like Buddhism and Jainism, divinity is said to be immanent within us; it is 'you' (*tvam* in Sanskrit). But there are problems with both these views. Where god is understood to be the perfect existence outside of us, his existence itself remains doubtful because there is no direct way of knowing that he actually exists. And when god is said to be within us, our own existence is of course doubt-free but then we are all clearly less than perfect. So we get stuck between the perfect but doubtful and the doubt-free but imperfect. It is only advaita Vedanta which shows us how to arrive at perfect existence which is also doubt-free. While we will not get into how this is done, it should be mentioned that the purpose of a mahavakya like *tat tvam asi* (which means 'you are that') is to help us make this unique reconciliation.

Another feature of the Hindu religion is the availability of a wide variety of scriptures. These nurture different minds at various levels of emotional and intellectual development, with material appropriate for them. From dramatic epics like Mahabharata & Ramayana to fable-like stories in the Puranas to intellectually-challenging contents of the upanishads and a vast range of literature in between, there is something for everybody here.

Further, our primary scriptures do not list out inflexible *do's* and *don'ts* like the Ten Commandments. While there are many codes of conduct (such as the Manu Smriti), they were never meant to be blindly applied for all times or irrespective of context. Though such codes and social constructs like the *varna-ashrama dharma* (incorporating the caste system) have obviously been misused by some people, such use was never the intent. For instance, the now infamous caste system was not designed to lock a person in a pigeon-hole forever, based purely on the accident of his birth. People were to be classified and evaluated based on three factors: birth *(jati)*, personal qualities *(guna)* and actual occupation *(karma)*. Of these three, the family you were born in was to be given only limited weightage and could be out-weighed by your qualities and actions. In this context, there is an often re-told incident of Shankaracharya (a *brahmin*) declaring a *chandala* (belonging to the lowest of the four castes) a guru, because of the chandala's remarkable spiritual knowledge. And it is indeed unfortunate that reprehensible practices like child-marriages and female foeticides still continue. But these have no sanction in the original Vedic scriptures and, sadly, terrible social practices (such as slavery or female genital mutilation) have occurred in other cultures as well.

The karma theory and the idea of *adrishtam* (the relationship between causes and effects, even when their connections are not apparent to us) are other useful features in this religion. They suggest a credible explanation for apparently random things which affect our lives; they also encourage good ethics and provide hope in adverse circumstances.

The Vedic religion, unlike many others, is not based on the words of a single messenger or prophet. And unlike other major religions where faith is the corner-stone and where scriptural contents have to be accepted because they are scriptural contents, the higher reaches of Vedic thought use a great deal of logic and analysis of our personal experiences. While to be formally called a

Hindu, the acceptance of the validity of the Vedas is considered to be of prime importance, nowhere do these scriptures say that freedom from all problems *(moksha)* is reserved only for Hindus. And even for those who accept the Vedas as a proper source of knowledge, questions and debates are encouraged and students are taught that no statement which is illogical or which contradicts valid experience should be accepted, irrespective of its source. This approach is both remarkable and refreshing.

There are many more features of Hindu religion and thought which makes these traditions special and valuable. So, if the notion of all religions being on a single indifference curve gets very wide-spread, there is a real risk of this entire religious culture dissipating and becoming irrelevant in a spate of apparent modernity. After all, why would anyone want to preserve something which has no special features?

One sentence from the Rig Veda which is often quoted by the proponents of 'many paths to the same goal' is: *ekam sad vipra bahudha vadanti* which is translated as 'one truth called differently by seers'. If one looks at this sentence in the context of the entire scheme of the Vedas, it becomes clear that what is sought to be conveyed is that there is only one reality though it may be given different names. This is a statement regarding the singular nature of the absolute and should not be interpreted to mean that all paths lead to the same goal.

Tolerance, open-mindedness and respecting the freedom of choice of others does not mean validating or adopting all contradictory ideas. And when ideas oppress & hurt others, even tolerance can be questioned. We tend to be sanguine about differences when we don't realise that glossing over them does insidious harm to an ancient and valuable culture which has so much to offer. Unless we understand the full breadth and the unique vision of the Vedas and communicate this in a manner appropriate to current times, we will lose something of value to all of mankind in a rush of misplaced universalism.

The study of Vedanta requires a teacher.
There are, unfortunately, quite a number of people waiting
to exploit the faith and vulnerability
of seekers looking for a guru. It needs to be kept in mind
that the spiritual market-place
needs as much care and caution
as any other market, perhaps more so.

CAVEAT EMPTOR!

India has some of the oldest scriptures in the world and they contain, amongst other things, a treasure-trove of spiritual insights. We also have ancient and yet effective teaching traditions for transmitting these insights. And, even in our modern society, those on a spiritual path are usually given adequate space and support in this pursuit.

Current spiritual teachings and methods derived from Hindu scriptures can be broadly classified as:

Jnana or knowledge based,
Bhakti or devotion based,
Yoga or meditation based, and
Tantra or rituals based.

These spiritual streams have completely different goals and methods which have led to ongoing debates. But the common focus of such traditions and their lineage of gurus has always been the genuine welfare of seekers; their objective has never been the glorification and enrichment of individual teachers or the growth of their cults.

During the last century or so, the original nature of these traditional insights and teaching methods have been tweaked by some non-traditional teachers. Many of them have chosen to deliberately water down or hold back the finer aspects of spiritual wisdom because these may overwhelm and put off casual or unprepared students. (As one contemporary teacher put it, *"I initially give them what they want so that they finally want what I want to give!"*) Some other recent gurus have been those rare ones who have personally succeeded in obtaining great insights without having been systematically exposed to our scriptures and their traditional teaching methods. Such gurus naturally cannot use materials and techniques with which they themselves are unfamiliar. While one can argue about the pros and cons of such developments, their underlying intent still remains the genuine welfare of seekers.

However, there is now a disturbing and growing rise in a newer breed of spiritual teachers whose primary goals are personal property, power and prestige. For them, their followers are merely the means to achieve these ends. This exploitation of followers, for the personal benefit of the teacher and his coterie, is aided by the increasing number of seekers who:

- are unduly fascinated by the magical and the mystical,
- look for quick fixes,
- have a high emotional quotient which needs a constant psychological crutch, especially when faced with reverses, and
- have touching faith in anything which claims to be based on ancient traditions or blessed by divinity.

How does one go about figuring out whether a particular guru and his institution are dubious or not? The problem becomes vexing because spirituality is an ambiguous term and a fresh seeker is himself none too clear about spirituality's real goals or methods.

To compound this, our traditions do require respect for and faith in spiritual teachers. But, while there are such mandates, it is wrong to conclude that we are therefore required to forsake our common-sense and objectivity. Spiritual gurus and their teachings undoubtedly need to be approached with an open mind and be given the initial benefit of doubt as we try to learn something outside our usual frames of reference. However, after a fair trial, our traditions have never advocated continuing to accept teachings which contradict our valid experiences or violate logic—a teaching can be supra-logical but should never be illogical. And a magical-seeming outcome of an esoteric method should be taken as being genuine only if not accepting it would be even more incredulous.

Further, during the process of being exposed to spiritual insights, one should keep in mind that a real guru does not try to hold on to his disciples by making them dependent on him. He does not exploit a seeker's distress, gullibility or trust. He regularly acknowledges that what he teaches comes from an ancient chain of earlier teachers and that he is only the current link in that unbroken chain.

A proper guru should not only have adequate grounding in the scriptures and their teaching methods but he must also actually live the values and life-style he is advocating. In the context of spiritual teaching, this includes a certain amount of simplicity, non-acquisitiveness, lack of ego, no hankering for wealth & fame; there should also be genuine concern for the welfare of every one of his students, irrespective of a student's wealth or status.

In contrast to this, it is worthwhile noting some common methods and characteristics of teachers whose intentions are suspect; this may help a genuine spiritual seeker to be on guard against exploitation by such 'gurus' and their cults.

Manipulative spiritual cults usually have a charismatic leader who is eloquent and quick-witted. The ability of such a 'guru' to hold and enthral a large number of people with his magnetism is the corner-stone of these movements.

Such 'gurus' are self-appointed and often award themselves grandiose titles. Their choice of clothing can be striking, not necessarily in keeping with any tradition or norm. The terminology they use is often non-standard and self-invented.

They promise people a vast change in their lives, culminating in 'enlightenment' but if, and only if, they unquestioningly follow him and his secret techniques; these apparently esoteric techniques are not to be shared with anyone outside the cult.

They cultivate a band of devoted followers, quite in love with their leader whom they would not dream of doubting or challenging. If anybody does this, he is mocked, ignored or pitied as being unfit for evolution.

They produce a strong group environment using stories, music, dance, rituals and a unique terminology. With great care, a 'feel-good' atmosphere is nurtured within their gated *ashrams*, where a captivating emotional charge is created.

A large amount of public service work, using an army of volunteers, is undertaken, reflecting innocent concern for the people and the planet. But, behind this screen of good work, the leaders and their cults accumulate large sums of money, extensive property, great personal fame, powerful political ties and dominant influence.

Given the problems and ignominy faced by some of the more flashy cult leaders in the past, the current crop of leaders of such cults are being more clever and circumspect in their doings—for instance, a 'guru' will now hesitate to flaunt a fleet of the most expensive of cars. But, in any case, the more gullible adherents will follow their leader even after he steals money, sleeps with his followers or does even more perverse things, none of which are in keeping with the values he is expounding.

Having garnered a certain recognition in India, these teachers are quick to establish outposts in countries like Switzerland and the U.S. (presumably because people in these countries are in more dire need than people in Nepal or Uganda).

In fact, one can find several parallels between such 'spiritual' institutions and commercial corporations: both look for the best markets to sell their products & services at a profit, both build brands & distribution, both are secretive & protective about their know-how, both use a part of their resources for social service and, in both, the owners & senior management profit the most.

Do these teachers and their institutions do any good at all to their followers? To answer this, a distinction must be made between their public teachings meant for casual followers and their restricted teachings which are reserved for those who show more commitment to such 'gurus'.

The more generalised and public teachings here are based on selected portions of ancient wisdom from a variety of traditions and scriptures, even though these sources are not acknowledged. To these are added elements based on keen observation of current societal patterns, psychology, medicine and science. This potpourri is intelligently put together and contains some useful truths which have immediate appeal; the appeal is enhanced by the oratory, personality and showmanship of the master.

Because these teachings have a certain amount of logic and the ring of truth, they are useful to many people. They bring in some needed discipline in the lives of many followers, by encouraging them to be regular in carrying out prescribed practices. Further, public service work supported by such organisations undoubtedly benefits several needy people.

Despite the good which is done by their activities, such 'gurus' put serious seekers (who are given more detailed teachings) on a false and frustrating path. The 'advanced' teachings of such cult leaders lack real substance, often being actually misleading. The genuine growth of students is not their primary objective. The example set by the personal lives of such teachers is at variance with true spirituality. Because of such reasons, seekers are not led to the level of peace and fulfilment they are seeking. In fact, because of their disappointment with this kind of experience, where they have been misled, they may never explore other sound and valid approaches to spiritual growth because they are now put-off for good.

Some other seekers in such cults may become so mesmerised by the master's personality that they lose all objectivity and the ability to think for themselves; they can become bigoted robots who will blindly do the leader's bidding and brook no doubts about the cult's doings.This then permits some 'gurus' to exploit the bodies, emotions and property of individual followers in ways which, in the extreme, can be illegal and immoral.

The spiritual arena is not regulated by internal governance (unlike the medical profession, for instance); it is also not governed by law on misrepresentations and unsubstantiated claims, unlike normal commercial transactions. Here, promises, processes and results are entirely dependent on the knowledge, intention and character of the teacher; his followers have no safety-net or recourse, even if they have been led up the garden path.

This is why the old Latin maxim of *caveat emptor* (buyer beware!), which applies to all market-places, applies even more so in the guru or spiritual market.

We are often made to feel that we have become very demanding and expect too much from life. But the actual problem is that we set our sights too low and short-change ourselves.

ARE WE ALL ASKING FOR TOO MUCH?

There is a general consensus that many problems arise because, under the pressure of our unending desires, we demand too much of everything. This conclusion is supported by pointing out facts such as:

- We have become insatiable consumers, wanting more, bigger and better at an exponential rate.
- We are never grateful, no matter what we have and nor do we pause to savour whatever has been obtained, because of the furious race to obtain even more.
- We have a strong sense of entitlement that the world owes us security, comfort and pleasures which we take for granted.
- We rarely pause to evaluate the appropriateness of our desires or consider toning them down; our entire focus is on fulfilling every desire which arises in our minds, whatever that desire may be.

All these are listed as major causes for both the degrading state of our planet as well as for our increasing personal disquietude. There is, of course, a lot of truth in this. Rapacious use of natural resources undoubtedly has grave consequences. And, despite being the most comfortable and the most empowered generation in the history of mankind, we yet lack peace and a sense of fulfilment. These are real problems and paradoxes but does their actual cause lie in our asking for too much?

Conventional wisdom would say 'yes' and then suggest that we curtail our desires or, better still, stamp them out to reach a state of no desires. However, barring in the cases of an exceptional few, desires keep arising in us despite all the advice and teaching we receive. And, anyway, even wanting to be without desires is itself a desire.

In this context, while Vedanta does initially focus on moderating, refining and balancing our desires, its ultimate teaching brings in a completely different perspective. In Vedanta's view, the real problem is not that we desire too much; the problem actually is that we desire too little!

Our incessant need for something more is driven by our little-understood but fundamental need to be without any limitations or boundaries. It is because of this natural urge that the most successful, the most powerful of people yet seek something different, something more. The most powerful of our politicians want more power, the most popular of our entertainment stars want more popularity and the wealthiest amongst us work even harder for more wealth.

We attempt to address this powerful and grand urge, the urge to be without any boundaries or limitations, with petty offerings of a little more money, a different vacation, a better relationship, some increase in fame or power and so on. Though these crumbs bring temporary relief, they can never satisfy our basic hunger which is to be free of all limitations.

Once we understand the futility of our usual attempts to fulfil this urge, we have to turn to Vedanta's wisdom for a radically different solution. Vedanta tells us that the urge to be limitless cannot be dismissed by calling it an aberration or an impossibility. This hunger is natural & universal and there is no hunger in nature without the means to satisfy it.

From this starting point, the core teachings of Vedanta take us on a journey of exploration of the reality underlying the entire world as well as our own selves. In this process we learn that we are much more than our body and mind. We discover that we are, in fact, the awareness in which and because of which everything exists; the very concepts of time and space themselves exist in this awareness. Our real nature is timeless and boundless. And it is so, here and now. We don't need to wait or to make an effort to create it, we only have to recognise it by proper understanding.

By wrongly limiting our identity to our bodies and minds, we are reduced to looking for small gains which lie within the scope of our limited efforts while the truth of what we are is already immeasurably vast and needs nothing more to be done or achieved.

By desiring limited goals, by desiring too little, we ruin our external and internal environments without ever reaching a state of true fulfilment. It is only when we desire much more, the limitless and the infinite, that we open the door which lets us discover that we already are the whole: boundless, ever-existing consciousness. This approach of Vedanta may sound quixotic, dreamy and impractical till we apply ourselves diligently to its amazing teachings with the help of a proper teacher. The journey of Vedanta can be demanding and time-consuming but then the pay-off is equally vast and the loss in not embarking upon it is incalculable—how does one value the limitless?

Even after the message of Vedanta has gone home for us, our life at the level of body and mind continues and we have wishes and preferences which we cater to, like any other person. The real transformation is not external but internal, where our desires are now not compulsions any more but just harmless preferences. It is nice if preferences are catered to but there is no anxiety, anger, hurt or pride whether they are fulfilled or not. And it is now possible for us to take the agendas centred around our bodies and minds lightly because we are firm in the knowledge of our own true nature which always remains unaffected.

So let's ask for and work towards much more than what we have been asking for so far—let's ask for freedom from any compulsion by discovering the reality of our own selves.

Some of us are sold on the idea that we have only this one life,
which must be used to experience pleasures
as rapidly and as frequently as possible.
This then becomes our foundational philosophy for living.
Though appealing, this 'philosophy' needs examination.

YOU ONLY LIVE ONCE

YOLO is the rather mellifluous term used on social media for *You Only Live Once*. This conclusion, that we all only have this one life, leads many to see pleasure as the primary aim of living. The young use it to rationalise impulsiveness or recklessness. For the aging, such thinking brings greater focus on their so-called 'bucket lists', more so when they see their peers getting sick or dying.

That life should be lived for pleasures, without concern for other goals and consequences, is not a new idea. The Latin phrase *carpe diem* (seize the day) comes from a pre-Christian Roman poet and echoes the same thinking: enjoy yourself while you can.

Even more telling is the following advice from the much older Indian philosophy of materialism (called *caravaka darshan*):

> *yavat jivet sukham jivet rinam kritva ghritam pibet*
> *bhasmi bhutasya dehasya punar agamanam kutaha*
>
> Live a pleasurable life till you live; drink ghee even if you have to incur debt.

Once your body is reduced to ashes, where is the question of coming back?

This, of course, is advice to concentrate on having a good time and forget other concerns or long-term consequences. In Sarva Siddhanta Samgraha (a work attributed to Adi Shankaracharya), the caravaka position on living for pleasures alone is set out even more graphically as:

> *"The enjoyment of heaven lies in eating delicious food, keeping company of young women, using fine clothes, perfumes, garlands, sandal paste... while moksha is death which is cessation of life-breath... the wise therefore ought not to take pains on account of moksha.*
>
> *A fool wears himself out by penances and fasts. Chastity and other such ordinances are laid down by clever weaklings."*

This line of thinking is convenient and pleasant (*caravaka* means 'agreeable speech') for the many who don't want to look beyond immediate pleasures. It, of course, has had a large line of adherents over the ages and its obvious appeal continues.

The conflict between indulging in what is merely pleasurable (*preyas*) and doing what is truly good (*shreyas*) is age-old and enduring. We experience this daily in both superficial as well as in more serious matters: Stay on at the party for a few more drinks or head home to be up for gym the next morning? Watch a mindless serial or read a thought-provoking book? Indulge in more fashions and gadgets for ourselves or contribute to a worthy cause? Cheat to make some quick money or live in keeping with the value of honesty? Work on finding a meaningful purpose to our lives or spend all our time in hedonistic pursuits and endless accumulation?

In most sections of society today, there is an accelerating shift, away from the good and towards the pleasurable. This is partly driven by marketing blitzes of economies which need to keep growing—they achieve this by keeping us dissatisfied with whatever we have and by continuously arousing new desires within us, irrespective of their validity or utility. To compound this, we get smitten by the onslaught of social media which creates for us an unrealistic view of life filled with perfect health, picture-postcard vacations, unending pleasures and no pain; this traps us into seeking a life of more & more, without any denials, without any postponement of gratifications and without any negative experiences.

Many of us have now been made to see such make-believe lives not only as real but also as our birth-right; we are driven to seek and expect non-stop superficial pleasures as both the norm and our entitlement. And it takes a rare one to caution against such unreal expectations. (An example is a leading Bollywood actor who debunked the myth of her own picture-perfect appearance by publicly saying, *"It takes an army, a lot of money, and an incredible amount of time to make a female celebrity look the way she does when you see her. It isn't realistic, and it isn't anything to aspire to."*)

What is the problem in seeking pleasure from a life which you only live once? On one plane, nothing at all. It is natural for us to seek pleasurable experiences and we undoubtedly experience satisfaction when our desires are fulfilled. But problems arise when we focus entirely on pleasures as the source of our fulfilment. These problems arise both from the limitations of pleasures themselves as well as from lack of balance between our obvious need for pleasure and our less obvious but more fundamental need for deeper meaning.

We know from our own experiences that while the world offers variety, novelties and pleasurable experiences, it unfortunately does not have stability. Nothing in this universe (from stars to atoms, from volcanoes to rainfall, from health to emotions, from wealth to love) is constant or dependable and this lack of stability denies us peace and security

Further, our experiences of pleasure are always at the mercy of the condition of our bodies, the state of our minds and the environment in which we find ourselves. A great music programme is not enjoyable if we have a splitting headache, a gourmet dinner provides no pleasure if we are engaged in a massive row with our companion and an outing is not fun if we are being constantly attacked by mosquitoes. As such matters are not always in our control, we frequently remain helpless onlookers as they rob us of our happiness.

But happiness, peace and security are our fundamental needs which can never be addressed by depending upon the unpredictable, the uncontrollable and the undependable. However, this is precisely what we do when we lead a life focused on drawing pleasure from the world.

Another issue is our unending sense of being wanting. However successful we may be, there is always something more we could do with or something which we would be happier to be rid of. Maybe more money, more fame and more hair on the head or less weight around the midriff, less conflict in relationships and less pollution in the environment. But try as much as we can, there is no end to the things we want more of and less of. So, the problem of want dogs us to the end of our days.

Also, whatever we achieve invariably comes with attendant problems which ultimately negate our sense of fulfilment. To obtain anything involves effort as well as something else forgone. Having achieved what we wanted, we are then saddled with the need to protect it and the fear of losing it. To add to this, once we achieve something, the initial pleasure soon wanes, our minds get bored and we start seeking higher or different avenues of pleasure and excitement. And when things pass, as they all do, there is of course pain and regret.

So, basing life on only grabbing pleasures and excitement is not enough unless we are content to accept a continuous see-saw of pleasure and pain.

And, even more fundamentally, a life focused on pleasure-hunting masks our basic problem which actually is wanting to be without any bounds or limits whatsoever. Whether we realise this or not, we are all naturally driven to seek total freedom—freedom from any limitations. This is why the sense of fulfilment we obtain from any limited achievement is only temporary; as someone once said, if we were made the owners & rulers of the entire earth, it wouldn't be too long before we would start hankering for domination over other planets!

Unfortunately many of us don't recognise this problem, which is the real problem behind all our other apparent problems, because indulging in pleasures temporarily provides an escape from our sense of want. But no amount of our limited efforts (no matter how much we accumulate and how many avenues of pleasure we find) can take us to our actual goal of limitlessness.

In this context, a great teacher of Vedanta, Swami Dayananda, used to tell a story about the ocean and its waves. In this story, individual ocean waves have human minds. These waves see from afar that all waves finally hit the shore and die, breaking up and completely losing their identity. Upon realising this, some waves accept their lot and passively wait for the end, others struggle in a futile attempt to avoid hitting the shore and some others devoutly pray to the ocean-god to save them. But the majority of waves, instead of taking cognisance of their impending end, turn their minds away from the inevitable; instead, they focus on enjoying the ride and having a good time while they can.

Only a few waves have the opportunity to be guided by a rare wise wave (a guru wave!) who explains to them that the reality of all waves is nothing but water. And water remains water, whether it is in the form of the ocean itself or in the form of individual waves or in the form of droplets & spray or as rain which feeds rivers and oceans. Upon becoming enlightened by such knowledge, these few waves then enjoy their life-span, secure in the knowledge that their real nature – water – will continue to exist even after their form as a wave is gone.

Just as in this story, many of us restrict ourselves to having a good time (using the YOLO rationalisation) and deliberately shut our eyes to the fact that our short lives will surely end. As Yudhishthir said in the Mahabharata, the greatest wonder in the world is that while all people know they will die, they carry on as if they will live forever. And many of us contribute to this wonder.

The only valid solution for a wave is to discover that its reality is water; similarly, our only real answer lies in realising that what we truly are is unchanging and boundless consciousness. Our individual bodies and minds are only temporary forms which appear in and of this consciousness, just as waves arise in and of water. Just as water remains water even when a wave is destroyed, our underlying truth of consciousness remains unaffected no matter what happens to our bodies and minds.

The discovery of this fact is a possibility uniquely available to us as humans.Our highest potential is not fulfilled by just surviving, breeding, enjoying ourselves or by accumulating possessions. It is only when we stop being preoccupied with our hunt for temporary pleasures that we can rise to the zenith of our growth and understanding; once this happens, we become free of fear and insecurity and, while we can still enjoy our usual pleasures, they no longer remain necessities which completely drive our lives.

The turn towards discovering our highest nature does have an element of luck or grace in it—the scriptures themselves tell us that to be born a human (*manushyatvam*), then to have the desire for liberation from all limitations (*mumukshutvam*) and then, finally, to find a proper teacher to help us obtain this freedom (*mahapurusha samshraya*) are all dependent on grace (*Ishwara anugraha*).

But this is not a prescription for sitting back and waiting for the doors of grace to open by themselves. Our traditions have again and again emphasised the role of wilful effort (*purushartha*) in our quest for ultimate freedom (*moksha*).

The same scriptures which mention the role of grace in our journey also say that a person who does not strive for self-liberation is like a person who commits suicide because he destroys himself by clinging to the unreal and impermanent; they further ask who could be more foolish than a person who neglects his own true good. So, both traditional wisdom as well as our own self-interest should impel us to make efforts which go beyond just picking up bits of passing pleasures.

Finally, questioning the wisdom of the 'eat, drink and make merry' line of thinking does not mean proposing asceticism and denial of all forms of pleasure. What is in question is living for pleasure as a primary approach to life. Usual forms of pleasure and satisfaction are perfectly normal as long as they are legitimate and within our proper means. However, as we grow up (hopefully in maturity as well as in age), our focus should change to deeper and more permanent avenues of fulfilment, culminating in proper self-knowledge which finally erases all notions of limitations and bondage.

There are many things that can bring great benefits as well as great trouble. For example, antibiotic drugs have saved countless lives but their indiscriminate use has now produced drug-resistant pathogens which cause untreatable disease. Our sense of individuality is also equally capable of taking us to the pinnacle of our growth or of totally blighting our lives.

THE PRIVILEGE AND THE CRUSHING WEIGHT OF INDIVIDUALITY

The sense of individuality (the sense of 'I-ness' or ego) which we all have is a unique aspect of our make-up as humans. And it is an aspect which drives us powerfully; it results in many of us spending our lives catering to this identity of ours which constantly demands fulfilment in one form or the other.

When our individuality assumes disproportionate importance, it becomes a fulcrum around which we expect the entire world to function. With self-centeredness which becomes overgrown, our individuality becomes a liability, a crushing weight under which we labour till the end of our days.

Our traditions help us to moderate the negative effects of an overblown ego by a set of religious and secular mechanisms, broadly termed *karma yoga*. In addition to the valuable prescriptions of karma yoga, we can also use our current knowledge of science to retain perspective of our place in the grand scheme of things and help us to temper our excessive self-importance. In this context, let us remind ourselves of a few aspects of astro-physics and quantum mechanics which could be helpful.

Cosmology tells us that the earth is about 4.5 billion years old. We, *Homo sapiens*, showed up less than 300,000 years ago and our entire recorded history is only 5,000 years old, a period which is barely measurable on the cosmic scale of things.

In the very brief time that our species has been around, we first thought that our planet was the centre of the universe. We then learned that the earth is only one of the mid-sized planets orbiting the sun. We next thought that at least our sun was unique in its size and power till we figured that it was an unremarkable star in one of the arms of a galaxy of several arms.

Our galaxy, the Milky Way, is reckoned to have more than 100 billion stars. Many of these stars have planetary systems of their own, just like our sun. Some of these planets in other solar systems resemble the earth in overall properties and could potentially harbour life. So, from the perspective of just our own galaxy, our own solar system is not particularly noteworthy.

We had also once presumed that our galaxy was the entire universe, till we discovered that the Milky Way is merely an ordinary galaxy in an undistinguished portion of the known universe. Our universe is currently estimated to have some 100 billion galaxies or more.

Apart from the stupendous number of galaxies it contains, our universe is also vast in terms of distances—it is currently thought to be 92 billion light years in diameter. One light year is almost 10 trillion kilometres so this size is well beyond our usual comprehension.

We also now conclude, based on theoretical science, that apart from visible matter and measurable energy, the universe must also contain mysterious (unseen and unmeasurable) dark matter as well as dark energy which far outweigh the matter and energy apparent to us.

Finally, scientists are now grappling with the idea that just as the known creation is not restricted to a single planet or to a single solar system or to a single galaxy, it is entirely possible that the totality of creation is much more than a single universe. There may be countless other entire universes, the so-called multiverse, which we know nothing about.

And there is an equally fantastic set-up at the other end of this gigantic scale: the quantum world. Here invisible atoms resemble minute solar systems, subatomic particles are mysteriously waves at the same time, and where things are measured on the unbelievably small Planck scale. Here the conventional laws of physics cease to operate (for instance, in a phenomenon called quantum entanglement, two separated particles communicate with each other faster than the speed of light) and matter can be converted into energy.

In this incredible range of scales and unfathomable complexity lives an individual – the super-special, the super-important 'I' – whose dreams, achievements, emotions, relationships, possessions and problems are so, so important. So very important that they eclipse the magnificence, mystery, scope, scale, variety and beauty of the entire cosmos.

Our blind rush to shore up and defend our fragile ego-driven lives makes us lose our connection with the larger whole. We forget that everything, including us, is made from the same star dust, that the molecule of oxygen in our lungs right now was once part of a dinosaur or the emperor Akbar. And the very same molecule will remain even after we die, as part of some future object or living being. Our egos also make us forget not only the insignificance of our individual lives but that our entire human race may only be a fleeting and quirky wrinkle on the fabric of creation, which may be ironed out in a jiffy, without any real meaning or consequence.

Another interesting aspect of an ego-centric life is a great deal of concern with our prospective non-existence in the form of death, but no concern about our non-existence prior to our birth. If we are fearful about missing out on all the experiences after we die, should we not also be concerned about all that we missed before we were born? There is immeasurable time both before and after our own life-times; our lives are only momentary flickers in this vastness of time but they assume unwarranted importance because of an overdeveloped sense of individuality.

Does this mean that we should give up all aspirations, forsake all activities and wallow helplessly in our insignificance, fatalistically waiting for our death? Not at all. On the contrary, the privilege of human life, however brief, has to be used for exploration, joy and fulfilment. But here lies the rub: in which direction, by what method and towards which goal should we look for these things?

Our usual tendency is to look outwards, to look for fulfilment from the world. Our usual methods are to accumulate and protect what we like and drive away what we dislike. Our usual goal is to cater to the desires of our bodies &

minds and, most of all, of our egos. However, these tendencies, methods and goals are both petty and temporary—the sense of fulfilment we experience by employing them never satisfies fully or permanently. But full and permanent satisfaction are our fundamental needs, hard-wired into us. So we land up in a situation which is untenable.

Restricting our focus to just 'I', 'Me' and 'Mine' is not a simple error which we can gloss over because 'everybody else is doing the same thing'. It has two sets of consequences, one of which is apparent and the other less apparent, though more fundamental.

The apparent consequences include fear, struggle, living for the approval of others, anger, hostility and regret. We fear disease, loneliness, loss of money, loss of reputation and, of course, death. We constantly struggle to accumulate, to enjoy and to protect. We become petty, filling our time with superficial pleasures & concerns, upset by the smallest of irritations, lacking empathy for others and having no sense of connection with a larger whole.

Because we lack a greater purpose, because we fail to find worthwhile meaning and because we never experience satisfaction which is complete and lasting, we judge ourselves as constantly lacking. The resulting insecurity makes us seek reassurance by the approval of others in what we wear, where we are seen, with whom we associate and even in the way in which we think. Frequent disappointment & anger are our reactions to not being able to mould the world to our wishes and to our frustrating lack of total happiness. Hostility towards others, whom we see as the cause of our plight, and regret for not having handled things differently naturally follow.

More fundamental than all this is another consequence of our infatuation with our own individualities: our ego-based preoccupations deny us the opportunity to discover the truth of our own real nature. We can spend our entire lives wrapped up in our egos, fully occupied by our efforts to pander to them. We can then end up with ongoing emotional turmoil as a result of our continuous strife to extract joy from a world which is often not co-operative. This leaves us with no time, energy or openness to look at a different perspective of life and of our true place in it. We miss out on making the most remarkable of all discoveries—the truth of our own selves. And this loss is all the more tragic because we humans, with our special sense of self-awareness and high intelligence, are the only beings capable of this discovery.

And this is where Vedanta comes in. It first helps us to get less obsessed by our petty needs and motivations, all of which are centred on our egos. Once this is done and some balance and openness are restored to us, Vedanta offers its amazing insights into the truth of ourselves and our world. Its vision is unique and its assimilation requires an eligible student, guided by a competent teacher using a time-tested teaching methodology.

At the end of this process we realise how pathetically wrong we were in letting ourselves be stage-managed by our egos when our truth is so much above and beyond our ego-based fears and wants.

It is not that the knowledge imparted by Vedanta will erase all the problems or the wants of our individualities. What it does is to expand our perspective so that we realise our truth to be ever-existent and boundless consciousness. Once this becomes convincingly clear, issues revolving around our individuality are no more seen as viscerally vital matters. We find freedom not by denying or solving all our usual problems but by rising so far above them that problems at an individual level lose their importance.

As children we may have been really upset by the loss of a toy but the same event leaves us unruffled as adults. Or, it may seem dark and gloomy under an overcast sky till we fly up through the clouds to be in bright sunshine. It is growth in maturity and expansion of perspective which converts problems into non-issues.

It is up to us to carry our individuality as a crushing weight under which we fruitlessly labour our entire lives. Or we can use it as a privilege to be used for gaining true freedom—freedom by growth in our knowledge & perspective, by gaining proper understanding of our own real nature which is not restricted to the bag of skin, memories and emotions which we wrongly take ourselves to be. The choice is ours.

On the face of it, the Vedic religion seems to support belief in a bewildering array of gods and goddesses. It is therefore considered polytheistic and contrary to the monotheism of the Abrahamic faiths. But the truth is different and not even many followers of the Vedic religion appreciate it.

HOW MANY GODS?

One Size Does Not Fit All

When it comes to providing its concept of god, the Vedic religion does not go by the 'one-size-fits-all' model of many other religions. Being flexible and practical, it recognises that people have different needs, depending upon their emotional and intellectual development. These needs are unlikely to be met by a single god. It, therefore, provides three separate concepts of god, pitched at differing levels of understanding. Its three presentations are of god as:

- *Eka roopa* (single form),
- *Vishwa roopa* (universal form), and
- *Aroopa* (formless).

Personal God

The *eka roopa* or single form of god is the easiest to relate to. Here, the idea of god is personified and captured in the form of deities like Vishnu, Laxmi, Shiva, Paravati, Ganesh, Rama and Krishna. These are shown as individual gods with human forms and qualities. They often display extraordinary features (such as four arms or an extra eye) and supernatural powers. Many stories conveying ethical values, centred around such gods, are found in popular scriptures like the Puranas, the Ramayana and the Mahabharata. These deities portray very different personalities and one is free to pick a version which suits one's psyche, for the purpose of worship and emotional connection.

Universal God

Vishwa roopa or the universal form is a more evolved concept of god as the entire universe. Here, god is understood as both the material cause and the intelligent cause of creation (*jagat nimitta upadana karanam*)—if we were to take the example of a pot, it would be like combining the clay and the potter into one entity. In this vision, god is not limited to a single form but is seen as the totality, as the basis of everything which exists. He is often referred to as *Ishwara* and is seen to pervade the entire world. In this concept, which is unique to the Vedic tradition, there are not many gods, there is not even one god—there is only god, there is nothing but god.

As such a universal god is the material and the intelligence behind every single object and phenomenon, there is nothing which is profane. Because everything is part and parcel of divinity, everything becomes sacred. Based on this understanding, one can anoint one's own forehead with a *tilak*, greet others reverentially with a *namaste* (from *namas* meaning 'bowing' and *te* meaning 'to you'), place a stone on an altar for prayer, treat plants & animals as divine and deify the sun, the moon, stars, rivers and mountains. It does not matter what one chooses for worship when one recognises that everything is based on a single cause.

Ultimate Divinity

Beyond this, the final and the most evolved concept of god is *aroopa*—without the limitation of any form. Here, god is not even seen as the basis of the universe. In this highest vision of god, the universe itself is understood to be unreal, being only a temporary and insubstantial superimposition on a fundamental reality. This fundamental reality is the only thing which actually exists. It is changeless and boundless consciousness which is without any attributes *(nirguna)* and form *(aroopa)*. It is the only truth, the truth of the universe and the truth of us, the individuals. This is the highest form of divinity in the vision of our sages. And being attributeless and formless there is no way in which we can conceive of it or transact with it, not even by prayer. The only thing for us to do with this exalted idea of god, labelled as *brahman*, is to recognise it as the truth of our own selves and abide in it in a state of peace and fulfilment.

The Nataraja Tells All

All these three concepts of divinity are beautifully portrayed in the figure of the Nataraja which is possibly the most evolved icon in our culture. The Nataraja is a representation of Shiva and its idol supports multiple ideas and messages at different levels of complexity.

The Nataraja As Personified God

At its most basic level, the Nataraja is the image of the god Shiva in the form of a dancer. We turn to any god because he is powerful, majestic, benign and protective. And the Nataraja depicts all these qualities. His power is apparent in many ways. He casually lets fearsome snakes entwine his body. He wears the moon itself as a mere bauble on his head-gear. He stands unharmed within a circle of fire and holds a flame on his bare palm. He pins a demon underfoot.

His majesty is shown by his crown, his ornamentation and his assertive stance. His benign and protective nature is depicted by the benedictive gesture of one hand (known as the *abhaya mudra*) and by his trapping an inimical creature underfoot. He re-assures us by his serene face with a gentle smile. He invites us to seek the shelter of his feet by the fingers of another hand pointing to his raised foot.

The Nataraja, as god in a single form, provides a great idol for worship.

The Nataraja As Universal God

The imagery of the Nataraja gets more complex at the next level—of god in his universal form. Let us begin with how the Nataraja shows god as the substance of entire creation. One of the models of the universe which our scriptures hold out, lists five primary elements as the constituents of everything which exists. These are earth *(prithvi)*, water *(apa)*, fire *(agni)*, air *(vayu)* and space *(akasha)*. The Nataraja shows all these five elements: earth is represented by the very material of the idol, water by the small feminine figure of the river Ganga in his hair, fire by the flame which he is holding, air by the wind which makes his hair fly and, finally, space by the drum in his hand (because a drum's sound can be heard only if propagated through space). In this way, god is shown as the material cause of the entire creation.

But what about god as the efficient or the intelligent cause of the universe? This is cleverly shown by the dance of the Nataraja, which represents creation. Dance is not random movement but involves intelligent order. Dance is the creation of a conscious dancer. But the dance analogy tells us much more than god being like the potter who is the intelligent cause behind the pot.

Unlike the pot where the material cause (clay) is different from its intelligent cause (the potter), dance is nothing but the dancer as it exists only in and through him. Here, there is no separation between the material and intelligent causes. Further, while dance is totally dependent on the dancer, the dancer is completely independent and continues to exist even when there is no dance. Thus, the Nataraja's dance symbolises creation to be dependent on and subsumed by its intelligent creator, Ishwara, who himself is entirely independent. As there is no part of the dance separated from the dancer, there is nothing in the universe which is not Ishwara. It also shows us that, just as a dancer has full knowledge of and control over the dance, Ishwara too has all knowledge and power to generate, pervade and dissolve the universe. Another important feature that the Nataraja highlights through his dance is our tendency to get taken in by name and form rather than substance. We can get so captivated by the movements of the dance and so engrossed in its enjoyment that we begin to look upon dance as if it is a substantial and independent entity; but dance is actually just a name given to a form of the dancer. Through this example, the Nataraja reminds us that the world too is just names and forms and we must not lose sight of Ishwara, the underlying reality. (As we will see later, Ishwara is held out as the reality behind the world only as an interim step before we realise the ultimate reality, brahman.)

How To Live

The Nataraja also provides several valuable lessons about how to live in this world. The basis of a well-lived life is a life of *dharma*, a life in keeping with natural order and universal values. The demon shown beneath the foot of Nataraja is called Apasmara and stands for our ego, *adharmic* propensities and negativity. By keeping him pinned down, the Nataraja tells us that we need to keep our undesirable qualities in check. This is easier said than done and the difficulty of leading a life of dharma and the skill required to do so is shown by the Nataraja dancing on just one foot, while his other foot is subjugating a writhing demon.

A life of dharma is necessary but not enough. To reach our highest potential, we need to go beyond dharma, to something higher. This is shown by the raised foot of the Nataraja, pointed out by one of his hands. This is a pointer to something beyond this world, to something which transcends our usual life. This is a call for a journey of spirituality, a journey to discover the truth of ourselves, of the world and of god—a journey to brahman. Such a journey is a demanding one, requiring not only control over our negative qualities but also energy, discrimination and insights.

Energy is represented by snakes coiled on the Nataraja and these snakes stand for the coiled (latent) energy within us. Discrimination is portrayed by one of his hands which resembles the extended trunk of an elephant—the elephant is considered to be the wisest of all animals and its trunk is a powerful and sensitive instrument of discrimination. Further, the Nataraja's third eye in the centre of his forehead, also speaks of extraordinary sight or insight into things beyond the obvious. All these are important resources required for our spiritual journey.

The Nataraja As Brahman

We finally come to god as being without any form, attributes or boundaries. This is obviously impossible to depict in a positive way so the Nataraja shows us this highest truth of divinity, called brahman, by showing opposing qualities which cancel out each other. The opposing qualities which are displayed by the Nataraja to convey the idea of no qualities are:

- Male vs Female—these opposite aspects are shown by the different earrings worn by the Nataraja on each one of his two ears, where one ring is more ornamented & feminine and the other is simpler & more masculine.
- Action vs Inaction—action is depicted by the dance and the hair flying in a frenzy of activity while rest is portrayed by a remarkably serene face and hooded eyes.
- Creation vs Dissolution—creation is shown both by the dance (a creative effort) and by the drum signifying the sound of *Om*, the primordial sound with which creation is stated to have started; the polar opposite of dissolution comes from the all-consuming fire surrounding the idol as well from the Nataraja's third eye which represents Shiva's destructive power (in addition to his power of insight).

Further, the Nataraja also mirrors the assertion of the upanishads that brahman is *satyam jnanam anantam* (unchanging existence which is conscious and boundless). The idol's very presence denotes existence. Next, dance involves knowledge & action which are associated with a conscious being; so, by his dance, the Nataraja displays the consciousness aspect of brahman. Finally, for a thing to be limited it must have some attributes which give it limiting characteristics and boundaries; the Nataraja, by displaying attributes which cancel out each other (as we have just seen), indicates the boundless nature of brahman. The consequence of being without limits is total fulfilment (because nothing more can be added to the limitless) and this too is shown by the Nataraja's smile and his joyous dance called the *ananda tandav*.

More Than Meets The Eye

At first glance the Vedic religion appears to be polytheistic with a confusing array of many gods, including some which appear bizarre; people are also puzzled by its apparently primitive aspects of animal and nature worship. It is only when we understand the rationale behind why and how divinity is portrayed in so many different ways in our culture that we are able to appreciate the practicality and the sophistication behind this multi-layered presentation.

The journey of Vedanta is supported by a meaningful relationship with Ishwara. *In this relationship, we often expect an infallible* Ishwara *to give us what we consider to be our fair and just dues. When this does not happen, we begin to doubt his infallibility and justness.*

INFALLIBLE *ISHWARA*

All creation needs two types of causes. If we look at a clay pot as an example of a creation, both the potter (the intelligent cause) and clay (the material cause) are needed. Further, in our experience, both these causes are always different—the potter and clay are not the same.

However, when it comes to the entire universe, advaita Vedanta has a different view: in its vision, the creator of the universe (who is termed *Ishwara*) is both its intelligent and material cause rolled into one. We will not get into the reasons for this view because that is not the topic here. Suffice it to say that having a material cause which is separate from the intelligent cause, for creation taken as a whole, would raise serious logical problems. Leaving aside these issues, it is easy to see that if we accept Ishwara as the combined intelligent and material cause of everything, he must necessarily have certain extraordinary qualities.

Any intelligent cause must have knowledge of what is to be created—the potter must have pot-knowledge in order to make the pot. So, the creator of the entire universe – Ishwara – must have knowledge of everything. Thus, omniscence becomes a necessary quality of Ishwara.

Next, the material entirely pervades whatever is made out of it—there is no part of the pot where clay is not present. Similarly, there can be no part of the universe – the good, the bad or the ugly – where Ishwara is not present. In other words, Ishwara has to be all-pervading. (When a scripture like the Bhagavad Gita has Krishna declaring that among immovable objects he is the Himalayas and the Ganga among rivers, this should not be taken to mean that Ishwara does not pervade a small clod of earth or the water in a drain. Such statements are poetic and designed to glorify divinity for the purpose of worship—it is far easier to have a worshipful attitude towards divinity which is compared to the Ganga than to drain water.)

Further, the material cause is independent of creation while creation is entirely dependent on its cause—clay can exist on its own but the pot cannot exist without the clay. Similarly, the universe is entirely dependent upon Ishwara but he remains independent of the universe.

Ishwara's nature is beautifully shown by some forms of divinity in our culture, such as the Nataraja. Nataraja is depicted as a dancer and there is purpose behind this depiction. The dancer has full knowledge of the dance, he pervades the dance and yet he is independent of the dance—the dancer exists even when he is not dancing but there can be no dance without the dancer. In a similar way, in relation to the entire universe, Ishwara is omniscient, all-pervading and independent.

The dancer analogy shows one more aspect of Ishwara: that Ishwara is all-powerful. Just as a dancer can choose to dance or not to dance, how to dance and when to stop, Ishwara too has all power and control in relation to the universe.

So we now have an idea of Ishwara who is all-knowing, all-pervading, all-powerful and independent of the universe. With all these qualities in limitless measure, Ishwara is then naturally understood to be infallible—he can never fail to do whatever he wants to do.

To be able to emotionally relate with Ishwara (during worship, for instance), we find it useful to envisage him as a person who rules his universe with human qualities like judgement, preferences and the ability to make choices. And because we see this supreme person as being infallible, we expect him to deliver our desired results, as long as we fulfil what we think is our part of the bargain with him.

So, as we pray to Ishwara, make him offerings and lead an ethical life, we expect to be rewarded by circumstances conducive to our desires. This, of course, does not always happen and we face disappointment when we can't have what we want or can't get rid of what we don't want. When faced with such disappointments in major areas of life, many of us feel let down—an all-knowing, all-powerful, compassionate and fair creator & ruler of our universe could have and should have supported us.

The idea of an infallible Ishwara, unless properly understood, can easily get linked to our frustrated desires, creating some serious misunderstanding. Our disappointments can take us to the point where we now see him as cruel or capricious or indifferent; we may also begin to doubt his very existence or decide that even if he exists, we don't want to deal with him. It is in this context that we need to properly understand what the infallibility of Ishwara actually means.

Contrary to our notions, the infallibility of Ishwara is not reflected in our expectations or in future events but is manifested in each and every actual happening. To put it in different words, **Ishwara is infallible in the sense that the infallible is Ishwara.** And the only things which are beyond doubt or failure are things which have actually happened. So, Ishwara's infallibility is expressed in actual events and situations, in things which have already come to pass.

What does this mean for us in practice? This means that we should learn to accept every result, every situation and every event that has actually happened as Ishwara's giving, as his *prasada*. When these results are not to our liking, we should accept them without asking '*Why me?*' or complaining about injustice. It is interesting to note how we resent happenings which are not in line with our wishes, even as we seem to readily accept Ishwara's doings. So, when something that we want happens we say "It is Ishwara's *grace*" but when something unwanted happens our statement changes to "It is Ishwara's *will*".

In this context, we have to realise that though we look upon Ishwara as a person for our emotional needs, he is actually not an individual like us, doing things based on personal choice. Ishwara is the impersonal order which runs through the universe, producing appropriate effects as a consequence of innumerable past actions. And this chain of causes and effects is very complex, affects everything and can be spread over a very long period of time. It is not possible for us to identify what causes led to a specific event which we may be experiencing now.

And this order is impartial, infallible and appropriate. So, as we grow in our understanding and in emotional maturity, we begin to serenely receive results even if they are contrary to our expectations. In fact, if we are truly committed to our own evolution, we should look upon unpleasant outcomes as opportunities for our internal growth. Whatever be the results we enjoy or suffer, we learn to take them with equanimity because they are our *prasada* from Ishwara, the universal order. This graceful acceptance of what actually happens is the real acknowledgement of Ishwara's infallibility. This is a very important part of an enriching set of actions and attitudes called *karma* yoga.

We can, of course, choose to believe that there is no such universal order and it is only randomness which sometimes gives us desirable situations and sometimes the opposite. If we want to ignore the order visible in every aspect of creation, from the functioning of subatomic particles and living cells to stars and galaxies, nothing much more can be said. However, if we recognise and appreciate this infallible order, we acknowledge Ishwara for what he really is; and, even more important to us personally, we can begin to relax in the knowledge that what has happened had to happen and what will happen in the future will not be random or unfair. We may not get what we desire but we will get what we deserve.

This understanding of Ishwara as universal order does not mean passivity and fatalism. Our actions do have consequences either sooner or later. Therefore, there is every reason for us to do, with vigour, whatever is right and appropriate in a given situation. Appropriate action is in our domain but we do not have total control over their results because results are affected by a whole host of past actions which we cannot even remember, as well as by the actions of others.

Here, we should bear in mind that any form of prayer is also a volitional action which will have its effect, in some form or the other, now or later. Therefore, prayer is both beneficial and an intelligent activity: beneficial because it adds one more element of action towards our desired goals and intelligent because it acknowledges that there is always that 'x' factor in our affairs, beyond our knowledge and control, which we try to get on our side through prayer.

Later, when we study Vedanta further, we come to realise that the entire universe does not possess absolute reality for reasons which Vedanta goes to great lengths to explain. As a creator and his creation share the same level of reality, the universe's lack of absolute reality also extends to Ishwara. In other words, like the universe, Ishwara too is not absolutely real. And while Vedanta does state this (blasphemous as it may sound), we cannot use this statement to circumvent the necessity of our relating to Ishwara.

Why do we need to bother about an Ishwara who is not absolutely real? The reason for this is simple. Ishwara is as real or as unreal as the universe. We, the individuals, are an integral part of this universe. To deny absolute reality to the universe (which is what Vedanta ultimately does), we also have to deny absolute reality to our individual selves. But it is very difficult for us, at least in the early stages of our spiritual journey, to not take our plans, hopes, fears, desires and emotions very seriously. And the moment we give validity to our individual selves, we simultaneously impart the same reality to the universe and to its creator, Ishwara.

Further, in order to clearly appreciate Vedanta's teachings, we need to cultivate a mind not rent by overpowering likes & dislikes and not buffeted by uncontrollable emotions. To achieve this we all need a way to process our emotions; relating to Ishwara, who provides an altar where we can voice our hopes, fears and resentments without inhibitions, is invaluable in this process.

In our journey towards the recognition of *nirguna brahman* as our reality, we need the help and blessings of *saguna brahman* – Ishwara – whom we pray to and whose infallibility we properly understand.

Teachers and books start the teaching of Vedanta using different topics like happiness, god, the meaning of life and so on. Why are different starting points used? Does it matter for what personal reason we initially take interest in Vedanta?

UNRAVELLING THE KNITTING

Pulling on any one strand of yarn is enough to ultimately unravel a whole sweater. Our ignorance of matters related to Vedanta is also like a knitted garment—all its strands are inter-connected and tugging on any one of them leads to the undoing of the whole. This is why teachers of Vedanta can pick up any of our questions or problems to start their teaching.

What are the usual strands which are selected to commence an inquiry into Vedanta? They are many and varied, depending upon the specific issues bothering an individual student or an aspect that the teacher himself chooses to use as a launch-pad. Let us look at some of them.

Happiness or Fulfilment: This is probably the most common thread leading to Vedanta. We all look for happiness or fulfilment. We of course experience happiness from time to time but it is never complete and permanent. We are constantly looking for more joy, peace and contentment; we also want to get rid of fear, anger, regret, guilt, insecurity and hostility. When our search for happiness is not fully catered to by our usual means then we may knock on the doors of Vedanta to find a solution. We are further tempted when we hear words like supreme bliss and *ananda* used in the context of Vedanta. Such words lead us to hope that Vedanta may succeed where all our other efforts have failed. Also, apart from the lure of usual joy, we are further intrigued by the notion that Vedanta may give us an experience of some rarefied and extra-ordinary level of joy, hitherto not experienced by us. Thus, our search for happiness is probably the most common starting point for many Vedantic journeys.

Mortality: To exist, to live on is a primal urge in all human beings. One reason why a few voluntarily seek death is excessive pain or unhappiness which militates against the equally visceral urge to be happy. Some others willingly go to their deaths for a larger cause, dedicating themselves to which gives them a special sense of fulfilment. Apart from such extraordinary situations, everyone wants to live. So, the fear of death and the need to know what (if anything) happens after death become compelling reasons for some to take interest in Vedanta. On top of this, when we hear that Vedanta claims that our true self is immortal, that provides another strong reason to check out Vedanta.

Perennial Questions: There are some age-old questions which occur to all of us from time to time. For some of us these questions go beyond occasional doubts and become serious enough to warrant significant effort in trying to find answers. People with this bend of mind often turn to Vedanta to see if they can find satisfying solutions here. Let us take a quick look at some of these perennial questions:

Who Am I?

Many of us wonder who or what we actually are. Are we limited to a body and mind which goes into oblivion upon death? Is there a soul which survives death and continues either in a different world or is re-born in this world with a new body? There are conflicting answers to these questions. Also, we sometimes find ourselves happy and sometimes miserable, sometimes angry and sometimes peaceful. Are we this continuous flux or is there a steady basis to us? We naturally want to know the truth of our own selves and turn to Vedanta in the hope that it will provide clear answers.

Is There A God?

Our religions tell us that there is a creator who created the world and supervises its running. But different religions have very different ideas of who or what god is. So which one is true? And as we don't actually see god, we can only infer him from his orderly creation, much as we can infer a potter when we see a pot. But this analogy has problems. The potter has clay available to him but, before any creation, from where could god get his raw materials? Also, if god is all-merciful, all-powerful and all-knowing (as we are told), why are there defects, problems and evil in god's creation? So, *"Is there a god?"* and *"What is the nature of god?"* are questions which have perplexed humans from time immemorial and a search for answers here leads some of us to Vedanta.

What Is The Goal Of Life?
For some people making a living, fulfilling the obligations of their various social roles, taking the dog for a walk, being entertained by events on a screen before going to bed and repeating this cycle the next day seem to be enough. They are not troubled by the need to find a larger context or meaning for their lives. But some others cannot help being afflicted by existential doubts and they have to find out whether their lives are just short and banal incidents or are they part of a grander, more meaningful scheme. Such questions again open the door to Vedanta.

Are Our Lives Run By Fate Or Free Will?
This question also has been the subject of countless debates without a clear conclusion. Many events in life seem to happen purely out of blind chance or destiny. A child is born with a horrible disease, someone is struck by an accident despite being cautious, some people are gifted with exceptional beauty and skills, somebody wins a large lottery prize not only once but twice! In all these matters, our free will and effort clearly have no role. On the other hand, there are so many areas where our free will has the determining role. Should we be vegetarian or non-vegetarian? Sleep for that extra half an hour or get up and meditate? Stay on with that comfortable job or take a risk with something entrepreneurial? In all these matters we clearly experience our free will. So questions remain. To add to this confusion we hear about the karma theory which brings in both free will *(purushartha)* and fate *(prarabdha)*. And if it is both, then which is more dominant? Once again, Vedanta looks like a promising door to knock on for answers.

What Matters
Finally, what really matters is entering the edifice of Vedanta. The door chosen for entry is not important because once we get into Vedanta and apply ourselves diligently to its teachings with the guidance of a proper teacher, the ignorance which Vedanta targets will unravel.

Traditionally, three scriptures are considered crucial for the study of Vedanta. A look at their place in Vedanta's scheme is useful.

THREE GATEWAYS

The teachings of Vedanta are contained in a large collection of Sanskrit literature. The apex of this collection is three scriptures which are of prime importance. These three are the upanishads, the Brahma Sutras and the Bhagavad Gita. In the study of Vedanta, they are collectively referred to as *prasthana trayi*, meaning three gateways. (The direct meaning of *prasthana* is leaving or departing but the implied meaning here is entering a gateway or starting a journey and these three scriptures are considered to be the principal entrances into Vedanta.)

The upanishads, which are portions of the Vedas themselves, are the first and foremost out of this prime set of texts. The Vedas are the oldest and the most authoritative scriptures in our tradition. They are not ascribed to any known authors and are looked upon as revealed texts because the knowledge contained in them became available to ancient *rishis* by what tradition regards as divine revelation.

The upanishads are the origin of and the undisputed authority for Vedanta's insights. In fact, as far as Vedanta is concerned, the upanishads are the only full-fledged and unique means for knowing the true nature of our own selves. Within the prasthana trayi, the upanishads are known as *shruti prasthana* (revealed texts) or *updesha prasthana* (injunctive texts).

A total of 108 upanishads are yet available to us though the original number, now lost to time, was far larger. Ten of these upanishads are considered to be principal upanishads because Adi Shankaracharya wrote commentaries on them.

Next in the hierarchy of the prasthana trayi come the Brahma Sutras. An ancient sage known as Badarayana reduced the essence of the upanishads to concise and logically arranged aphorisms and this collection of 555 brief statements is known as the Brahma Sutras.The Brahma Sutras are termed *nyaya prasthana* or *yukti prasthana* because of their extensive use of arguments and logic.

Even though the Brahma Sutras are well-organised, they are still very difficult to understand because of their brevity and references to the contents of the upanishads in a way which is not apparent to the lay reader (a bit like French wine labels which are fully intelligible only to aficionados who already know facts not made apparent on these labels!).

The last (but not least) in this set of three scriptures is the well-known Bhagavad Gita. It is termed as both *sadhana prasthana* (practical text) and *smriti prasthana* (remembered text).

The Gita, which has 700 verses, is a small part of a very large work of 100,000 verses called the Mahabharata, authored by the famous sage Vyasa. The Gita is much easier to read and to understand compared to the upanishads and the Brahma Sutras; its setting and tone are more practical and readily applicable to daily life and its problems. A significant portion of its contents deals with preparatory matters like devotion and proper understanding of actions and their results. Because of its qualities, its beautiful poetry and emphasis on the concept of a personified god, for a majority of Hindus the Gita is the only Vedantic text that they ever get exposed to.

All the founders of the three major schools of Vedanta (Adi Shankaracharya, Ramanujacharya, and Madhvacharya) wrote *bhashyas* (commentaries) on these three texts. Of these, Shankaracharya was the most prolific *bhashyakara* (commentator) and we have available to us his bhashyas on ten Upanishads, the Brahma Sutras and the Bhagavad Gita. These are invaluable materials for understanding the original texts.

In addition to bhashyas, teachers and commentators have produced other types of works such as *karikas* which are independent expositions on an original text. The Mandukya Karika, which expounds on the Mandukya Upanishad, is one such important work containing the pinnacle of Vedanta's insights; it is the only work written by Gaudapada (who was the teacher of Shankaracharya's teacher) which is available to us even now.

Apart from the prasthana trayi, there is another whole category of writing which revolves around a specific subject, as against the contents of an original text. Works in this genre are called *prakarana* and they are in the nature of a dissertation on a chosen topic (which could be just one facet of Vedanta or its entire scope). They can be very long and detailed (like Vivekachudamani – attributed with controversy to Adi Shankaracharya – which has 581 verses); others can be concise and yet encapsulate the basic teachings of Vedanta (like the 53 verses of Vakya Vritti also ascribed to Shankaracharya). Prakarana books exist in large numbers and grow continuously by works of new authors in every age.

In addition to the traditional listing of categories of Vedantic texts mentioned above, we also have some modern works which do not fall within these categories. These books are compilations of conversations with men of great wisdom who had full understanding of the deepest teachings of Vedanta, but who did not focus on producing elaborate and formal texts. These collections are put together by students and translators associated with men like Ramana Maharshi and Nisargadatta Maharaj. Some works of this category contain piercing insights which ring so clearly of timeless truths that they are a joy to read

How does one approach or start with this mass of Vedantic literature? There are no simple answers here. The primary texts, the upanishads, were never meant to be available for study by any curious passer-by. They are couched in such language and have such a mystical flavour that for any beginner to just read their bare texts is not only quite meaningless but could also lead to premature and false conclusions or bring about disdain for their contents.

The upanishads are more like a collection of snapshots of great truths rather than structured arguments. They contain transcendental flashes of spiritual brilliance. But, contrary to popular belief, every sentence in the upanishads is not a statement of the final and absolute truth. There are many tentative approaches, interesting debates as well as stories and anecdotes, many of which emphasise questioning and seeking more than just providing bald answers. Their unusual and subtle truths are meant for those who combine a driving thirst for their knowledge along with a level of intellectual and emotional preparation; others are likely to fail in understanding their true message and also face the risk of drawing wrong understanding.

The best thing of course is to have selected upanishads gradually and consistently unfolded to us by an illumined teacher from the basis of his personal experience; this is how they were designed to be taught. However, given the difficulty in spending too much time with a teacher and the ready availability of scores of books on the upanishads, it would be unrealistic to suggest that one should read nothing on one's own. If possible, only what is recommended by the teacher should be read. If one must read in an unguided fashion then one should begin with prakarana works like Atma Bodha, Vakya Vritti and Vivekachudamani; in due course, one can then try and read some of the shorter main upanishads along with Adi Shankaracharya's commentaries.

Even though the Brahma Sutras are very concise and logically arranged, attempts to read them on one's own can be even more frustrating than in the case of the upanishads — their very brevity and a different style of writing and arguing make the Brahma Sutras much more abstruse and are best studied only under the personal guidance of a proper teacher.

The Bhagavad Gita lends itself to much easier reading as it is supposed to; with a commentary, it can be an exceptionally valuable text combining, as it does, many of the preparatory and core teachings of Vedanta in a work of beauty and practicality.

More modern books containing conversations with and answers from truly evolved persons of this century can be rewarding reading. Apart from books, we also now have available audio and video formats of teachings of some current teachers of Vedanta. The calibre of such material obviously varies with the teacher concerned. These media provide a practical and valuable supplement to traditional learning but they are not substitutes for live interaction with a teacher. Further, some of this modern material deviates significantly from the traditional teaching methodology of Vedanta and reliance on it can derail a newcomer. So care is needed in deciding what to use and, that too, at what stage in our journey.

In whatever reading we do, we should bear in mind that there will be many areas of confusion and apparent contradictions even in authoritative material. Traditions try to help us derive the right message from our scriptures. One such traditional mechanism is the *shad linga* (six signs or pointers) test which is drawn from *purva mimamsa*. These signs are meant to assist us in arriving at *shruti tatparyam* or the highest and core message of the scriptures. The shad lingas are:

- *upakrama upasamahara*. Find out what is stated both at the beginning and at the end of the scripture. This indicates the real intent of that scripture. (Even a lot of contemporary writing is based on the technique of "*first tell them what you are going to tell them, then tell them and, finally, tell them what you have told them*"!)
- *Abhyasa*. If some statement is repeated several times (such as *tat tvam asi* which is repeated nine times in the Chandogya Upanishad), it indicates the scripture's central message.
- *Apoorvata*. The upanishads are independent and primary means of knowledge in their field and so their essential teachings should be novel and unique; they should not be covered by other means of knowledge. Statements which fulfil these criteria are the crucial ones. So when an upanishad says *ayam atma brahma* (brahman is your truth), we have to see this as its core message because we cannot arrive at this conclusion with certainty by other means of knowledge.
- *Phalam*. The result of understanding the primary message of the scripture should be of great benefit. In the case of the upanishad it is, of course, moksha or attaining freedom from any sense of limitation. A statement leading to moksha should be considered prime.
- *Arthavda*. That which is praised in the scriptures by statements like 'by knowing which everything becomes as good as known' or 'the knower of brahman attains the highest' indicates the real message of the scriptures.
- *Upapatti*. The deepest message of the scripture may not be established by reasoning alone but it should be supported by logical arguments and should not offend reason or valid experience.

Some confusion about what the scriptures actually want to tell us can be avoided by recourse to such analysis and the guidance of the teacher but some of it is unavoidable—it almost seems that the struggle and frustration in trying to arrive at some clear and meaningful vision is part of the admission price!

Finally, the entire treasure of Vedantic literature is so vast that one can only hope to read and study a small fraction of it; however, it is reassuring to note that, for a prepared student, just the Gita and a few upanishads studied and understood well are enough to dispel all his self-ignorance and help him find release from unnecessary suffering.

Why is it necessary to read a large number of long-winded books on Vedanta? Can't we have its teachings in a crisp summary?

CAN'T WE HAVE VEDANTA IN A CAPSULE?

- *Swimming is the sport or activity of moving through water by moving your arms and legs.*
- *Music is vocal, instrumental or mechanical sounds having rhythm, melody or harmony.*
- *The world is an insubstantial appearance and brahman is the only reality which is not different from you.*

There! In these three short statements or capsules we have the essential features of swimming, music and Vedanta. But what good are these capsules? Can we derive any real benefit from them?

Swimming can be learnt only by getting into the water and personally working on the acquisition of a new skill. And a bare description of music neither connects us to its magic nor explains why it affects our emotions so deeply.

The point in saying all this is to emphasise that some things are not mere information but a journey to be personally undertaken, a path to be actually walked. In our highly cerebral and rushed world today, there is a tendency to look for short-cuts which are primarily intellectual. With this orientation, some of us look for a primer on Vedanta, hoping that an overview of its essential features will bring personal benefit. But a summary of Vedanta's vision is as useful as the definitions of swimming and music we saw earlier. What needs to be understood is that Vedanta is not a quick-fix, not entirely an intellectual exercise and not merely data which can be conveniently reduced to a set of bullet-points.

It is, in fact, a long and subtle journey of exploration, of examining and peeling away layers of wrong conclusions. It involves the modulation of our emotions, the re-formatting of our priorities & life-styles and of letting proper knowledge seep into the deepest recesses of our minds. Merely reading a snap-shot of Vedanta's teachings does not bring us closer to its real objective any more than reading a map gets us to our actual destination. And Vedanta's objective is not to provide us with information but to bring us the personal realisation that we are the unchanging awareness in which all objects exist and without which nothing exists. This realisation takes both effort and time because it initially seems to contradict our experiences and goes against our habitual reactions.

For these teachings to make a real difference to us requires exposure to enough of them, over a period of time. We need a certain critical mass of these teachings for them to actually work. An analogy here is of a nuclear device where smaller pieces of fissionable material are initially held separated from each other. When this device has to be detonated, these smaller pieces are brought together by internal mechanisms so that they combine into a single large piece. Their combined mass then leads to a rapid and self-sustaining chain of fission which results in a tremendous release of energy—a nuclear explosion. The key to this is creating a critical mass of the nuclear material; if the quantity of the material is less, the desired release of energy will not happen.

This analogy becomes particularly relevant in current times where we have easy access to a huge variety of information on all aspects of religion and spirituality, combined with lack of time and short attention spans. In this environment, if we briefly dip into many and varied sources, we will pick up a lot of ideas, new terminologies and interesting concepts but not enough on any one path to make a real difference to us.

Unless we accumulate a sufficient amount of the knowledge that Vedanta has to impart, the needed inner transformation will not happen. The required critical mass will not be created by quick and intermittent dips into Vedanta's waters. Swami Dayananda used to humorously use the analogy of a rasagulla.

This spongy Indian sweet has to be kept submerged in syrup for sufficient time for sweetness to permeate it—a quick dip in and out does not work. In Vedanta too, we need to stay with consistent teachings over a sufficient period for them to enter us in a meaningful way.

There are, of course, capsules which contain the essence of Vedanta's vision. A mahavakya or a great sentence from an important upanishad says: *tat tvam asi* meaning *you are that* and there are many other similar statements in the Vedic scriptures. Such statements contain great truths in a very condensed form. But just as Einstein's famous equation *(E=MCsquared)* conveys no real meaning to the average person, such Vedantic capsules do not become personally relevant unless one goes through systematic and consistent study, under the guidance of a competent teacher, over a sufficient period of time. Further, to benefit from this study, one also has to cultivate certain personal qualities and skills.

Without meeting all these conditions, and merely reading such capsules, is only of very limited use. In fact, such a summary approach can be damaging either because it may lead a person to think that there is no need for further study or because he may conclude that Vedanta doesn't work because he does not experience the promised results of Vedanta.

A brief overview of Vedanta is of course useful for introducing the subject to a new-comer and capsules of its key-points come in handy as *aide-memoires* for students who are in the process of learning. Problems only arise when we try to find clever short-cuts or have false expectations. At times, these false expectations are promoted by advertisements which promise the *Discovery Of Your Eternal Self* over an expensive weekend retreat in Goa or in California! Only if such a thing was possible…

People who are happy coasting along with a conventional life without asking fundamental questions will not be inclined to walk the rather long and demanding path of Vedanta. This also applies to those who believe that the solution to their problem lies in the next level of wealth or better relationships or better health or new sources of pleasures & entertainment. Curiosity or the need to appear knowledgeable may get them to look at Vedanta but not as an irresistible calling. But, with such an approach, the real benefits of this ancient wisdom will remain away from them till they are ready to put in the effort and time which Vedanta requires.

Vedanta is stated to be a spiritual pursuit and its goal is said to be moksha. *However, both spirituality and moksha are words whose meanings are often neither clear nor consistent amongst those who use them.*

SPIRITUALITY & *MOKSHA*: THE BLIND MEN'S ELEPHANTS

We all know the story in which a group of blind men comes across an elephant for the first time. Each one of them touches a different part of the elephant and comes to his own conclusion about the creature. The person whose hand lands on the elephant's trunk concludes that it is like a snake. For another one whose hand reaches its ear, it seems like a kind of fan. For yet another person, whose hand is laid on the elephant's leg, thinks that the animal is like a pillar. The blind man who places his hand upon the elephant's side finds that it is like a wall. And the last man, who feels its tail, describes it as a rope.

Spirituality and *moksha* are two commonly used terms in the course of studying Vedanta which are subject to similar confusion and misunderstanding. Our understanding of both these terms can vary as widely and be as much off the mark as the blind men's conclusions about an elephant.

The term *spirituality* was originally used within early Christianity to refer to a life oriented toward the Holy Spirit of its scriptures. However, in modern usage spirituality has both religious and non-religious connotations, with its non-religious usage getting more popular. We, therefore, now have an increasing number of people who say "*I'm not religious but I have a strong sense of spirituality*". In this modern sense, spirituality involves a feeling or belief that there is something greater than one's individual self, something more to being human than sensory experience, and that the greater whole of which we are part is cosmic or divine in nature.

For many, of course, their understanding of spirituality still continues to have a large religious component; to them, it means belief in god, usually accompanied by prayer, rituals and pilgrimages. For some others, spirituality means association with gurus; for them, paying obeisance to every passing guru and listening to sporadic teachings, irrespective of their context or consistency, is spirituality. And for yet others, regular chanting of mantras, daily meditation and occasional yoga retreats constitute the heart of spirituality. Then there are those who have no truck with any of these things and are convinced that they have paid their dues towards spirituality by leading ethical and compassionate lives. And there are also those who look upon communion with nature in any form as spirituality—for them, experiences in a forest, on a mountain-top, at the ocean's shore or during a starry night are all spiritual.

Moksha also means different things to different people. The idea that many have here is that moksha is the cessation of all suffering in our lives. For some, moksha also carries the alluring expectation that it will bring an experience of extraordinary joy, never tasted by us so far. For some others, moksha is the release from the cycle of births and deaths and a permanent place in heaven in the loving presence of almighty god. For yet others (such as some Buddhists) moksha means a state of oblivion or nothingness; this is contrary to other beliefs (such as in Jainism) where moksha is a mortal individual becoming an omniscient and eternal being by getting rid of his impurities.

But all these are either wrong ideas or, at best, half truths at least in the context of Vedanta. We need to be clear about what these terms actually mean for us. Let us start with a short meaning of spirituality for us: Spirituality is whatever that propels us towards moksha. This of course makes it apparent that unless we are first clear about what moksha means, we will remain unclear about what spirituality is.

The essence of moksha is encapsulated in the powerful Upanishadic statement: *tat tvam asi* (you are that). What this cryptic statement means is that the truth behind an individual and the truth behind the rest of creation is the same. Fully understanding the scope and nature of this single truth frees us from all our fears & insecurity; and such freedom is moksha.

Another way to look at moksha is by way of a simple definition provided by Osho who said that moksha is knowing your being and remaining centred in it. Because the truth behind all individuals and behind all other objects in the world is the same, moksha here too means proper understanding of this single truth.

The understanding that a single reality is all that actually exists automatically reduces everything else which we deal with to a lower level—a level where things only appear to be real but actually lack independent and absolute reality. Recognising such non-reality of the objects and individuals in the world – *mithyatvam* of jagat – is an essential feature of moksha. A further corollary to this is discovering that *mithya* objects can never affect my reality; this discovery, when it is doubt-free and settled, is moksha.

Moksha can also be expressed by its effects in our lives. In this sense, moksha can be seen as arriving at the clear understanding that happiness represented by security *(artha)*, pleasures *(kama)* and righteousness *(dharma)* – the three primary human pursuits – is already within ourselves. This, in turn, means that moksha is total independence because there is no need to depend upon people, possessions and situations or even the gods for happiness.

We should also be clear about what is not moksha. As we just saw, being dependent on or beholden to anything or any one (including god) is not moksha.

Further, moksha is getting over our false identification with our bodies and minds; therefore, hanging on to our sense of individuality or improvements at our physical and emotional levels are not the primary features of moksha.

Also, while moksha certainly changes our understanding of suffering at the worldly level, it does not erase worldly problems—a person with the full knowledge of Vedanta will continue to experience physical pain from a disease and experience natural sadness at someone's untimely death. The primary effects, both physical and mental, of unfortunate occurrences cannot be eliminated. But moksha eliminates what Buddha called the second arrow: the subsequent waves of anguish, anger, hostility, guilt, regret and personal suffering which continue to afflict most of us for much longer and more powerfully, well after the initial effects of an unfortunate event.

Coming to joy, all experienced joys (however exalted) are only passing events in the mind and they are not moksha. Moksha is to see our reality as beyond and far more immense than our bodies and minds; the result of this is not an experience of bliss but a state of tranquillity and fullness upon recognising our reality as unchanging and boundless consciousness.

While Vedanta does go along initially with the idea that moksha is a release from the ongoing cycle of several lives of an individual, its ultimate teachings make it clear that our reality has nothing to do with births, deaths or re-births. Moksha is seeing that what we truly are always remains unaffected and is beyond the bounds of time and space. This makes the issues of births, deaths and rebirths irrelevant. Our bodies and minds are subject to these events but these are only passing superimpositions on our reality.

With this understanding of moksha, let us now come to spirituality. To repeat, spirituality in the context of Vedanta, is anything and everything which leads us to moksha—full understanding of the only truth which really exists. The emphasis here is not so much on the process selected for obtaining this understanding but on the end objective which is abiding knowledge of this truth. Because this truth happens to be our own real nature, the same objective can also be stated as obtaining proper self-knowledge. Processes which can truly be included under the heading of spirituality can vary but they must all prepare us for self-knowledge and lead us to this goal.

Things included in a spiritual journey guided by Vedanta can be looked at in many ways. Vedanta requires an eligible student, an *adhikari* who is equipped with the necessary qualities (*sadhana chatushtaya sampanna*). So, spiritual sadhana includes our efforts to obtain these preparatory qualities.

Looking at spirituality from the point of the three primary qualities present in all of us, the spiritual journey can be seen as moving upwards from a life dominated by our baser qualities (*tamoguna pradhanam*) to more normal human qualities (*rajoguna pradhanam*) and then to cultivation of divine qualities (*sattvaguna pradhanam*). (*Tamas* is a quality dominated by dullness, inertia and ignorance. *Rajas* is the quality of energetic desires and actions. *Sattva* is characterised by knowledge, harmony and contentment.) It should be noted that cultivating sattva is a means, not the end; a sattvic mind is needed to understand and absorb Vedanta's real teachings which take us to a perspective where even sattva is seen to be part of mithya jagat and, therefore, of limited relevance.

Another way to look at spirituality is that it is a process of *mala, vikshepa* and *avarana nivrutti*. Compulsive desires, negative emotions and non-constructive attitudes are like dirt (mala) in our minds. Excessive activity and excitability lead to a mind which is fragmented and in turmoil (vikshepa). And ignorance veils our own true nature (avarana). Getting rid (nivrutti) of mala, vikshepa and avarana are all part of our spiritual journey because these are the basic impediments to self-knowledge.

Spirituality can also be stated as moving from an *artha-kama* focus to a *dharma-moksha* focus in our lives. For many of us the pursuit of security (artha) and pleasures (kama) are the primary goals of life. When the inadequacy of these goals dawns upon us, the consequent turn towards a more balanced life with increasing focus on finding more fundamental answers is the turn towards spirituality.

Yet another way to see spirituality is that it is a move away from a predominantly *pratibhasika* life (a subjective life dominated by strong personal like & dislikes, prejudices and ill-founded conclusions) to a more *vyavaharika* life (a more objective life less coloured by personal aberrations). When the impetus behind this is the urge to obtain knowledge of the ultimate reality (*parmarthika satyam*), this move can be termed spiritual.

These are some of the things which can be seen as spiritual processes and efforts.

To recap, moksha is arriving at the doubt-free and stable knowledge that there is only a singular truth behind all existence and the spiritual way of life includes everything which propels towards the acquisition and assimilation of this knowledge.

Either out of genuine hesitation or as a convenient excuse some people say that Vedanta requires capabilities that they do not possess. While Vedanta does require preparation and commitment, so do many other things we undertake in our lives.

IS VEDANTA TOO CHALLENGING?

A refrain one hears from some people is that Vedanta is too difficult a project to embark upon. For a number of people the put-off is the amount of commitment they think it requires. For others, the hesitation stems from a self-perceived lack of intellect to grapple with Vedanta's unusual concepts. Yet others say that they are not ready to forsake life's pleasures which, according to them, Vedanta requires. A different genre of objections claims that it is better to help fellow-human beings or spend time connecting with god instead of the impractical and self-centred occupation with Vedanta's academic concepts.

An interesting thing about these conclusions is that they are often arrived at without actually giving Vedanta a fair trial or making serious inquiry into what it really entails. This is a bit like a business executive who once told me *"If I can't see anything out of the window, how can the pilot?"* to explain his refusal to take night flights!

Leaving aside preconceived notions and snap judgements, does Vedanta really require extraordinary effort, exceptional intelligence or complete disengagement from the world?

The answer to this question lies in the traditional list called *sadhana chatushtaya*. The translation of this Sanskrit term is 'the four means' and covers the initial qualities needed in a student, if Vedanta is to work for him or her. They are:

- Discrimination
- Dispassion
- A set of six disciplines & qualities*
- Intense longing for freedom

One important thing to note here is what this list does *not* mention. Words like *medha* (incisive intellect) or *sanyasa* (renunciation) are not used here at all. Therefore, extraordinary intelligence or turning away from the world were never held out to be prime requirements from everyone who wants to study Vedanta.

Actually, most of the qualities which are mentioned in this list are not unusual. Discrimination and a certain amount of dispassion are helpful in both our professional and social lives. And who can question the utility of a tranquil mind, controlled senses and other similar disciplines in anything that we do?

The only quality which may seem unusual is the last one: an intense longing for freedom. And this is also the most important of the four pre-qualifications for entering Vedanta. We all are, of course, used to longings in many forms: for money, for pleasures, for security, for health, for relationships. However, the longing referred to here is longing for freedom from longing itself. This freedom is termed *moksha* in Sanskrit and the longing for it becomes paramount only when one has realised the limitations inherent in our usual pursuits.

To be drawn into Vedanta we need to realise that what we want is not more security or more pleasure, but freedom—freedom from compulsive desires. When a mature person analyses his experiences, he discovers that behind his pursuit of security and pleasure is a basic desire to be free from all insufficiency, to be free from incompleteness itself; a basic desire which no achievements can fulfil.

And until this realisation dawns, our minds will encourage tremendous effort in other pursuits like money, fame, health and relationships; but the same

---

* (These six are *sama, dama, samadhan, uparati, titiksha* and *shraddha*—control over one's mental and physical reactions, attentiveness while learning, cultivation of liking for what is being taught, the ability to put up with some inconveniences and initial faith in the validity of the teaching.)

mind will continue to throw up a series of objections in respect of Vedanta, such as Vedanta is too difficult or only needed for those at the fag-end of their lives. So, the realisation that all our longings are rooted in the longing for the ultimate freedom is really critical. And this longing cannot remain cursory but has to grow to become burning.

What about working for the good of others or religious activities? Are they not on a different footing than self-centred occupations like amassing personal wealth and fame? Will such efforts not provide us complete and lasting fulfilment? The fact is that no one does anything unless it brings him or her a personal sense of fulfilment. As the Brihadaranyaka Upanishad says *...atmanastu kaamaaya sarvam priyam bhavati*—everything is done for the sake of a pleased self. So, whether we are saints or sinners, our activities are fuelled by first judging ourselves to be lacking in some aspect and then working towards whatever we reckon will address our need to be fulfilled. And none of our activities, however noble or religious, will get us off the treadmill of always feeling limited, always being compelled to seek something more or something different. So, while doing good to others and relating to god are beautiful and useful, they do not address our fundamental problem fully and permanently. We have to turn to Vedanta to find the proper solution.

Vedanta, even when pursued properly, does not actually give us anything beyond what we already have. All it does is to make us see how wrong we were in judging ourselves as being small and limited; it opens our eyes to our truth which is limitless and timeless. Vedanta also does not deny our natural and legitimate wants or desires. It only removes the internal pressure which makes our wants compelling; we stop being slaves and become masters of our desires.

Vedanta certainly requires effort and commitment but most of us, who have business or professional careers or responsibilities of running a home, put in as much or even more in these occupations compared to what is required for Vedanta.

Further, the qualities required from an eligible student (the sadhana chatushtaya list we saw earlier) does not mean that we have to achieve perfection before we start. All that is required is a reasonable amount of these qualities so that we have a state of mind, time and energy which are enough for the teachings of Vedanta to seep in.

We should not let some terminology which may be initially daunting or distortions caused by incompetent or self-serving 'teachers' obfuscate the true nature of Vedanta which is elegant, simple, practical and immensely valuable. Our real problem is not lack of time or abilities but lack of conviction regarding the insoluble nature of the problem we are all trying to solve. We keep on hoping that our usual methods will somehow and some time deliver a solution but, unfortunately, a full solution never comes from these methods.

One issue which is pointed out by many who are hesitant about investing their effort and time in the pursuit of Vedanta is the undeniable fact that out of all those who take to Vedanta, very few actually succeed in reaching enlightenment in its fullest sense. This may suggest that Vedanta is an effort doomed to be fruitless for the majority of us. In this context, at least three factors can be pointed out to provide reassurance:

- Ultimately (maybe even in a future birth!), everyone does get enlightened because nobody can be indefinitely kept away from his own reality.
- The journey of Vedanta is enjoyable in itself and after we give it some time and effort, we will find that no other pursuit is as engaging and satisfying.
- Much before we complete the full journey of Vedanta, we will obtain many smaller but very valuable gains which will make our lives simpler, lighter and more free.

Finally, until we actually apply ourselves diligently and systematically to Vedanta, under the guidance of a competent teacher, we will continue to struggle for crumbs of fulfilment through our usual methods while, ironically, absolute fullness remains our own true but unknown nature.

Experiences enrich us but they become even more valuable when we see their limitations and look beyond them to find something more fundamental and more valuable.

REAL VALUE OF EXPERIENCES

Experiences are life itself because what is life other than a series of physical and mental experiences? Our joys & sorrows, our possessions & relationships, our pleasures & pains are all only available to us as experiences.

We live in a wonderful world of magnificence and opportunities. We are blessed with physical & mental abilities to experience its variety and utilise its resources. However, many of us deny ourselves an opportunity to experience much greater variety in our lives, either out of lethargy or because we are diffident about trying something new. Such restricted mind-sets make us miss the magic, the learning and growth which a larger variety of healthy experiences can bring to us. To remain fresh and receptive to new experiences, it is useful to periodically ask ourselves, *"When did I last do something for the first time?"*. The answer may surprise us!

We can also make the mistake of painting ourselves in a narrow corner by looking only for the big and grand. In some of our minds, the only meals worth talking about are at restaurants helmed by Michelin-starred chefs, our clothes & accessories must bear names of designers in vogue and our holidays have to be at locales currently considered to be the most exotic. There is nothing wrong in enjoying great cooking, having well-designed wardrobes and exploring novel destinations. However, there is a tremendous loss if, as a corollary to this, we ignore and eventually lose our ability to equally enjoy simpler and less complicated joys which life brings to us much more often.

Another factor which prevents us from extracting the maximum from any experience is our tendency to continuously trawl the past or worry about the future. History does teach us useful lessons and it is undoubtedly sensible to plan for the future. But this should not be at the cost of not fully experiencing whatever is on hand. A new house can be enjoyed in the present without wasting emotional energy in regretting, *"I would have enjoyed this so much more if I could have afforded it when I was younger"*; an exhilarating hike up a challenging mountain need not be tainted by wondering whether my advancing years will permit me to repeat this experience later. By not remaining in the present, we deny ourselves the full joy of the current experience because of lack of focus and dissipation of emotional energy. On the other hand, if we live our lives totally in the present, we draw so much from all our experiences, possessions and relationships that even when they pass (as they all must), we are not left thirsting because we have already drunk so deeply.

We often also let the joy from an experience be affected by comparisons, instead of enjoying that experience in itself. A car can provide pleasure by its styling, performance and comfort but we can mar this by making a comparison with a newer & fancier model which our undeserving neighbour has now acquired. And the damaging habit of comparisons is also applied in respect of our own past—we are capable of selectively recalling some high-points of our past and then trashing the present by comparison (*"The new artist's Darbari raga was nice but nothing in comparison to the old master's rendition which I had heard ten years ago"*).

One other thing which takes away from the full joy of experiences is a false sense of entitlement which is often combined with a *blasé* air of "been there, done that". Pleasant experiences are privileges and gifts—the world does not owe them to us and we should accept them with a sense of gratitude and humility. And being cynical or indifferent merely causes a loss to ourselves. It is only by being sensitive and receptive to all that comes our way can we fully enjoy the pleasant and even use the unpleasant to our benefit, by drawing some lessons which adversity can teach.

But more important than anything said so far is the fact that, if properly used, experiences can bring home to us the limitations of experiences themselves. And this can provide some remarkable learning opportunities.

What are the limitations of experiences? There are many.

First, we all have limited resources of money, time and energy. Anything we choose to do is always at the cost of something else foregone. For the moment, a particular choice which we have made may bring us satisfaction but, in the long run, the price we have paid for that choice in terms of resources expended and other opportunities foregone comes to haunt us. So, ultimately, everything ends up being a zero-sum game and this is why we remain unfulfilled even after a life-time of efforts and successes.

Then, no matter how great and exciting our experiences, our minds still get bored or fail to find continuing fulfilment. It is as if once we experience a certain level of security and joy, our mental thermostats reset themselves to a higher level and render the current level inadequate. This is why our chase for fulfilment is like a chase for the horizon which constantly recedes and remains away from us, no matter how fast we run.

The next important limitation of experiences is what we have already seen: comparisons. Julius Caesar felt that all his achievements were meagre compared to what Alexander had achieved and, that too, at a much younger age. And all of us today enjoy powers and comforts which Alexander could not have even imagined and yet we do not feel particularly blessed just because others around us have the same privileges. In fact, many of our desires which drive us towards experiences are mimetic; they don't emerge from within us but are based on imitating the desires of other people. As the French thinker Montesquieu put it, "*If we only wanted to be happy, it would be easy; but we want to be happier than other people which is almost always difficult because we think they are happier than they actually are.*"

Further, to enjoy any experience needs not only the experience itself but also a suitable condition of our bodies and minds. A beautifully cooked & presented meal provides no joy to an overweight man trying to deal with his hypertension and diabetes. And a sublime concert does not even register in the mind of a person agitated by a massive row at work or at home. Unfortunately, the states of our bodies and minds as well as the actions of other people are never entirely in our control.

For all these reasons our efforts to experience pleasures, security and fulfilment are neither predictably successful nor lasting. While we want only the pleasant, the unpleasant also occurs with regularity, as if it is the flip side of the same coin. This interplay of good and bad has an emotional impact on us, ranging from peaks of joy and a sense of pride to depths of anger & depression along with hostility and a feeling of being victimised.

Some of us see the futility of this emotional up-down and realise that depending upon experiences as the primary source of our joy and security is a faulty premise. But this conclusion does not bring an answer to our inborn need for joy, security and fulfilment. If not from experiences, then from where do we satisfy our natural hunger in these matters?

It is at this stage that our sincere search for a different type of solution and a dose of good luck may propel us towards a teacher of Vedanta. And it is Vedanta which helps us question our long-held notions about ourselves, about the sources of our happiness and about the world in which we live. It takes us beyond experiences, to an understanding of consciousness which is the unvarying presence behind all experiences. We then make the startling discovery that all the joy we derive from any experience doesn't actually come from the experience itself. All that an enjoyable experience does is to temporarily reveal our own nature which is permanently fulfilled. To be in touch with our real nature all the time, what we need to do is to get rid of wrong understanding and the pressure of likes & dislikes from our minds. We will then find ourselves to be peaceful and content, irrespective of any experience, because that is our innate nature.

The ultimate value of experiences is in their turning our minds away from outside experiences to an inquiry into the experiencer. So, we should pray not only for pleasant experiences but also for wisdom which lets us see the limitations of even the best & holiest of experiences and opens our eyes to something much more fundamental and permanent. Our experiences are many but *they are known, they do not know*: a perception cannot see a feeling and a feeling cannot perceive an image. There is something in us which is aware of all our experiences. This awareness is the common factor in all our experiences but does not share the qualities and limitations of any particular experience. We need to turn our attention to investigating this awareness.

It is easy to mistake emotional maturity as being the end of the road for the journey of advaita Vedanta. Vedanta's goal is larger and goes well beyond this.

EMOTIONAL MATURITY AND ADVAITA

There are many people who have never studied Vedanta but display remarkable good sense as they deal with the ups and downs of their lives. They remain pictures of equanimity and grace, even under pressure. They willingly do more than their fair share in shouldering burdens. They are empathetic and helpful to those in need. They are able to accept the failings of others without becoming judgemental. Even when fate inflicts misfortunes upon them, they continue to do the best that they can, without lamenting "*Why me*?". The prospect of their own imminent deaths does not appear to disturb them.

The company of such people is a matter of joy and privilege for the rest of us —we not only get help from them but also draw inspiration, humility and the reassurance that the world yet has a lot of good in it.

A question which arises from these examples is that if people can possess such qualities without studying Vedanta, why bother about Vedanta at all? Perhaps one would be better off in trying to cultivate these practical qualities instead of struggling with the academic-sounding concepts of Vedanta.

In this context, we first need to remember that visible equanimity in people is not always a mark of their maturity. At times it can be apathy or fatalism. Some others accept circumstances without evident reaction because they are diffident by nature and hesitate in showing any kind of emotion. Yet others have psychological complexes which make them adopt the roles of perpetual martyrs; not only do they passively accept the 'injustices' done to them but parade them, almost like badges of honour. In our discussion here, we are not talking of such people but of those who are genuinely mature. It is in cases of truly balanced people that we need to understand how the effects of emotional maturity and the effects of imbibing the vision of Vedanta are so very different.

To understand this difference in simple terms, emotional maturity helps people to live a better life while Vedanta enables them to see life itself as a game. While this sounds simple, the difference is fundamental and with major consequences. But, first, let us look at a common-place analogy to portray the difference we are talking about.

You are playing a game of tennis with a friend who is an excellent player. You, too, are good and are able to make your friend struggle hard before he finally wins. Both of you then walk off the court laughing, saying "*What a great game!*". In this scenario, your ability to play the game well would be the equivalent of having emotional maturity and your being able to laugh, despite losing, would be the equivalent of you having imbibed the vision of Vedanta.

While you played the game of tennis seriously enough to put in your best effort, you were able to take your loss lightly because, after all, it was only a game and your real life remained unaffected by this loss. Vedanta brings about this combination of seriousness and lightness in respect of our entire lives. And it does this by helping us understand our real nature which remains unaffected by the successes or failures in our lives as well as by the good or bad states of our bodies and minds.

Vedanta helps us to see that by restricting our identity to our bodies and minds and seeing the world as the cause of our pleasures and pains, we are making a cardinal mistake. And it is this mistake which makes us take our personal agendas so seriously and converts our lives into do-or-die struggles.

We won't go into the reasons why this error occurs or the ways in which Vedanta helps us overcome it. But one pertinent thing which needs to be brought out here is the important role of emotional maturity which is required as we study Vedanta.

Why is emotional maturity required for someone who wants to pursue Vedanta seriously? The reason is simple: to understand our reality, which happens to be very much greater than our bodies and minds, we need to shift our attention above and beyond our physical and mental attributes. But we can transcend these attributes only when they are not holding us back by continuously shouting for our attention. A knee throbbing with pain will rivet our attention to it; it will recede in our mind and permit us to move on to other matters only when it is relatively healthy and pain-free. In a similar way, without adequate emotional maturity, the demands of our bodies and our over-reactive mental processes will continuously buffet us, fritter away our time and energy and prevent conditions which are conducive to our understanding and assimilating the vision of Vedanta.

Healthy bodies and mature minds are supported by *ashtanga* yoga, *dharma* and *karma* yoga which tools exist in our tradition primarily to prepare us for the journey of Vedanta. These important tools produce a degree of maturity for us to use for a bigger purpose. But, confusingly, a further increase in emotional maturity also happens to be a by-product of progressing on Vedanta's journey. Because people who have completed Vedanta's course do display great emotional maturity, this can be wrongly construed as Vedanta's objective. But, as we saw earlier, a refined and balanced mental state is a prerequisite; it is only the journey's starting point, not its end.

Why should one strive for Vedanta's knowledge? Why not stop after cultivating emotional maturity which brings balance and ease in our lives? The answer is that emotional maturity, though beautiful and valuable, suffers from two major drawbacks.

First, it does not take us to the full solution of the fundamental human problem. This fundamental problem manifests itself in all of us in three facets: mortality, deficiency of knowledge and a sense of limited fulfilment. Or, to put it differently, we all want to live, to know more and to be happy, without any limit. However, our deaths are inevitable, our knowledge is always limited and our happiness is neither total nor permanent. And no amount of goodness, religiosity or maturity solves this problem fully.

There are, of course, many people without exposure to Vedanta who are at peace with their limited lives and go to their end without their equanimity appearing to be unsettled. A couple of things should be kept in mind here. No one can know what is actually going on in someone else's mind and it is possible that a tranquil facade covers disquietude which is not apparent. Further, we are all able to handle certain levels of deficiencies and reverses in our lives. If we are fortunate enough to pass through life without those levels being breached or without our vulnerable trigger points being pressed, it may appear that we do not need Vedanta to sail through life smoothly. But this conclusion, based on what we see of the limited examples of others, is as dangerous as not buying insurance just because our neighbour never had an accident throughout his life!

The second, and even more fundamental issue in ignoring Vedanta is the non-fulfilment of our highest potential. Just as playing a game well does not provide a higher purpose to the game, living a sensible life does not explain our existence or its purpose.

We human beings are unique because we have a high level of intelligence, a capacity to be self-judgemental and a sense of free will. Because of these abilities, it is not possible for us to ignore questions about the nature of the world we live in, about its creator and about the real purpose of our existence. Just emotional maturity and conventional knowledge cannot answer these questions. It is only Vedanta which takes us to a different level of understanding, a whole new perspective where these questions are fully dealt with. It is in doing this, where we use our unique mental faculties to resolve uniquely human longings, that we reach true fulfilment of our potential.

One mistake that some students of Vedanta make is to take emotional maturity and the resulting equanimity of mind as a primary goal. The real goal of Vedanta is the definite and constant understanding that the only reality is *nirguna* and *nirvikalpa atma* and everything else (including one's body and mind) is only a dependent appearance of no real significance. One should, therefore, not get too focused on completely eliminating the ups and downs of the body and mind as they are affected by *prarabhda*, age and surroundings. One should also not make the error of evaluating the progress of one's Vedantic journey only by this parameter.

Therefore, while we should greatly value emotional maturity and work towards acquiring this asset, we must not confuse means with ends and lose track of our real goal: freedom by knowledge of our true nature.

The twists and turns on the path which leads us to Vedanta are many. But while the journey may take a lot of time and effort and while luck may play a considerable role, there is every reason for us to start and persevere.

ROAD WITH MANY FORKS

You Are the Queer Duck!

When students of Vedanta begin to realise the value and beauty of this ancient wisdom, they naturally want to share it with those around them. But then they find that most people are disinterested, sometimes dismissive; even the more polite one seem to merely indulge the Vedanta student's enthusiasm—much as we indulge a child's latest fancy, in the expectation that he will soon grow out of it.

When I first encountered such reactions, I mentioned them (in a tone of both complaint and smugness) to a wonderful teacher of Vedanta, Swami Tadatmananda. Swamiji then gently chided me, "*Always remember, YOU are the queer duck, not the others*". This statement continues to caution me against having an inflated self-opinion just because I happen to be interested in an uncommon subject.

Uncommon Seeking

But, while false pride is clearly misplaced, the fact is that spiritual seeking is rare and has been so over the ages; as the Bhagavad Gita says (in the 3rd verse of its 7th chapter): *manushyanam sahasreshu kashchid yatati siddhaye...Out of many thousands among men, only one may strive for perfection...*

Turning to Vedanta requires specific choices at a number of junctures in our lives. And without the benefit of good guidance, good sense and good luck (the last one also being remarkably important), we are more likely to make choices which actually lead us away from Vedanta. This is why relatively few people reach a point where the journey of Vedanta becomes the central theme of their lives.

Disenchantment With the Usual

For most of us the first important juncture in our lives, where we have a chance to pick a path leading to Vedanta, comes after we have pursued the conventional goals of pleasures and security, with the usual mixture of successes and failures. At some stage in this process, it strikes a few of us that there is perhaps more to life than continuously chasing success in terms of wealth, fame, power, experiences and relationships.

Such a doubt does not arise for many of us because the pace of our lives often makes it seem unnecessary to stop to re-assess the validity of our original goals & assumptions. Further, the wealth we have accumulated, the honours we have garnered, the poems we have written, the technologies we have invented, the families we have raised, the social causes we have contributed to and the duties that we have performed all reassure us that we are on the right track. So, we continue with our old plan of life, perhaps with greater vigour and determination. And, for some others, the sheer struggle for survival is so all-consuming that there is no scope to think about any other thing.

However, if we happen to be one of those who sees at this stage that despite all that we have done, we still remain unfulfilled or insecure, this may provoke us to re-assess. As the Mundaka Upanishad (1.2.12) says: *pariksya lokan karmacitan brahmano nirvedamayan nastyakrtah krtena...Examining the worldly pleasures acquired by actions, the wise man gets detached from them since the eternal cannot be gained by actions...*

Religion

If we do get disenchanted with the usual "eat, drink and be merry" formula or fed up with the never-ending struggle to eke out more from life, we come to another choice. Here, in trying to find a different approach, some turn to *bhakti* or to techniques like *samadhi* meditation, awakening the *kundalini* and the like. Often, the expectation here is of obtaining some supra-normal results which will either miraculously change things for us or provide us with the comfort of a psychological crutch. Religion as well techniques of yoga and *tantra* can be valuably used and Vedanta encourages them but these do not permanently solve the fundamental human problem of never reaching total fulfilment.

The Real Solution: Knowledge

At this stage, a few of us come to the tentative conclusion that perhaps what we need is not some esoteric solutions but a new perspective. It strikes us that new understanding might solve our problem of continuously feeling limited & wanting, which problem we have not been able to address despite our best efforts so far.

This, then, brings us to wisdom which is meant to give us greater insight into the truth of things. Here again we come to another choice: do I look for new understanding about my life from Vedanta or from a number of other Indian view-points or from western philosophy?

Divisions Within Vedanta

If, for whatever reason, we choose to look at Vedanta, we are again confronted with a further choice between its three major (and widely differing) interpretations: *advaita Vedanta* as championed by Adi Shankaracharya or *vishist advaita* advocated by Ramanujacharya or *dvaita* propagated by Madhvacharya. And though all these three rely on the same foundational scriptures, their core conclusions vary widely.

Guru

Even after we pick advaita Vedanta to help us, we may decide to rely only upon our own intelligence to study this subject, without turning to a traditional guru. But, for Vedanta to truly deliver, some live interaction with a proper teacher is necessary. Therefore, self-study alone is unlikely to benefit us fully.

Of course, turning to a guru is no guarantee that he will honestly and competently make us see the vision of reality as envisaged by our sages. There are, unfortunately, many gurus who are incompetent or with ulterior motives or both.

Our Preparedness

And even if we have the good fortune of finding a proper guru of advaita Vedanta, this still does not ensure that we will acquire the emotional and intellectual qualities which are necessary to fully benefit from this guru. A student who does not fulfil Vedanta's eligibility requirements is unlikely to benefit greatly from even sound teaching given by a proper guru.

The X-factor

And, finally, there is that 'x' factor in all our lives – call it *prarabdha karma* or grace or luck or whatever else – which provides associations, surroundings and circumstances which can either make or mar our pursuit of Vedanta. We can use all our intelligence and efforts to do the right things but extraneous circumstances beyond our control can deny us the results we target.

In this context, our traditions refer to four *kripas* (events of benevolence or grace) which are needed by us:

- *Ishwara kripa* which brings in health, situations and associations which are supportive of our pursuit—for instance, continuous ill-health, grinding poverty, famines, floods, earthquakes & pestilences or toxic relationships can seriously impede our task.
- *Guru kripa* which results in our finding a proper guru who is available to us and willing to teach us.
- *Shastra kripa* refers to our being successful in drawing the right meaning from the scriptures which are capable of letting some people draw contrary or even perverse conclusions from their contents.
- *Atma kripa* which leads to being endowed with beneficial qualities of mind and heart, giving us the ability to stay the course and absorb the subtle teachings of Vedanta.

Without all these factors operating in our favour, our journey can get derailed.

Journey's End

So, with this large number of variables and choices, Vedanta has remained a subject of deep personal interest to only a very small fragment of society. And out of the few who take to Vedanta, an even smaller number are able to complete its entire journey. To once again quote verse 7.3 (its second half) of the Bhagavad Gita: *yatatam api siddhanam kashchin mam vetti tattvatah…* and amongst those who have achieved perfection, hardly one knows me in truth (out of those who strive for this knowledge, only a rare one truly gets it).

Start Now

What does this mean for us? Don't explore Vedanta because there are too many if's and but's? The journey of Vedanta is undoubtedly demanding and uncertain. But the pay-off is correspondingly vast and magnificent—the discovery of permanent security, fulfilment and peace.

We can, of course, choose to stick to safe shores and be content with our usual goals, cocooned by the familiar and by the safety of numbers of many others who have made the same choice. Or we can venture out to sea in the quest for new shores, taking some risks while looking for an entirely new perspective in our lives.

And the great beauty of Vedanta is that even a limited effort in its direction never fails to bless us with some benefits. So the fear of not being able to complete Vedanta's full journey should not stop us from beginning to explore the great insights and subtle truths which are the legacies of the Vedic tradition for all of us.

Encountering and overcoming obstacles is part of the Vedantic journey. Being aware of them is a step towards being prepared for them.

SPEED BREAKERS AND ROAD BLOCKS

Barring a few exceptional souls, most of us find that our Vedanta journey is slowed down and even stalled by a number of speed-breakers and road-blocks which we come across both before and after we take to Vedanta. The impediments which affect us before we turn to Vedanta are perhaps more critical because they discourage us from even looking in Vedanta's direction. These impediments are both self-made as well as thrust upon us by society and our living conditions.

One basic impediment which can prevent us from taking interest in Vedanta is the fight for survival. For those who have to struggle for subsistence or in lives which are blighted by oppression, painful disease or great mental imbalance, there is limited scope for Vedanta to find a place. In such a disturbed state, it is difficult (though not impossible) to relate to a way of thinking which requires some leisure and equanimity of mind.

But even others, in more fortunate circumstances, just cannot or will not think of anything beyond the common-place. As Bertrand Russell once said (rather superciliously), *"Most people would die sooner than think; in fact, they do so."*

Mesmerised by usual pleasures, which are incomplete and temporary, many yet choose to ride their inevitable yo-yos of pleasure and pain. Despite the fact that all their efforts have always left them thirsting for something more or something different, they battle on unthinkingly, letting their hopes overrule their own experiences.

This approach, of relying on passing episodes of pleasure, becomes all the more acceptable when it is seen that the majority of people have chosen to sail in the same boat—there is both comfort and a misplaced sense of safety in numbers. Personal laziness also contributes to our choosing the path of least resistance, by going along with the general tide.

And indifference towards Vedanta can also arise because we have, over time, gotten so used to our usual mode of life and so inured to the swings between pleasure and pain that the need to do anything different does not strike us—like the fable of the frog in water which is gradually heated so the frog does not realise that the temperature is reaching scalding levels.

Further, societies as a whole evolve taboos in respect of some matters which they consider unsuitable for open discussion; just as in many sections of society it is bad form to talk about sexuality or your religion or your wealth, there also seems to be an implicit embargo on questioning the validity of our usual approach to life. This societal norm mostly succeeds in keeping uncomfortable questions nicely tucked away and in discouraging us from looking for new answers.

Religion and devotion to God or preoccupation with other righteous activities are further reasons which stop many from looking at Vedanta. While there is a lot to commend in a religious and ethical life, what is lost sight of is that even the holiest and the most exemplary of lives is still a limited life—like all lives, limited by mortality, limited by ignorance and limited by inadequate fulfilment. Our usual methods never succeed in helping us to fully overcome these limitations but we console ourselves either by surrendering to the almighty or by becoming so impressed by our own goodness that exploring a different direction never occurs to us.

And fervour bordering on religiosity also occurs to some of us in the area of making a living or making a home. We start with whatever occupation we have chosen to meet our commitments and as a means for finding personal fulfilment. Nothing provides us full and unchanging happiness which is what all of us need. But, instead of realising the limitations of what we are doing, we end up elevating our usual occupations to holy grails and stop looking further. In such a state, we don't pause to evaluate the validity of the limited goals which our current trajectory is leading us to.

Preconceived notions or unfounded prejudices are other powerful reasons which hold us back from Vedanta, without giving it a fair trial. These issues manifest themselves by us saying that this is the way life is and there can be no solutions other than the ones we have been using so far; or we can dismiss Vedanta out of hand, on the assumption that it is impractical or too abstruse.

At times, we do get a nagging feeling that we should be looking at some alternatives to our current tactics. But then there is trepidation in seriously checking out something like Vedanta lest it undermines our whole superstructure of values, dreams and relationships. Any radically new thought can be subversive as it can challenge established norms, comfortable habits and accepted privileges; this possibility causes fear.

Lack of appropriate role models which inspire emulation and lack of good teachers to guide us are other important reasons which act as road-blocks, especially in current times.

Finally, in all our affairs, there is always that indefinable but critical factor which we label as luck, grace or *karma*. This can play a role in turning us away from Vedanta. (Here, it must be said that nothing is likely to be achieved by just relying on our luck or by moaning about it; the only useful thing to do is to apply ourselves as diligently and as intelligently as we can to our own long-term good and pray for success.)

In the context of those for whom the turn to a new direction has not yet occurred, Khalil Gibran had the following beautiful words to offer:

> *In your longing for your giant self lies your goodness: and that longing is in all of you.*
> *But in some of you that longing is a torrent rushing with might to the sea, carrying the secrets of the hillsides and the songs of the forest.*
> *And in others it is a flat stream that loses itself in angles and bends and lingers before it reaches the shore.*
> *But let not him who longs much say to him who longs little, "Wherefore are you slow and halting?"*
> *For the truly good ask not the naked, "Where is your garment?" nor the houseless, "What has befallen your house?"*

The fact is that each and every one of us is looking for freedom—freedom from want, freedom from lack of fulfilment. And this is Vedanta's goal too—to help us find total freedom. So, whether we realise this or not, we are all actually on the path of Vedanta. We begin by looking for fulfilment by either obtaining something that we desire or by getting rid of something that we dislike. In time, some of us see the futility of these efforts and move on to try and discover fulfilment which is not external but which is already integral to all of us.

But even after we turn to Vedanta to discover our inherent wholeness, we can still run into a number of other speed-breakers and road blocks. For Vedanta to work for a student, he needs to fulfil certain eligibility criteria. A straightforward list of four qualities (*sadhana chatushtaya*) is available for our use from scriptures. These qualities cover discrimination, dispassion, the longing to find total freedom and a set of certain basic intellectual & emotional attributes. Not having sufficient eligibility will certainly mar our progress.

Another way to look at this is via an analogy often used by teachers of Vedanta. In this analogy, our mind is like a pot of water and the knowledge of Vedanta is like the sun shining in the sky; and the goal here is to obtain a proper reflection of the sun in the water (copy Vedantic knowledge to our minds). What could be the possible problems here?

The first is impurity or *mala*. If the water is turbid, with dirt suspended in it, then such water obviously cannot reflect the sun. So our task here has to be its purification. In the case of our minds, impurities are primarily caused by over-powering likes and dislikes and the preparatory teachings of Vedanta prescribe *karma* yoga as a mechanism to minimise these impurities.

The next problem is continuous disturbances, *vikshepa*. Even if the water in the pot is clear, it will not be able to reflect anything faithfully if it is agitated because of non-stop movements. A similar problem occurs in our minds if they are hyper-active in chasing endless desires and in a continuous struggle with our environment. Here Vedanta offers *upasana* yoga (devotion and meditation) as a way of toning down ceaseless mental movements.

Finally, even pure and still water will not reflect anything if the pot is covered with a lid, *avarana*. For us, the lid here is our ignorance and the way to remove it is regular study of the scriptures, under the guidance of a proper teacher, by a qualified student over a sufficient period of time. Only this *jnana* yoga will remove the ignorance covering our minds.

All these issues can stall our progress unless we sincerely implement the appropriate solutions for each one of them.

But even an eligible student with proper exposure to Vedanta may yet not derive full benefit of his new knowledge. Becoming eligible for knowledge (*jnana yogyata*) and then acquiring knowledge (*jnana prapti*) need not necessarily lead to the fruits of such knowledge (*jnana phala*).

The student who has received his full dose of Vedantic knowledge may continue to have doubts about the real and ultimate point that the scriptures want to convey. The scriptures talk about a wholeness, a unity, a oneness which negates any subject-object distinction. But our experiences are always exactly the opposite, all based on the perceived distinction between the subject 'I' and everything else. We live in duality, we think in duality, we feel duality. There is thus a huge gulf between what we have been taught and what we experience every moment.

Even after we are able to bridge this gulf (by seeing that advaita is a matter of understanding and not a matter of experiencing), our habitual reactions and thinking still run our lives and deny us the peace and undisturbed fulfilment which Vedanta is meant to bring to us.

To overcome these problems, our traditions prescribe two more processes to be employed after receiving proper knowledge: the removal of doubts by thinking & discussion and the internalisation of Vedanta's vision by repeated contemplation. Or, to use Sanskrit terms, *shravana* has to be followed by *manana* and *nidhidhyasana*. Without these two further processes, mere exposure to knowledge will not deliver the goods because that knowledge will remain diluted by doubts and lack of full integration.

It is, therefore, important to keep in mind these impediments so that our own journey does not suffer from avoidable slowing down and stoppages.

At first glance it may be difficult to see the connection between our personal relationships and our efforts to study Vedanta. But who we associate with and what expectations we harbour as we relate with others have a great impact on our inner growth.

RELATIONSHIPS

We seek companionship of fellow human beings because that is natural to us. As Aristotle put it, *"Man is by nature a social animal; an individual who is unsocial naturally, and not accidentally, is either beneath our notice or more than human."*

Most of us find it impossible to lead healthy and meaningful lives without relating to others. And relationships, especially close ones, greatly affect the quality of our lives—good ones can make our lives heavenly while bad ones can create hell for us, right here on earth. Apart from this, to accomplish something worthwhile, cooperation with others is usually necessary and that involves relationships.

While acknowledging the important place of relationships in our lives, we should derive an important message from the teachings of our scriptures: never look upon relationships as a means of happiness, only as a means of growth. Such a message may sound innocuous but, in fact, it is vital for all of us. This message of the scriptures is based on wisdom and concern for our individual good. Experience tells us that our happiness depends on countless factors with many of them being beyond our control. If happiness was in our control, would any one of us be unhappy for even a moment? Our happiness is unpredictable and fragile, it comes and goes on its own terms. The experience of happiness is affected by the state of our own bodies and minds as well as by the behaviour of others and the environment in which we happen to be. Further, what is a source of joy today can become a matter of indifference or even of grief tomorrow. Given this fickle nature of happiness, relationships based primarily on happiness expected to be derived from them will also be correspondingly unpredictable and fragile.

If we are looking for happiness which is stable and dependable, our objective should not be relative happiness born out of relationships but finding the very source of permanent and unalloyed happiness which, Vedanta says, is internal. As a Sanskrit saying states,"*sarvam paravasham dukkham sarvam atmavasham sukham*"—anything dependent on anyone or anything else is a cause of sorrow, real happiness can only come from within us.

Proper self-knowledge is required to discover that happiness is actually integral to us. Vedanta is meant to give us this knowledge but, before it can do so, it needs a certain level of preparedness. Important elements of this preparedness can only come from relationships. Let us look at some of these elements. One basic thing necessary for our inner growth, in the direction envisaged by Vedanta, is reasonable physical and mental health. There is credible evidence to show that good interpersonal relationships positively contribute to a healthy body and a healthy mind. And this applies even to *sanyasis* who, despite having given up most worldly connections, are encouraged to maintain nurturing relationships with their gurus as well as with their chosen deities (*ishta devatas*).

Growth and maturity also involve us becoming more of contributors rather than just perpetual consumers and this calls for relationships with others. Even the basic level of an individual's contribution to society expected by the Vedic tradition (*pancha maha yagnas*), needs co-operation of and interaction with others. And greater contribution beyond the minimum, for the good of society as a whole, requires involvement of a larger number of people and a lot of team-work. This, again, brings in relationships.

For those who go by the model of *karma*, the consequences of many of our past good and bad deeds (*punya* and *papa*) can only be exhausted via specific relationships which are needed for both pleasurable and painful experiences. Finally, relationships are necessary for us to learn the lesson of forbearance *(titiksha)* and for ego modulation. Bad relationships can cause suffering which becomes all the more acute when it comes from a near relationship—as Shakespeare said, "*Lilies that fester smell far worse than weeds*". But suffering is an integral part of life and it requires a certain amount of forbearance and softening of the ego if we are to gain and grow from it. Without this, our minds will remain too disturbed to draw the most valuable lesson from suffering—the lesson that it is futile to rely on anything external for our happiness. (To see the potential value of suffering in a humorous light, we can turn to Socrates who, when asked by a young man whether he should get married or not, is reputed to have advised, "*By all means, marry. If you get a good wife, you'll be happy; if you get a bad one, you'll become a philosopher*"!)

Titiksha becomes all the more important in our old age. This is when flagging mental and physical energies reduce the role of free will *(purushartha)* and restrict our ability to change things to our liking. Consequently, our lives become more dominated by destiny (*prarabdha pradhanam*). An important aspect of living in freedom at this stage is our acceptance of the increasing role of destiny. And we should be doing this not out of resignation or with resentment but out of wisdom, without unnecessary resistance.

This of course is not to suggest that our traditions advocate the supine acceptance of all bad relationships and situations. What to do with unpleasant relationships depends on the nature of specific cases—the level of toxicity generated by such relationships, the assessment of the differing levels of suffering caused to the parties involved when relationships are altered and the level of maturity of those individuals. There are undoubtedly circumstances where a larger good is achieved by walking away from some relationships. In the modern context this could involve divorces or cutting off the apron strings for irresponsible & exploitative children. Even in the past, the taking to renunciation *(sanyasa)* by an individual driven by the need for inner growth, led to the erasure of many relationships but this was applauded as it was seen to be in the interest of a larger cause.

Finally, whatever may be an individual situation, we must always bear in mind the fundamental advice in respect of any relationship which we saw earlier: never look upon relationships as a means of happiness, only as a means of growth. If we keep this principle in mind, we will continue to mature irrespective of the nature of our relationships, including the problematic ones. And without inner growth and maturity, we will not be able to properly relate to even our own selves, much less with others.

The teaching of Vedanta uses many analogies including the rope-snake, the ocean and its waves, clay and clay objects and so on. However, the most important analogy is the one where the world is compared to a dream. This comparison leads to many doubts and questions.

IS THE WORLD A DREAM?

The texts and teachers of advaita Vedanta often compare our waking world to a dream. This comparison brings out different reactions from students, at times of incredulity and even of derision. The reasons for such disbelief are simple—just look at the differences between our waking lives and our dreams:

- Dreams are purely personal and subjective while the waking world is experienced and shared by many others.
- Dreams are experienced by us for a very brief period while the waking world exists for us throughout our lives.
- Dreams are disjointed and disconnected, with an impossible juxtaposition of time and place; for instance, in a single night's dream you could be in New York and Mumbai as well as having a conversation with a dead friend. On the other hand, our waking experiences are logically connected and they work in a cogent manner.

How, then, can we accept that our waking world is like our dream world? We, therefore, remain convinced that our waking experiences are real while the dream ones are not and it appears unreasonable to draw any parallels.

The first thing which we should note here is that none of these differences between our dream experiences and waking experiences are problematic issues while we are dreaming. The dream world is as real and cogent as our waking world, while the dream is going on. It is only upon waking up that we find problems within our dreams and dismiss them as being unreal. Vedanta says that our waking state is also like a dream, though at a different level. So we will find everything to be real in our waking state but only till we wake up from here to an even higher level of reality. This waking up is not a physical awakening but a cognitive one. It is a release from our ignorance, in the light of Vedanta's knowledge. Only then will we understand that our waking world is also unreal.

But leaving this aside, let us understand why the teaching tradition of Vedanta uses the seemingly inappropriate dream example. For this, we have to understand the limitations of comparisons in general and also be clear about what Vedanta means by the term 'real'.

Let us first look at the limitations of comparisons. For this purpose, let us take the example of England's King Richard I (of the Crusades fame) being described as 'Richard the lionheart'. And, in India, we sometimes hear the complaint, *"This dal is like water"*. We can immediately find flaws in both these statements, if we want to. We all know that lions have tails, claws, fangs and fur; and we also know that water is transparent, odourless and tasteless. But King Richard had neither a tail nor the many other attributes of a lion. And even watery dal has colour, taste and smell. How then can we compare Richard to a lion or dal to water?

We can do this because, in any such comparison, the intention is never to imply that the two things being compared are identical to each other in every respect. If they were identical, we would not use a simile or a metaphor or an analogy; we would just employ another term which is synonymous, such as *H2O* or *aqua* for water.

But when we say *Richard the lionheart,* our limited intention is to focus on his lion-like quality of bravery and not on the fact that Richard lacked a tail. Similarly, our comment about the dal being watery is only to bring out the fact that it is too thin and runny, not to imply that the dal is devoid of all colour, taste or smell.

Now, coming to the statement that the world is like a dream, the intention is obviously not to suggest that our dream and waking worlds are identical on all counts. As we have seen, it is very simple to come up with several objections to this idea. (And it is also quite presumptuous to think that these obvious objections would not have occurred to the long lineage of Vedanta teachers.)

Our dreams and our waking world share some similarities but that does not mean that they are identical. We should therefore focus on the few important similarities which Vedanta wants us to draw lessons from, instead of getting ensnared in listing dissimilarities. What are those important similarities?

One important reason why Vedanta draws a parallel between our dreams and waking experiences is to bring our attention to the fact that just because something is experienced, it need not necessarily be real; we experience our dreams vividly but yet take them to be unreal. While Vedanta never denies our experiences, it says that we must not be closed to the idea of examining and re-interpreting even our waking experiences in light of better knowledge. If we are not willing to do this, we may as well continue to hold on to the conclusion that the earth is stationary and the sun rises and sets, because this is our daily experience. The dream analogy is only to caution us from hastily concluding that the waking world is absolutely real, just because it is experienced.

Further, we learn from our dreams that it is consciousness which is primary in our experiences and not our bodies. In our dreams, we fully experience actions and sensations even though our bodies are dormant and non-participative. So bodies are not necessary for conscious experiences. This understanding is developed further when Vedanta analyses our waking, dream and deep sleep states to establish the primacy of consciousness.

The next important idea which the dream comparison intends to convey is that there can be one underlying reality behind a number of apparently different things. The sky, mountains, rivers, flowers and people in our dreams are entirely formed out of just our thoughts, which are nothing but our consciousness; whenever we dream, it is only our consciousness which projects a whole world of variety, with its own frame-work of time and space. Vedanta uses this example to support its teaching that the reality underlying our waking world is also single, even though the world displays so many differences and varieties.

Another important factor which is relevant to this analogy is the precise and technical definition of the word 'real' in Vedanta. In the language of Vedanta, 'real' is something which always exists, which cannot be sublated in all three periods of time—the past, the present and the future. We write-off our dreams as unreal because their durations are very short relative to our whole lives. But, in Vedanta's definition, both our waking and dream states last only for a limited time (though the spans differ) and nothing that we know in either of these two states has unbroken existence in the past, present and future. Therefore, for Vedanta, though we experience our waking world to be more real than our dream world, they are both fundamentally unreal .

The dream analogy also shows us that it is necessary for things to be on the same level of reality (*samana satta*) to be able to affect each other. The water on our bedside table cannot quench our dream thirst and the tiger from our dreams cannot maul us as we lie asleep in our beds. The teachings of Vedanta show us that all the things in the world (including our own bodies and minds) lack permanent reality. But for anything which temporarily appears, there has to be a substratum, like the rope for the snake or our thoughts for the dream or clay for the pot. Vedanta tells us that the common substratum for the entire creation is consciousness. It is this consciousness which is the reality behind both an individual and the world he perceives. Vedanta goes on to show us that this consciousness, being independent and unchanging, enjoys a higher level of reality than the world and its individuals. If we get over our false identification with our bodies and minds and understand our own reality to be unchanging consciousness, we can stop taking our worldly problems so seriously. This is because consciousness, which is our reality at a more fundamental level, can never be affected by issues at the worldly level just as a dream fire cannot singe the sleeping individual.

Yet another interesting thing which our dreams bring out is the strength of our *samskaras*—the deep grooves of our habituated ways of thinking. Our dreams can have many weird and fantastic elements as well as unrealistic ideas of time and space. But, even in our dream fantasy, our strong identification with our bodies continues. A man will never dream of himself as a woman, much less as an animal because of his strongly-held identification with a male human body. This gives us some indication of the amount of work we need to do in nidhidhyasana to get over our patterns of identification and thinking.

It is also important to understand where the dream analogy fits in within differing explanations of creation provided by Vedanta. The teachings of Vedanta can, at different stages, talk of three apparently contradictory theories or views *(vadas)* of creation. These are termed:

Shrishti drishti vada: In this view, creation (*shrishti*) is primary and things are seen (*drishti*) only after they are created. Here the understanding is that first there was a universe in which life gradually evolved on our planet and, eventually, human life and human consciousness evolved. This is the most common-place view which, in Western philosophy, is known as the Realist view.

Drishti shrishti vada: In this view it is consciousness (*drishti*) that is primary and gives rise to the appearance of the world (*shrishti*). In this understanding, consciousness exists first and then this consciousness manifests the apparent world with its subject/objects duality. This is similar to what happens in our dreams. In Western philosophy this is known as the Idealist view of reality. Such a view is close to what is known as *vivarta vada* in Vedanta.

Ajata vada: *Ajata* means non-creation. This is the most radical view, unique to Vedanta, that there never was any creation at all, and that there is only one unchanging reality. The previous two *vadas* can be quite readily understood. *Ajata vada,* however, is a teaching that is relevant only at the paramarthika level and difficult to relate to at our vyavaharika level. It is usually associated with Gaudapada's *karika* on the Mandukya Upanishad but also features in several other scriptures such the Yoga Vasishtha and the Ashtavakra Gita.

Why are there such different explanations for creation is perhaps best explained by quoting the words of Ramana Maharishi as reproduced in Day To Day With Bhagavan:

> *"Ramana Maharshi: I do not teach only the ajata doctrine. I approve of all schools. The same truth has to be expressed in different ways to suit the capacity of the hearer. The ajata doctrine says, 'Nothing exists except the one reality. There is no birth or death, no projection or drawing in [of the world], no sadhaka [no seeker], no mumukshu [no one seeking liberation], no mukta [no liberated person], no bondage, no liberation. The one unity alone exists ever'.*
>
> *To such as find it difficult to grasp this truth and who ask "How can we ignore this solid world we see all around us?" the dream experience is pointed out and they are told, "All that you see depends on the seer. Apart from the seer, there is no seen." This is called the drishti-srishti vada, or the argument that one first creates out of his mind and then sees what his mind itself has created.*

To such as cannot grasp even this and who further argue "The dream experience is so short, while the world always exists. The dream experience was limited to me. But the world is felt and seen not only by me, but by so many, and we cannot call such a world non-existent," the argument called srishti-drishti vada is addressed and they are told "God first created such and such a thing, out of such and such an element and then something else, and so forth." That alone will satisfy this class. ... To such it is best to say, "Yes. God created all this and so you see it."'

Dr. M. said, But all these cannot be true; only one doctrine can be true.

Bhagavan said, All these are only to suit the capacity of the learner. The absolute can only be one."

This is why Vedanta teachings often start by working in a *shrishti-drishti* framework, which is the default conceptual framework of reality for most seekers, especially at the start of their journey. Then, the *drishti-shrishti* framework is introduced. Finally, the *ajata* or no-creation viewpoint is brought in when the seeker is ready, in stepwise progression depending on how the seeker is progressing with the teachings. The nature and content of teachings differ depending on what framework of reality is being used.

The limitations of examples while learning from Vedanta are not restricted only to the dream example. A teacher may use the example of a cinema screen and say that in a movie we focus on the unreal scenes projected on the screen and not take notice of the screen which is the only constant and real presence. Without the screen there would be no movie at all. The teacher may then go on to compare brahman with the screen and the world to the movie. If we do not limit this example to what it is intended to show, we may conclude that this example implies that the world is like a real movie, that we (the individuals) are like real movie-goers and that brahman is like the screen. There are three separate entities in this movie example: the movie-goer, the screen and the movie. But, at the full level of understanding of Vedanta's vision, brahman is the only thing which exists and the world as well as the experiencer of the world are all nothing but one and the same brahman. So the movie example should not lead us to believe that Vedanta accepts a real multiplicity of things.

Similarly, when Vedanta talks about original consciousness *(atma)* and reflected consciousness *(chidabhasa)*, we must bear in mind that such usage is only interim and designed to address a limited point. Reality is non-dual and all these explanations in response to our questions are useful only till our understanding reaches a certain level where we see the irrelevance not only of the questions but of the questioner himself!

The examples used in Vedanta give us many valuable messages. Amongst all the examples used, the dream example is particularly valuable. However, use of this analogy should be restricted to its intended purpose and not stretched beyond what it wants to convey. To avoid drawing wrong conclusions from such examples in the course of our study of Vedanta, we need a proper teacher whose guidance is indispensable.

An unremarkable experience used for remarkable teaching.

DEEP SLEEP: A PEEP INTO THE INFINITE

Avastha Traya

Vedanta uses many of our common experiences to help us relate to its subtle truths. One important and effective *prakriya* (mechanism or technique) used in the teaching of Vedanta is the *avastha traya* (three states) prakriya. These three states, which we go through daily, are waking, dreaming and being in dreamless sleep.

Dreams

The dream experience is very important and used often in the course of teaching. Dreams establish that just because things are experienced, they are not necessarily real; this we learn when we wake up and realise that what was so vividly experienced and seemed so real in our dream was actually unreal. Dreams further tell us that it is possible for a whole variegated world of objects to appear on the basis of a single and undifferentiated sub-stratum; this is shown by the fact that our dreams which, though as complex as our waking world, are only appearances in and of our own consciousness. Our dreams also tell us that things at one level of reality have no effect on things at another level just as a downpour in our dream will not wet us as we lie asleep in our beds.

Vedanta uses our dream experiences to derive these and many other useful lessons as it takes us to the proper understanding of the real nature of ourselves and of the world which we confront.

No Bodies And World In Deep Sleep

Like the dream state, the deep sleep state also tells us a number of vital things. Let us look at these in some detail. We can begin with the fact that in deep sleep there is total absence of our bodies, minds and of the entire world. All these are very evident in our waking hours and they are also evident, though in a different way, when we dream. But in deep sleep, when our minds shut down, our bodies and the whole world completely disappear. This makes it very clear that our perception of outside objects is only as formed and channelled by our minds. Such an observation is important in countering the notion which many have, that matter is the primary reality while a conscious mind is only a by-product; in fact, it is only because of a conscious mind that our own bodies and the entire world arise for us.

Sleep Is Identical For All

Another important aspect of deep sleep is that this experience is absolutely identical for all of us. We have no way of distinguishing tonight's experience of deep sleep from last night's. We also cannot tell the difference between our own experience of deep sleep from any one else's. Sleep is the same for the rich and the poor, for the strong and the weak, for the young and the old, for a man and a woman, for a learned person and an ignorant person.

Problems Disappear In Sleep

The uniformity of the deep sleep experience is accompanied by the fact that all our problems and limitations disappear in this state. This gives us an important pointer to the solution for our problems .

Our problems arise because we think we are a body-mind combination and identify with all the limitations of this combination. However, Vedanta teaches that our reality is not the body-mind combination but *sat chit ananda* atma which has no limitations, wants or problems. It is because of the false identification with our body-mind that we wrongly take ourselves to be mortal, ignorant and unfulfilled. Based on these mistakes, we make herculean efforts to perpetuate our bodies, to learn more and more and to seek the desirable while pushing away the undesirable. However, given the inherent nature of the body-mind combination, our efforts can never fully and permanently succeed. It is because of this endless struggle that we get tired.

In deep sleep, our minds stop functioning and their false identification with our bodies ceases. With this, not only do all voluntary physical movements stop but all fears, longings, self-judgements and regrets also vanish. Both our bodies and minds then get their much needed rest and we feel refreshed when we wake up. What this points to is that if we can minimise our false identification with our bodies even in our waking state, we will continually experience the peace and contentment which sleep brings to us intermittently.

Ignorance Continues In Deep Sleep

Because our problems disappear in deep sleep, we may think that our ignorance about the true nature of ourselves also disappears in that state. However, our ignorance continues in all the three states of waking, dreaming and deep sleep. The only difference is that while ignorance is active in waking and dreaming, it is latent or in seed form in deep sleep. This is why in the waking and dreaming states, active ignorance leads to the error of identification with a body-mind. But in deep sleep, where there is only latent and inactive ignorance, there is no error of false identification.

How do we know that ignorance is present in deep sleep? Because when we wake up our identification with a body-mind and all its attendant problems continue. The only way in which ignorance can be removed is by knowledge and obviously no new knowledge can be acquired in sleep. This is why Vedanta tells us *jnanam eva moksha;* our real solution is self-knowledge.

Problems Only Because Of Part Knowledge

Another important fact which is brought out by the deep sleep state is that our problems do not arise from *total* ignorance of our reality. And Vedanta tells us that once we have *full* knowledge of atma, our problems will again recede. Our problems arise only out of partial knowledge and partial ignorance of our true nature. This is why none of us have any sense of limitation or face issues in deep sleep, where there is total ignorance. And, based on the lives of enlightened masters, we see that the same freedom is available to those who have acquired full self-knowledge. Problems only affect the rest of us in our waking or dream states, till we are able to obtain and assimilate Vedanta's teachings.

Using the rope-snake example here, in complete darkness we do not see the rope at all – total ignorance – and so no snake appears to frighten us. In full light, we see the rope clearly so again no snake appears. The snake emerges only in half light when we see a coil of something without recognising it as a rope and then project a snake on this hazily seen something.

We have a similar situation in the case of atma. We have no doubt about its sat and chit aspects—we clearly know that we exist and that we are conscious beings. However, we do not know that our reality is unchanging and limitless. Despite this partial ignorance we do not conclude that our self-knowledge is incomplete. Just as a snake is wrongly seen in the place of a half-seen rope, we make the mistake of superimposing a limited body and mind on the partially known atma. We then suffer the consequences of this assumed limitation because no matter what we do and how much we have, we continue to remain limited by mortality, bothered by limited knowledge and suffer from limited fulfilment which always remain associated with an individual body and mind.

Therefore, Vedanta holds out full knowledge of our own reality as the only total and final solution to our fundamental problems.

Does Consciousness Exist In Deep Sleep?

The three states of waking, dreaming and deep sleep are temporary as they continuously interchange. Vedanta tells us that the only constant and unchanging factor across all these three states is consciousness because of which we know that we go through these three states. It is because of consciousness that we are aware that we are awake, that we dreamt and also that last night we slept dreamlessly. Vedanta therefore holds that our real truth is consciousness and the three states we experience are only temporary and passing projections in and of that consciousness.

But this explanation can raise some questions. How can we say that consciousness is present in deep sleep? The fact that we experience nothing in deep sleep could be because consciousness does not exist in that state. And if that is so then it cuts at the root of the statement that consciousness is the constant and unchanging witness of these three changing states.

Vedanta, however, tells us that the fact that there is no experience in deep sleep does not point to the *absence of consciousness*; it actually points to the *consciousness of absence* of anything to be experienced. This absence of anything to be experienced occurs not because consciousness disappears but only because our minds are temporarily non-functional in deep sleep.

The continuity of consciousness in deep sleep is supported by our own experiences. We do not feel that the person who wakes up is different from the person who fell asleep; there is a continuing identity in terms of the same ego, memories and desires all of which are rooted in a conscious mind. And we know that we slept dreamlessly as our own, direct knowledge, not by some inference or because of someone else's testimony; this again tallies with unbroken consciousness.

(For those who want to go into further and more technical details, another question can be raised here: Who knows we slept dreamlessly? It cannot be the *chidabhasa* or reflected consciousness which is not present when the mind, which is the reflecting medium, is covered in deep sleep. It cannot be original consciousness because it never directly participates in the act of knowing—knowing occurs only in a mind energised by the *reflection* of original consciousness. Then who knows? The knower of our deep sleep experience is the innermost layer of our body-mind complex, which is called the *karana sharira* or the *anandamaya kosha*. This layer consists of ignorance which, though latent, has seeds of *tamas*, *rajas* & *sattva* which are dynamic and capable of recording the fact of no experience. Upon waking up, this subtle impression is handed over to the ego which arises with chidabhasa. The ego, though not present in deep sleep, now falsely claims "I slept soundly".)

Valuable Lessons From Deep Sleep

As Vedanta tells us, consciousness is our constant and unchanging reality and the three states of waking, dreaming and deep sleep are passing events lacking intrinsic reality. Our deep sleep experience is crucial in supporting this conclusion; it also gives many other insights into our problems and their solutions. It takes Vedanta to derive such learning from a daily and commonplace experience like sleep.

The mind is both our problem and, paradoxically, also the solution to our problem.

MIND THE GAP

London's underground railway (the Tube) has signs saying *'Mind the Gap'* all over its stations to warn users about the danger of falling into the gap between trains and platforms. We could use this phrase in Vedanta too, and with two different meanings.

In our first use, we understand this phrase to mean that our mind is the gap—the gap between the fulfilment we seek and the lack of fulfilment we experience. We can say this because the mind is always present whenever we experience lack of fulfilment. On the other hand, in a 'no-mind' state (such as in deep sleep or when fully absorbed in an activity like meditation or a peak experience), we do not feel any lack or the need to bring about changes in ourselves. We feel insecure and incomplete only when our minds are active and not fully absorbed.

If the mind is the source of our discontent, what should we do about it? One theoretical solution, which is absurdly impractical, is *manonasha*—destruction of the mind. This 'solution' (of something like a permanent coma) would reduce us to the state of a rock which, too, has no problems. But who would want to be without a mind—to be permanently without thoughts, emotions, feelings, experiences and functionality? A less drastic variation on this theme is an altered state of mind achieved by the use of drugs. But here, while mental faculties are available, they are distorted and abnormal; useful functioning and inter-actions are not possible. Our minds are a natural part of us and doing away with the mind's function, even in part, cannot be a meaningful solution.

The next solution, which is supported by many traditions, is *manolaya*—temporary dissolution or absorption of the mind. A prime example of this solution is *samadhi* meditation where, with effort and practice, one can achieve a 'no-mind' state. But the absorption of the mind it leads to is only temporary. The mind with all its issues is present before the meditation begins, it is only suspended during the period of meditation and returns with full force when that episode of meditation ends. The stillness of mind experienced during meditation can cause good effects even after the meditation is over. Some of our negative emotions can get sublimated, the hyper-activity of our mind may find a rein and our instant reactivity to situations may reduce. While all this is very helpful, it does not address our basic problem which is the problem of duality—the problem of the 'other'.

The upanishads tell us that the root of all our problems lies in *dvaita*—when we see other people and objects which constitute our world. The moment we conclude that there are real entities apart from us – the 'other'– problems of both fear and limitation arise. Other people can cause pain and things in the world can afflict us with disease, accidents and uncomfortable comparisons. All things outside of us can be potential threats to our sense of well-being by their presence or by their absence. They limit our happiness because we could always do with more of something we like and with less of something we don't like. These problems arise only because of the perceived presence of the other.

If duality is real then there is no real solution to these problems of fear and limitation. But the upanishads go on to make us understand that the world of other people and objects we perceive is not absolutely real; their teachings lead us to see that there is only one reality which is the basis for the appearance of the entire world, including our own body and mind. Without real duality, our fear and sense of limitation no longer have any basis.

This insight of the upanishads needs an active mind which is capable of thought and understanding. Temporarily quieting the mind by techniques like meditation is no solution to a problem rooted in ignorance. To know the truth behind the world and ourselves we don't need to destroy or suspend anything. What we need is a change in our understanding to recognise that the duality we transact with is not real. We need to delete duality only in our cognition, not in our experiences. This is similar to enjoying a sunset while understanding that the sun does not set. Such negation of false experience by understanding is termed *badha*. And this is the method of Vedanta—to use the mind's power of understanding to remove specific ignorance in the mind without any change in our surroundings and without erasing the mind. As has been often said, the problem is the mind and the solution is also the mind.

In order to do its task, Vedanta first concentrates on moderating our egos and modulating our emotions so that our intellects are not unnecessarily hindered in the process of understanding Vedanta's message. Unhealthy egos and uncontrolled emotions can create so much turbulence and opacity in our minds that the subtle truths of Vedanta have difficulty in striking home.

But just receiving Vedanta's teachings in a prepared mind, though vital, is not enough. Here the warning, 'Mind the Gap', needs to be repeated but with a different meaning. At this stage of our spiritual journey, where we have already put in significant effort in studying Vedanta, we need to be mindful or careful of another gap. What gap? The crucial gap between knowledge and deliverance.

There are many students of Vedanta who have studied this subject for several years, who have clearly understood its message but are yet not able to experience the freedom and fulfilment which are Vedanta's promises. Why is that? Because there is a gap between what they have understood and the reactions of their egos and emotions, which are still not in line with this new understanding. This is a bit like an overweight man reaching for a large dessert or avoiding gym work-outs despite being convinced of the benefits of a healthy regime. He continues with a damaging life-style not because he does not know better but because habitual ways over-power his knowledge. In Vedanta, too, a similar problem arises because our reactions continue to remain in the deep grooves formed by past habits and conditioning. Just intellectual clarity about the message of Vedanta does not necessarily mean that the rest of the mind will fall in line.

How do we bridge the gap between what we know and what we actually feel and do? There are two aspects to the answer here. The first is to make sure that we do have sufficient amounts of the qualities required for Vedanta to work; we need to be *adhikaris* with *sadhana chatushtaya*. Many of us diligently work on understanding what Vedanta teaches without making changes in life-styles or without focusing too much on watering down strong likes and dislikes. Lack of dispassion and lack of a certain amount of disconnect with the world is a big impediment to deriving real benefit from Vedanta.

Assuming that this has been dealt with, the next aspect of the answer is in the final process which Vedanta lays down for our use: *niddhidhyasana*. Niddhidhyasana is translated as contemplation and refers to repeated dwelling on the already known teachings of Vedanta with the objective of converting second-hand information into personal conviction.

This process is long; it also lacks the intellectual stimulation which comes from the acquisition of new knowledge because, here, we are repeatedly traversing ground which is already known. And even teachers are of limited help in this process, unless we have an old and on-going personal relationship with a proper guru.

The importance of nidhidhyasana is brought out by Swami Sarvapriyananda (of the Ramakrishna order) by using an interesting metaphor from medicine. He compares the introduction of the novel insights of Vedanta into our minds with the transplant of a donated organ, such as a kidney, into our bodies. After a new kidney is implanted into us, we have to exercise regularly, control our diets, avoid polluted or crowded places and take a daily dose of immunosuppressants. If we do not follow this regime, not only will the transplant operation not give us the desired benefit but will also ultimately result in the rejection of the foreign kidney by our own bodies. Similarly, without proper and continuing nidhidhyasana, the newly implanted knowledge of Vedanta will not work properly and will ultimately be overcome by our past habits and tendencies.

There are many ways in which niddhidhyasana can be practised. One way, of course, is regularly sitting down for formal contemplation. This may appear to be identical with the practice of meditation in yoga. But it is, in fact, quite different. In Vedantic contemplation, our objective is not to have a mind empty of all thoughts (it is not *citta vritti nirodha* as stated in Patanjali's Yoga Sutras); in our contemplation we repeatedly go over any one or more aspects of Vedanta's teachings mentally, with a quiet and focused mind. Our aim is to see the truth of the teachings for ourselves again and again so these truths completely seep into us. Continuing to read and listen to the teachings of Vedanta, even after having understood them, is also another way of niddhidhyasana. Writing, discussing and sharing with others is yet another way. In short, anything which keeps us in regular touch with the teachings of Vedanta is useful in this process.

How long should this process continue? Until we bridge the gap, till the wisdom of Vedanta becomes integral to us, available instantly and without conscious thought or effort. It is only then that peace, security and contentment actually become ours.

And if we don't complete this crucial last step, we may end up being scholars of Vedanta but never closing the gap between superficial information and the personal transformation which is needed to bring home the real fruits of Vedanta.

Many ideas put forward in the earlier parts of the teaching process of Vedanta, later get replaced by other ideas which are contrary to the initial teachings. This leads to doubts and questions.

DO THE TEACHINGS OF VEDANTA SPIN YARNS?

In a word, *yes*! This fact, of course, seems startling and disappointing. After all, one would not expect ancient and much-admired teachings to lead one up the garden path. But the truth here is beyond a simple 'yes' or 'no' answer.

There are three major factors which make Vedanta appear contradictory and even misleading at times. These factors are the existing world-view of the student, his limited receptivity to radically new ideas and the lack of a proper teacher. But, before we go into these matters, let us look at some examples of Vedantic teachings which are apparently based on contradictions and can cause confusion for a student.

Elements of Creation

The initial portions of Vedanta talk about five basic elements (*pancha mahabhutas*) and the process by which they mix in different ways to create the universe. The five elements are space, air, fire, water and earth (*akasha, vayu, agni, apa and prithvi*). But this model of creation is not only contradicted by science but also by the scriptures themselves when, in other places, they tell us that it is *brahman* which is the basis of creation, not these five elements.

Brahman

To make this worse, the teachings which hold out brahman as the cause of the universe (*jagat karanam*) later overturn this also, by stating that brahman is neither the cause nor the effect of anything.

Size and location of atma

There are mentions in the scriptures of *atma* being the size of a thumb and of it being located in the heart. But the same scriptures, in other portions, repeatedly deny any attributes (such as size or location) for atma.

Karma and re-birth

The *karma* theory, wherein the results of many of our actions are said to be carried forward to future births, is a significant part of Vedantic teaching. Scriptures also reassure us that any spiritual effort we make is never wasted and if it has not produced fruits in this lifetime, it will do so in a subsequent one. However, in an apparent volte-face, we are later told that our world and our own individualities have no absolute reality and that the ideas of birth, karmas and re-births are only relevant at a level which is not the highest level of truth.

Ishwara is *mithya*

Ishwara plays an important part in the Vedantic journey, especially in the preparatory stages, where he is held out to be *sarva shaktiman, sarvajna* and *sarva vyapi* (omnipotent, omniscient and all-pervasive) as well as *karma phala data* (the giver of the fruits of our actions). But later, when we are told that the world is *mithya* (without independent reality), we are told that Ishwara, as the creator and ruler of this world, is mithya as well.

Moksha is conditional and prospective

Perhaps the most frustrating aspects of these apparent contradictions, especially for advanced students of Vedanta, are the different ideas put forward about Vedanta's holy grail: *moksha* or liberation.

A student's ultimate objective is to find freedom from all limitations, which the proper assimilation of Vedantic wisdom promises. He is told that this liberation is dependent on his cultivating specified qualities & disciplines (*sadhana chatushtaya*), adopting a certain life-style (of *karma* and *upasana* yogas) and going through prescribed learning processes (of *shravana, manana and nidhidhyasana*). He is further told that this prospective liberation can happen either during his current lifetime itself (*jivan mukti*) or after his death, post a suitable stay in a higher realm or *loka* (*videha mukti*). Once liberation occurs, the student is told that he will be permanently released from the cycle of births & deaths and the attendant suffering of being in *samsara*.

But, even though many students (including senior ones) gloss over this point, the real fact is that *mukti* is not a *sadhya vastu* but a *siddha vastu*—it is not something to be achieved but it is something already achieved. Our liberation, though obscured by our misunderstanding, is an already accomplished fact which is neither subject to the student's efforts nor is it a future event. This, of course, seems to make cruel mockery of the student's great and long-drawn efforts to attain liberation and goes against all that he has been led to believe during his journey of Vedanta.

Why These Contradictions?

Why do the teachings and teachers of Vedanta play around like this? Why do the traditional teaching processes rely on making statements which are not entirely true, only to replace them later with truer statements? For answers to this, we have to go back to the three factors which were mentioned at the outset: the existing world-view of the student, his level of preparedness to be receptive to radically new ideas and the lack of a proper teacher.

Our Usual World-view

We all see ourselves as separate and limited individuals confronting a vast and complex world which we have to handle in order to obtain happiness. In fact, many of us have a view of reality which consists of three completely separated elements: the individual 'I' *(jiva)*, the world *(jagat)* and the creator *(Ishwara)*. But Vedanta's core teaching is based on advaita or non-duality which denies absolute reality to individuals, to the world and to the creator. Such a contrarian view clearly goes against our experiences and our conditioning. If it is put forth at the outset, it would stretch a student's credulity and faith beyond breaking point. This is one reason why the full extent and implications of advaita are not fully set out initially. The teachings of Vedanta start by provisionally accepting the reality of the individual and the world he confronts; the truth that the only reality is brahman, and the far-reaching consequences of this truth, are later disclosed and, that too, in small and gradual steps.

The Student's Level

Further, different students come with different needs, abilities and levels of intellectual & emotional preparedness. The speed of their progress and their ability to stay the full course are not certain. This is another reason why the teaching methodology deliberately starts with what may be euphemistically called 'watered-down truths'. The idea is to lead someone deeper in gradual steps and to not completely demolish his existing beliefs because, should the student stop enroute, he should not be left high & dry, without any support from his old and comforting ideas.

Actually, our traditions once restricted exposure to Vedanta to *sanyasis* who had already committed themselves to a life-time of study, without any other agenda and who had the requisite emotional and intellectual abilities. Even then, exposing them to the truth only in gradual stages was considered important. Today, when all of us have full access to Vedanta irrespective of our eligibility or commitment, we randomly expose ourselves to different levels of teaching. For us, an understanding of this technique of Vedanta, where different levels of teachings are used at different stages of learning, is even more important.

Lack of a Teacher

This brings us to the need for a proper teacher in our Vedantic journey. To find a proper teacher and establish an ongoing relationship with him over a sufficient period of time is a great blessing. Such a teacher assesses our abilities and preparedness as he leads us from the initial teachings to subtler and truer depths, in steps specifically meant for an individual student. Because a teacher discriminates between the calibre and progress of his students, he can give different answers to the same question, depending upon the level of the student asking that question.

A student starts his journey with wanting freedom *for* his body-mind but Vedanta's purpose is freedom *from* the body-mind and the teacher has to skillfully lead him through this transition. But, today, we often have only sporadic exposure to a teacher (often, several different teachers) and rely on books and audio/video recordings without the benefit of meaningful live inter-action. And the consequences of this approach are often confusion and frustration.

We need to understand that the problems of life that we all are trying to solve are centred on our bodies and minds. As bodies and minds are part of the mithya *jagat*, they can only be affected by a solution at the same level. So Vedanta is also at the level of mithya. Therefore, it has no relevance to the real truth behind any individual because this truth is always limitless, unchanging and unaffected. Vedanta is only for the false 'I' which sees itself defined by a body, a mind and their possessions, relationships and attainments. However, there is no point in emphasising this just as a doctor does not tell a patient that he is getting a placebo. During our journey on the path of Vedanta, *samsara* is very real for us and so are the conditions of Vedanta such as *adhikaritvam, jeevan mukti & videha mukti:* necessary, useful white lies.

The teaching techniques of Vedanta like *adhyaropa apvada* (making a statement which is not the whole truth and, later, replacing it with a truer statement) and *adhikari bheda* (calibrating the teaching to suit individual needs) are part of the meta-teachings of advaita—they are meant for teachers and are not often explicitly discussed and explained to all students. But in situations where we do not have the guidance of a proper teacher on a regular basis, it is important to recognise these aspects of the traditional teaching methodology, to avoid unnecessary impediments in our journey.

Newer Approaches to Teaching

To further complicate matters, we now have newer methods of communicating the message of Vedanta, which are very different from the traditional teaching methodology. These newer methods come in different shades and with different names such as Direct Path Advaita and Satsang Advaita. These techniques alter traditional processes and also short-circuit eligibility requirements. Some of these modern versions present bald truths in an immediate and brief way, to all comers. Instead of systematically dismantling the seeker's pre-existing beliefs, they attempt to supplant them with radical new views. These new views are contrary to everyday dualistic experiences and not enough rationale is provided for them. The results of such approaches, though initially appealing, are often not helpful in the long run. As Denis Waite wrote in his Book of One, *"But simply stating how things are, is not going to have much effect upon those minds that have been habituated since birth to separation and an egotistic outlook on life. Furthermore, if a seeker accepts the truth of the statement that they are already free and nothing needs to be done (or can be done), they are left in an impossible situation. They are still suffering but can do nothing to alleviate it."*

The traditional teaching methodology of Vedanta, including its apparent contradictions, is intelligently designed and time-tested; all it needs to deliver its real results is an eligible and committed student, guided by a proper teacher over a sufficient length of time.

According to critics of Advaita Vedanta, the concept of maya/avidya *to explain the appearance of an unreal world is its weakest link.*

CAUSE OF THE WORLD'S APPEARANCE

Advaita Vedanta's real answer to the question, "Why is there a world?" is: *There isn't!* Vedanta's basic teaching is that there is only one reality which exists. This of course flies in the face of our experience because we continuously experience a tangible world of many different objects, all of which are very real to us. But Vedanta reiterates that the reality which exists is single. There is no other reality of its own type: it is not like one tree amongst many other trees. There is no reality of another type: it is not one type of thing, different from other types of things (such as animals being different from rocks or trees). Further, being a homogeneous whole, it also has no divisions or parts within itself: it is not like a tree which has distinct parts such as a trunk, branches and leaves. (This is put in Sanskrit as *na sajatiya bheda*, *na vijatiya bheda* and *na svagata bheda*.) Vedanta obviously then needs to reconcile our experience of plurality with its teaching of a single reality.

Vedanta goes on to explain that the world we transact with is undoubtedly experienced but what we experience has no intrinsic reality. It likens the world to our dream creation which is experienced without being real. Unlike our individual dreams which are a projection of our personal thoughts, this world is a projection of universal consciousness and we are all part of that impersonal projection. What causes this projection? As an answer, Vedanta holds out a power called *maya* which causes the world to appear; this same power resides in our individual minds as *avidya*. Maya is capable of both veiling and projecting (*avarana* and *vikshepa*). With this power, maya hides the true nature of our own reality and projects the appearance of a world which seems outside of us. Of these two powers, the veiling power is more problematic than the projecting one. After all, every time we see a movie we are subjected to a projection but this projection does not fundamentally affect us because it does not veil us—in a movie we do not forget that we are individuals outside of the movie. We, therefore, remain unaffected despite all that happens in the movie. However maya/avidya covers our true nature and causes us to falsely identify with a limited body-mind which faces what appears to be a real, uncontrollable and an immensely powerful world.

The concept of maya obviously leads to questions. What causes maya? Where is maya located? How is the existence of maya, which is different from brahman, compatible with a singular reality as claimed by Vedanta? The person who raised the most challenging questions about maya was Ramanujacharya (11th–12th century CE) whose views about the nature of reality were very different from Adi Shankaracharya's (8th century CE) views. The answers provided by later teachers of Vedanta to these questions are very detailed and technical so we will not get into them here. Instead, let us take a more generalised look at maya and the world's appearance.

The first and foremost thing we need to keep in mind here is that Vedanta's focus is not on explaining maya. Maya is brought out by Vedanta only as a temporary device for those who need an explanation for their experiences of a world of plurality when Vedanta repeatedly states that there is only one reality. Vedanta's real purpose is not explanations but to relieve us of unnecessary suffering. It recognises that all suffering arises because we take ourselves to be small and limited individuals pitched against a vast world. Its solution is to show us that neither we, the individuals, nor the world we face have intrinsic reality.

For this purpose, Vedanta guides us to see that there is an underlying common reality behind the appearance of both individuals and the world. This reality is without any boundary or attributes and remains completely unaffected even as it supports the appearance of the world and its events. To again use the dream analogy, our reality is like the consciousness of a dreamer which is not affected by all the objects and the ups & downs in the dream it projects.

Vedanta terms this reality as brahman or atma and says that the full understanding of brahman or atma as our own reality, addresses our problems at their fundamental level. And Vedanta goes into great detail to explain and justify this uncommon and radical view to us. However, there is not that much material to explain why such a reality should give rise to the appearance of the world. But we want to know why the world appears. In effect, we want to understand maya or avidya.

Vedanta starts by saying maya is beginning-less *(anadi)* and beyond explanation *(anirvachaniya)*. If something has no beginning, there is no question of determining its start time. To illustrate, if we don't happen to know the Mandarin language, can we find out when our ignorance of that language began? Our ignorance here is beginning-less because if it had started at a specific time, we would have known Mandarin before our ignorance of it began! If maya or avidya is without a beginning, can it have an end? The answer is yes, just as our beginning-less ignorance of Mandarin can come to an end upon our learning that language.

So, one can accept Vedanta's statement that maya is anadi, without a beginning, and with the possibility of an end. But how meaningful is it to call something anirvachaniya? Is it not evading the question? In the case of usual things it would be quite useless to say that there is something but then go on to say that nothing can be said about that something. In fact, Ramanujacharya (one of Shankaracharya's main critics, as stated earlier) pointed out that a thing can only be real or unreal, not anirvachaniya. He then said that if maya is real, then there are two realities: brahman and maya. This would put an end to the concept of advaita. And if maya is unreal, it would result in an untenable situation of unreal maya being the cause of an unreal world!

Here we must first remind ourselves that Vedanta is not a collection of answers to all questions. In this context, it is useful to repeat a story that Gautama Buddha is said to have told to one of his disciples. This student had question upon question about metaphysical issues such as what happens after death. In response, Buddha is reported to have told him the following story:

> *There was once a man who was severely wounded by a poisoned arrow.*
>
> *His family and friends wanted to get him a healer but the injured man refused, saying that he first wanted to know the name of the person who had wounded him, the caste to which he belonged and his country of origin.*

He also wanted to know if that person was tall and strong, if he had light or dark skin and whether his bow-string was made of hemp or silk.

He further wanted to know if the feather of the arrow belonged to a hawk, vulture or peacock.

And so on and so forth, till this man died of his wound, without knowing the answers.

With this story Buddha tried to show his student how we need intelligence to separate the important from what we can do without. It might be unconsciously, but sometimes we focus too much on questions that are actually unimportant out of fear of confronting the truly important ones. We leave the heart of the matter unknown, while we worry overmuch about issues that are less relevant.

What is vital for Vedanta's purpose is our understanding of the world's unreality and not getting mired in questions about why and how this unreal world appears. For achieving its purpose, Vedanta dwells on 'what is' rather than 'why is'. In this it is like science which tells us that gravity makes falling objects accelerate at the rate of 32 feet per second squared but cannot tell us why it is that rate and not some other rate. (While Vedanta does not and need not rely upon comparison with science to prove itself, it is interesting to note that some newer thinking in science – such as Einstein's relativity or Heisenberg's uncertainty – also points to the lack of absoluteness and determination in subtler areas of scientific knowledge.)

Despite all this, teachers of Vedanta recognise that our minds may still continue to have questions even though answers are not relevant to our real problem. Some explanations are therefore put forward, in the hope that we will then move on to what is actually useful.

The first thing we are made to recognise here is that maya is not an usual thing but the very cause of everything. Time, space and causality itself are all products of maya. Asking questions about the cause of causality is like asking what was before time or what is outside space. These questions can arise only if time and space are first accepted. Asking what caused maya is already accepting causality which is part of maya. Questions about cause and purpose can be asked within the maya-created world but not of maya itself. Such questions themselves are based on a defective premise and cannot be answered in terms of which they are raised. How does one answer the question, "Why is the earth flat?"!

Also, questions about the world's appearance only occur to us, individuals, who are all part of the world. Wanting to understand why and how the world appears while being part of the world is like a character in a movie or a person in our dream wanting to figure out why and how the movie or dream was made! Within the dream or the movie no good answer is possible and outside the dream or the movie there is no real question. After all, how much time do we spend in figuring out the cause for the rude behaviour of a person in our dreams or the cause of a fire seen in a movie, once we wake up from the dream or walk out of the movie?

But if provisional answers must be provided, one answer to the question about the world's appearance is *Why not?* There are only two possibilities for brahman (or atma): either it projects a world or it does not project a world. The question *why* can be raised with equal force in respect of both these possibilities so where does that take us? There is a *why* because the world appears but the same *why* could be asked if it did not.

Further, if we look at our own experience, we all go through the three states of waking, dreaming and deep sleep without asking why and how. In a similar way, brahman supports the three states of projection *(shrishti)*, continuation *(stithi)* and dissolution *(pralaya)* of the universe. Why do we have questions and problems here?

Finally, questions like *why* and *how* in respect of the world never arise in our moments of total joy. Are we bothered about these issues immediately upon winning a large lottery, falling deeply in love or becoming engrossed in soulful music? From this, we must realise that our real question is not why the world but why our unhappiness or why our lack of fulfilment. Our primary objective should therefore be to be rid of unhappiness and lack of fulfilment.

If these answers do not satisfy us, we should check to see if we are more satisfied by explanations for the cause of the world if it were to be real. If the world is not a projection as Vedanta says but it is real as claimed by Vedanta's objectors, a number of fundamental questions arise. Who created it? For what purpose? From what materials? And if we subscribe to the idea of a god having created this world, we are yet left with fundamental questions with no satisfactory answers. Before any creation, where was this god located and from where did he get the raw materials required for a real creation? What is god's purpose in having this creation? Why did he bring in evil, tragedies and suffering into his creation? Upon proper inquiry we will find that the only credible possibility for the world is for it to be a projection. We should also rely on the experiences of those exceptional people who have completed Vedanta's journey and who tell us that upon full understanding, questions about maya remain as relevant as questions about the source of the water seen in a mirage.

Instead of getting distracted by never-ending questions and arguments about matters which are not germane to our real issues, we should focus our time and energies in trying to solve our actual problems by understanding the nature of our own reality. As the Buddha pointed out, it is wise to pull out the arrow and heal the wound instead of speculating on the arrow-maker's ancestry.

There is a difference in the goal of meditation in Vedanta and in Yoga. Even within Vedanta, there are significant differences in the role assigned to meditation by traditional Vedanta and neo-Vedanta.

ROLE OF MEDITATION IN VEDANTA

The practice of meditation is best known from Patanjali's Yoga Sutras which list *dharana* (concentration), *dhyana* (meditation) and *samadhi* (absorption) as the final three steps of an eight-steps prescription. The ultimate objective of yoga, in Patanjali's own words, is *citta vritti nirodha* – cessation of the movements of the mind – and all his steps, including meditation, are geared to this objective.

However, rendering the mind inactive is not Vedanta's objective. Vedanta has a very different goal: proper understanding of our own reality, using an active mind.

This does not mean that Vedanta rejects meditation. On the contrary, Vedanta uses meditation as an important practice but not as an end in itself. For Vedanta, meditation is a preparatory practice which equips the student with a controlled and focused mind, a mind capable of absorbing the subtle teachings of Vedanta.

However, the use of meditation as a preparatory technique is only true of traditional Vedanta or Shankara's Vedanta as it is often termed. More modern interpretations of Vedanta (we will refer to these as neo-Vedanta) place a different emphasis on meditation. It is worthwhile to see the differences between these two approaches to meditation within Vedanta.

Let us first see where both traditional and neo-Vedanta travel together. Both agree that an ethical and a balanced life (a life of *karma* yoga) is necessary for a purified mind (*chitta shuddhi*); both also agree that worshipful meditation (*upasana* yoga) is necessary for a non-agitated and focused mind (*chitta ekagrata*). There is no dispute regarding such a prepared mind being necessary for the pursuit of Vedanta.

They both further agree that the goal of ultimate freedom *(moksha)* can only be achieved by obtaining a specific kind of knowledge—the knowledge of oneness (advaita). This is distinct from usual knowledge which is based on duality (dvaita). The most fundamental duality is between subject and objects or the knower and the known; the knowledge of advaita cognitively erases the perceived difference between the subject and objects. And it is agreed that this knowledge of non-duality is necessary for freedom.

Both also agree that advaita knowledge can only be obtained from scriptures *(shastra)*, with the guidance of a guru.

Finally, they both agree that advaita knowledge should be *aparoksha*—this knowledge should be immediate, direct & personal and not remote, indirect or second-hand. (Reading about Mumbai or having someone describe the taste of a mango would both be instances of remote knowledge; such knowledge would become direct and first-hand only upon visiting Mumbai or eating a mango.)

It is at this point - how to make advaita knowledge direct - that the two interpretations of Vedanta differ. Neo-Vedanta holds that advaita knowledge obtained during learning with the teacher is obtained in a state of duality: teaching necessarily involves duality (actually multiplicity) of the student, the teacher, fellow-students, books, talking, etc. Learning about non-duality while being in a state of duality is like getting information about Mumbai while being in New York or hearing about the taste of a mango without ever having tasted one—this is *paroksha* jnanam or knowledge which is second-hand and indirect.

According to neo-Vedanta, the only way to convert what it says is the second-hand knowledge of advaita (obtained from the scriptures) into direct knowledge is to get into the non-dual state ourselves. And neo-Vedanta holds that meditation is the only way to get into a non-dual state, where the subject-object division does not exist. Therefore, in this view, meditation is necessary after receiving knowledge, to convert sterile remote knowledge into live direct knowledge which will bring us the promised benefits.

Traditional Vedantins first counter this view of neo-Vedanta by pointing out that even during meditation, the subject (the meditator) and objects (the world) continue to exist as independent entities. Meditation, in this aspect, is comparable to deep sleep where the world is not perceived temporarily but is there in full force as soon as the sleeper awakens. Similarly, when the meditator comes out of meditation, he is he and the world is the world – both distinct and different from each other. So meditation is not a true non-dual state, it is only a temporary non-perception of duality. The answer given by the neo-Vedantins to this objection is that meditation is transcendental – beyond words, beyond worldly reasoning. But, they claim, it still works as is shown by the experience of many great mystics. So neo-Vedantins exhort students not to waste time in arguments but just focus on meditating.

Traditional Vedantins, however, have a more fundamental argument against meditation being necessary to make advaita knowledge direct and first-hand. They say that meditation is not necessary for *aparoksha* jnanam and all that is required for this knowledge is scriptural study guided by a proper teacher—guru *shastra updesha*. Advaita is a mental recognition of an already existing fact, not an experience of a new state. We cannot and should not try to experience advaita but, instead, focus on understanding that the truth behind all individuals and the entire world is common. Individuals and objects in the world do not have intrinsic and permanent reality (*mithyatvam* of *jiva* and *jagat*). This knowledge of non-duality is not obtained by deleting or blocking experiences of duality but by understanding that duality is not real. If, for instance, we are alone in a room with a mirror, we don't say that two people are present just because the mirror shows our reflection; the reflection, even though seen, is not to be counted. And for seeing the reflection to be unreal, it is not necessary to cover up or to break the mirror—just our knowledge is enough.

Therefore traditional and non-mystical Vedantins say that the knowledge received in a Vedanta class is not received in a dual state because duality itself is never real. Though it is perceived, duality is an error in our minds, it is *mithya*. So, *aparoksha* jnanam or direct knowledge is possible without needing mystical meditation—the only requirement is faith in the scriptures, a proper teacher and a qualified student spending adequate time and effort.

However, meditation is not discarded by traditional Vedanta. As we have seen, it is needed at the preparatory stage for mental tranquillity and one-pointedness. Further, for most of us, a type of meditation is also needed after receiving the teaching, to internalise the new insights by repeated contemplation in an appropriate state of mind. But this is not meditation to deactivate the mind or to get into a non-dual state; it is dwelling on the teachings in a calm and contemplative way as well as reviewing our habitual reactions to events, which are not yet in keeping with our new knowledge because of old grooves in our minds. (For those who are interested in more detail, Shankara's Vedanta, after his time, developed in two main and slightly differing streams known as Vivarana and Bhamati; the Bhamati school places much more emphasis on contemplative meditation compared to the Vivarana school.)

The stand of traditional Vedanta, that meditation is not required for acquiring knowledge of advaita, may seem like quibbling about an irrelevant point but, in fact, it is based on an axiom of great significance: **anything which comes in time will also go in time**. If non-duality is not real now, it will have to be brought into being by meditation. But then it is like other things which are all also created by effort and time and, like all other things, this too will cease to exist some time in the future. However, the promise of Vedanta is something uniquely different, something timeless, whose existence is uninterrupted and unconditional. This reality is our own truth and to realise it what we need is knowledge, not bouts of meditation.

The fundamental teaching of Vedanta therefore is that what we really are has been, is and will remain timeless and boundless and only knowledge can help us to remove the ignorance which keeps this fact hidden. And knowledge can only occur in a functioning mind. Meditation can give us a still or contemplative state of mind but it cannot take us to non-duality and nor can it remove ignorance which veils our truth.

The terms sat chit ananda *are regularly used in conjunction with the word* atma *in the teaching of Vedanta. It is important to be clear about the real purpose and the implications of these terms.*

SAT CHIT ANANDA ATMA

Vedanta tells us that there is only a single reality which exists. This common reality behind the entire universe is called *atma* or *brahman*. When the term atma is discussed in the context of Vedanta, it is described as *sat chit ananda*. These three words are translated as *unchanging existence*, *consciousness* and *bliss*. It is important to understand what this description implies.

Not Adjectives

First of all, we need to be clear that *unchanging existence*, *consciousness* and *bliss* are not adjectives which describe atma. We commonly use adjectives like *big* and *red* to describe an object such as a rose. However, atma is not one object amongst many where *sat chit ananda* can differentiate it from others; it is unlike a big red rose which has to be distinguished from a small yellow rose by the use of adjectives. As atma is the only reality which exists, there is no need to distinguish it from anything else because there is nothing else at atma's level of reality. Actually, these three words are completely integral to atma much as liquidity and wetness are not adjectives to water but the very nature of water (such words are called *swarupa lakshana* in Sanskrit). Because of this, it is equally valid to say:

- atma is unchanging existence which is conscious and limitless, or
- atma is consciousness which is limitless and unchanging, or
- atma is limitlessness which is unchanging and conscious.

(In terms of grammar, these three words – sat, chit, ananda – are said to be in essential apposition. This means that they are all nouns – not adjectives – and dropping anyone will detract from proper meaning.)

Why Any Terms?

Vedanta not only tells us that atma is the only thing which exists but also that it is without any attributes like size, shape, colour or location. It is somewhat like space which too has no attributes. But then why use sat chit ananda in respect of atma which has no attributes? The reason for such usage is that these descriptions counter our primal fears of death, ignorance and unhappiness. When we are told that our reality is *sat* this means that what we truly are is timeless and unchanging (that is what *sat* means). This, if properly understood, addresses our problem of mortality because the timeless and unchanging can neither deteriorate nor die.

When we are also told that atma is consciousness *(chit)*, it means that our reality is the basis of all knowing, because there can be no knowledge without consciousness. This fact resolves our problem of limited knowledge because while we, as individuals, will never know everything, we can be secure in the knowledge that our reality is what makes knowing itself possible.

Ananda is derived from *anantam* or limitlessness. Atma is termed ananda because no boundary is found for it and anything boundless has to be full & complete. When it sinks into us that our real nature is limitless, it takes away the pressure behind our getting something that we want or removing something that we don't want. After all, how can anything be in or out of limitlessness? And the proper understanding of the limitless nature of our own truth leads to peace and fulfillment which is captured by the term ananda.

So, *sat chit ananda* are not to be seen as a net of words capturing atma in its entirety but only as words highlighting aspects which are relevant to our basic problems. This is an important point because no words can fully describe or define atma.

Consciousness Emphasised

Now let us look a bit deeper into the consciousness aspect of atma. This is not because consciousness is more important than unchanging existence or limitlessness but because it is very often emphasised in the course of study of Vedanta. This emphasis is for the benefit of the student who recognises himself primarily as a conscious being and so he can easily relate to consciousness or awareness. The emphasis on consciousness when talking about atma can create areas of confusion as well as throw useful light on some of our problems.

The Meaning Of 'All Pervasive'

One area of confusion which can arise is when we are told that consciousness is all-pervasive. This may make us think of consciousness as being similar to perfume which pervades an entire room. But, in the case of consciousness, we need to understand that its all-pervasiveness is similar to the way in which gold pervades all gold ornaments. Ornaments such as bangles or rings are only names given to temporary forms of gold; without gold, ornaments have no existence. The ornaments are nothing but gold while gold exists even without being in the form of ornaments. Consciousness pervades everything because everything is only a projection in and of the single conscious reality.

Differences Between Objects

If everything is only consciousness, why are there such apparent differences between a stone, an animal and a human being? Vedanta explains that this is so because no object in creation fully shows all aspects of atma. Different objects display only limited aspects of atma, in different proportions, with the rest being covered. Thus, a stone exhibits only the existence facet of its reality and the consciousness & limitlessness aspects of the same reality are covered (by *tamoguna* if one goes by the *triguna* model). Animals display both existence and consciousness but the limitless aspect of their truth is covered (by a preponderance of *rajas* and *tamas*). However we humans are the only ones who, if we cultivate a sufficient amount of *sattva* and get the knowledge of Vedanta, can recognise our innate fullness.

Consciousness Is Not Anything

Further, because consciousness is the single reality behind everything, it can be said that everything is consciousness; but, paradoxically, it is also said that consciousness is not anything. Though this sounds contradictory, it is like saying that all waves are nothing but water while water is not a wave. Properly understanding this is important, especially in the context of some preliminary teaching techniques of Vedanta like *drik drishya viveka* (discrimination between the seer and the seen) where we are told that we are not the body-mind but the consciousness because of which the body and mind are known.

Here, one may falsely conclude that there are two things: the body-mind which is known and consciousness which is the knower. Vedanta initially uses this technique to counter over strong body-mind indentification. But it then goes on to tell us that there is only one unchanging and boundless consciousness which exists and all other things which appear to exist (including body-mind) are only temporary and insubstantial superimpositions on and of that single reality. However, just as clay is not the pot, unchanging and boundless consciousness is not body-mind; but, just as pot is nothing other than clay, body-mind is nothing other than consciousness. Consciousness is not any one thing. Consciousness is not nothing. Consciousness is but it is no thing!

Is Consciousness Personal?

Is it that each one of us has our personal blob of consciousness which is tucked away in our minds which, in turn, reside in our bodies? Actually, when we talk of *my consciousness*, it really means *the consciousness that I am*. It is not that our self is with consciousness, it is that consciousness *is* the self. Vedanta clarifies that there is only one universal, homogenous and indivisible consciousness which exists. It is not part, product or property of our bodies and is not affected by the presence or absence of our bodies. This consciousness is referred to as chit. Our bodies and minds are temporary appearances in and of this consciousness. However, our minds are capable of reflecting consciousness. What seems like our personal consciousness is this reflected consciousness (called *chidabhasa*) which enervates our bodies and makes our minds capable of knowing; it is like the consciousness of a person in a dream who seems conscious only because of the dreamer's consciousness. Our waking world is like a bigger dream at a higher level, where our individual consciousness is only a reflection of universal consciousness.

Just as a reflection is affected by the qualities of a mirror, the consciousness reflected in our minds is affected by the qualities of individual minds. However, just as original light is not affected by the different nature of its reflections in different mirrors, universal consciousness is not affected by the differing nature of chidabhasa created by different minds.

Problems Only With Chidabhasa

Understanding the role that reflected consciousness or chidabhasa plays in our lives is very important because our bodies & minds do not suffer from problems in the absence of chidabhasa. It is chidabhasa which generates our egos and also makes possible all our thoughts and perceptions. In a state of deep sleep, when our minds stop reflecting original consciousness, there is no chidabhasa, no sense of individual self, no perceptions or thoughts and, therefore, no problems at all. This is why deep sleep is a blissful state and it is the same for a king and a pauper or for a blind and a sighted person. However, as soon as we wake up and chidabhasa reappears, all our problems, issues and limitations come flooding back. While deep sleep is undoubtedly a state where we do not suffer from any sense of limitation, our ignorance about the nature of our reality subsists in it, though in a latent state. This is why all our issues re-appears upon waking up, when latent ignorance is once again activated. Therefore, Vedanta does not suggest a permanent state of deep sleep (or *samadhi* or being blissed out!) to solve our problems.

Incidentally, there are moments in our lives when our problems and limitations disappear even in the presence of chidabhasa. These are transcendent moments of pure joy and elation caused by experiences such as the first smile of a newborn or of falling deeply in love or of being overcome by the grandeur and mystery of a natural phenomenon. Such experiences are called peak experiences and give us moments of total fulfilment because our egos temporarily subside during them. Unfortunately these states do not last but, having tasted them, we yearn to regain the state of total freedom from all sense of limitations which we have experienced in those moments.

One other important thing to remember here is that if peak experiences or the knowledge of Vedanta give us a peaceful and contented mind, we should not conclude that we have *become* peaceful and content. We are always the unchanging, unaffected witness of both the miserable and the peaceful mind. Vedanta actually does not give us anything new but only helps our minds in recognising our own true nature which is inherently peaceful and contented.

Witness Consciousness

The term 'witness consciousness' (*sakshi chaitanya* in Sanskrit) is often used when speaking of atma. If atma is only a witness and it is the only thing which exists then who desires, who acts and who experiences? It cannot be atma if it is the uninvolved witness but, because nothing else really exists, it can only be atma! This conundrum has two different answers, depending on whether we are looking at it from the paramarthika or the vyavaharika level. It is easier to understand this by using the dream example. Within your own dream you, the dream figure, perform actions. However, once you wake up and realise that the dreamt individual was only an appearance and his actions had no reality, the very question (Who acts?) disappears.

But if one still wants an answer to what is behind the dream figure's actions then the answer is the dreamer's consciousness which is the reality behind the dream. The point to be noted here is that while the dreamer's consciousness makes the dream possible, it is not involved or affected by all that happens in a dream. And so it is in our waking state. The actions of our bodies and minds are possible only because of atma but atma itself does not get involved in and affected by what happens through them.This is why atma is said to be a witness. But we have to be careful here and not make the mistake of concluding that atma acts as a normal witness who registers what is happening. Atma is more like the light which illuminates the stage: without light, the play on the stage is not possible but the light is never involved in registering good actions, bad actions or no actions on the stage and it is completely unaffected by action or inaction on the stage lit by it.

Obstacles In Recognising Sat Chit Ananda

Vedanta wants us to recognise our reality for what it is—sat chit ananda atma. The teachers of Vedanta use a combination of scriptural material, logic and interpretation of our own experiences to lead us to the conviction that it is atma which is the only and primary reality. However, we face some problems in absorbing this teaching. First, there can be doubt that there exists, in fact, something like sat chit ananda atma. This difficulty is compounded by the majority scientific view which is that consciousness is not an independent reality but an epiphenomenon based chemical & electrical activity in individual brains.

Further, merely having conviction about the existence of atma does not take us too far. We need to take the next step to recognise that atma is not a remote object but our very own self, here and now. Without this recognition and personal owning up to our own reality, no amount of second-hand knowledge of atma will solve our fundamental problem. This is to be achieved by the last step in the journey of Vedanta – nidhidhyasana – whereby we have firm and first-person knowledge that our truth is nothing but unchanging and boundless consciousness and that consciousness is nothing but us.

But once we earnestly start on the path of Vedanta, our own efforts with the guidance of a teacher and the support of fellow students all take us to the full and proper knowledge of atma, our true self.

Advaita means non-duality.
If the truth brought out by advaita Vedanta is singular,
*why should it have different names—*atma *and* brahman?
And, that too, with different descriptions?

DESCRIBING THE INDESCRIBABLE

Many Questions

We learn from Vedanta that *atma* and *brahman* are just two different names for the same reality. We are further told that this reality is without any attributes so it cannot be described by words. But, in the same breath, we are presented with two different definitions for atma and brahman. Why should there be two terms for the same thing? How can anything beyond words have any definition at all?

However, teachers of Vedanta use both these terms—atma and brahman. Further, they describe atma as *sat chit ananda* but brahman is described as *satyam jnanam anantam*. This use of different terms and definitions needs some explanation.

The Purpose of Two Terms and Two Descriptions

The truth is that the single reality, which is the truth behind everything that appears in the world, can never be defined in any words. All that can be said about it is that it is not anything we know or we can conceive of; as an upanishad says, *'neti neti'*—not this, not this. But this negative description is not initially helpful to a seeker.

The teachings of Vedanta recognise that all seekers of its wisdom are rooted in experiences of duality. The most fundamental duality we experience is between us, the individuals, and the rest of the world—the subject and objects duality. Each one of us sees his or her own self as the subject (the knower) and everything else, including other individuals, as objects (the known). Vedanta therefore chooses to direct its inquiry into these two apparently different entities: an individual and the world confronting the individual.

When any object in the world is examined, it is found that each thing depends upon something else for its existence. For example, a shirt owes its existence to fabric, which in turn depends upon yarn and so on. This is true of every single object because everything depends on something more fundamental and that, in turn, depends on something even more fundamental and this chain of dependencies goes on and on, without an end. Logically, this chain must end with something which has an independent existence and which is the ground underlying the entire chain. If there was no independent substratum behind this seemingly endless series of dependencies, we would have an illogical state of infinite regress or the incredulous situation of a multi-level structure without any foundation. This necessary ground reality is called brahman. It is brahman which lends its existence to everything, much as water lends its existence to all waves. Brahman is the 'isness' behind everything which is.

Having understood brahman as the basic existence which supports the appearance of all the objects in the world, the next issue is whether brahman is inert *(jadam)* or conscious *(chaitanyam)*. Here, it is pointed out to us that consistent order is visible in all aspects of the world, from the cosmic to the sub-atomic and from the living to the non-living. Order involves knowledge which can only arise in consciousness and so the ground of everything in an orderly creation, brahman, has to be conscious.

Finally, just as clay does not have any shape of its own and can therefore become the basis of clay products of all shapes, brahman as the basis of creation of countless objects with varying attributes cannot have any attributes itself. But to define and limit something, attributes such as shape, size, colour or some other properties are necessary. So brahman without any attributes cannot be defined or restricted in any manner. Also, any change in something has to be with respect to some attribute in it which changes, such as black becoming white or hot becoming cold. Without any attributes, brahman has to be limitless and changeless.

Brahman, which exists independently and changelessly, is termed *satyam*. Because brahman is knowledge, it is *jnanam*. Because it is limitless, it is *anantam*. So, brahman is described as *satyam jnanam anantam*—independent and changeless existence which is conscious and unlimited.

We now turn to the individual who sees the world. An individual usually considers himself to be his body-mind complex: his physical body, thoughts, emotions, intellect and ego. But the teachings of Vedanta lead us away from this obvious conclusion by asking us to discriminate between the knower and the known (*drik drishya viveka*). In anything we know, the knower is always different from the known and what is known does not affect the knower. When our eyes see a red flower, they do not become a flower or turn red; they remain separate and unaffected by what they see. Because we know our bodies and the contents of our minds, we cannot be bodies and minds but we are the conscious knowers of our bodies and minds. So, our deepest truth as individuals is not the body-mind complex but the consciousness because of which we know our bodies and minds. This consciousness, as the underlying truth of us, the individual subjects, is termed atma.

That we exist and are conscious cannot be denied by anyone and therefore the words *sat* (existence) and *chit* (consciousness) are used in the description of atma. Further, our consciousness has no attributes and it is because of its lack of any attributes that we can become aware of the different attributes of all things. If our consciousness had its own attributes, those attributes would uniformly affect everything we know just as if our glasses were rose-tinted, they would make every single thing appear pink. As we saw earlier, a thing without any attributes cannot be defined or limited and so atma, our innermost truth, is unlimited. As nothing can be added to a thing without limits, limitlessness implies total fulfilment and so atma is described as *ananda* or joy (of being completely fulfilled).

Why is atma described as *ananda* and not *anantam* as in the case of brahman? Here, we should remember that atma is the self and we know from our own experience that we love anything else only for the sake of ourselves. Everything we do is to experience our own self without the obstruction of any want, lack or disturbance. Such a self, which is the source of all the joy we experience, has to be complete and fulfilled in itself. So the self or atma is called ananda but ananda here does not refer to the experiences of our usual joys; rather, it refers to fullness, peace and tranquility born out of the limitless nature of atma.

We should also bear in mind that the description of atma as *sat chit ananda* comes to us from a minor and later upanishad; such a description came into wide-spread use probably because of teachers who may have found it useful to attract and hold the attention of seekers—the promise to lead someone to joy is a much more attractive proposition than helping him to discover limitlessness, even though both are ultimately the same thing!

So, we now have brahman described as *satyam jnanam anantam* and atma described as *sat chit ananda*. Are these two things? Both are conscious existence without any limits. It is reasonable to assume that both are one and the same reality which is the basis for everything which exists in the world, including us, the individuals. Further, as both are limitless, it is difficult to accept the simultaneous existence of two limitless things because one would then limit the other. But while this is a fair assumption, this is not absolute proof that atma and brahman are the same, single reality. This is because, in logic, the absence of a thing is never positive proof. (Nobody in the Western world had seen black swans until they were first discovered in Australia in the 17th century. It had therefore been accepted till then that all swans are white. As it turned out, the absence of the colour black in swans seen till then did not prove the non-existence of black swans. Similarly, the absence of limits in atma and brahman does not conclusively prove anything.) This is where the upanishads operate as an independent means of knowledge, telling us something which we cannot definitely know otherwise: that brahman and atma are just two different terms for the same reality which is the common truth behind every single thing which exists.

The assertion of Vedanta that brahman and atma refer to the single truth behind everything which appears in the universe is corroborated by the fact that there is no appearance without our consciousness. We cannot experience anything (including concepts, emotions or memories) without the necessary presence of consciousness. If two things can never be seen separately (such as a wave which can never appear separated from water), then we must conclude that they are actually one thing (just as a wave is nothing but water). As nothing in the universe can be separated from the knower's consciousness, we have to conclude that the truth behind both the knower and the known is one consciousness.

If brahman and atma refer to the very same reality, why use two terms to begin with? Only to aid our understanding because different characteristics of the same thing appear more vividly to us, depending upon circumstances. If we are on a boat in choppy seas then the liquid nature of water is more apparent;

but if we are caught out in the rain without an umbrella, it is the wetness of water which comes to the forefront. Water is always both liquid and wet but one characteristic or the other strikes us more in a given situation. Similarly with the fundamental reality underlying everything. When it is associated with an individual, the aspect of consciousness appears to be more prominent. But when the same reality is seen as the truth behind the rest of creation, the aspect of existence seems to come to the fore. The two different terms – atma and brahman – and their descriptions capture these apparent differences.

So there is no real difference between atma and brahman but atma is more readily known to all of us because it is the ever-present consciousness principle reflected within us; it is that which gives us sentience and the capacity to know. This is why a lot of the teaching in Vedanta starts with atma—reflected consciousness experienced in ourselves is initially more accessible and understandable than consciousness in general.

How Is Definition Possible?

The final issue which needs to be addressed is how can there be any definition of consciousness which is stated to be without any defining attributes and beyond words.

The truth is that there can never be a complete definition of consciousness; it is because of consciousness that everything is known to us and, just as we cannot use our eyes to see themselves, we can never objectify consciousness to be able to define it. So the definitions given in the upanishads are not complete definitions. The descriptions which we are given only mention aspects which can help to address our problems of mortality, limited knowledge and lack of fulfillment. They only negate the most fundamental mistakes we make about our true nature.

Even as we study advaita Vedanta and begin to appreciate the truth of its insights, duality continues to hold us and creates doubts. Is it possible that duality or dvaita is the truth and advaita is only a fanciful concept? And even if advaita is the ultimate truth, what is wrong if we lead our daily lives in the acceptance of dvaita, without bothering about advaita?

ADVAITA OR *DVAITA*?

Advaita refers to the interpretation of Vedic scriptures according to which all that exists is a single reality. Everything else which appears and which is experienced – the entire world of objects and individuals – has no absolute reality but is just a temporary and insubstantial appearance, like a dream. The vision of advaita is best known from the works of Adi Shankaracharya.

Dvaita or dual, on the other hand, is a different interpretation of the same scriptures. Here, the world, its individuals and their creator are all given the status of reality. Thus, in this view, there exist multiple things which are all real, in keeping with our common experience. The two best known champions of the varying dvaita views are Ramanujacharya and Madhvacharya. (There are a number of other well-known names such as Nimbarka, Vallabha and Chaitanya whose views fall somewhere between the views of Ramanujacharya and Madhvacharya but all with elements of dvaita).

Many of us are drawn to the study of advaita because it is considered to be the pinnacle of thought in our culture. Further, because advaita is more commonly taught than other versions of Indian thought, it is easily available for study.

Also, it is intellectually fascinating and offers a more esoteric solution to our problems than the solutions offered within dvaita.

However, even as we study advaita and 'buy' its concepts intellectually, for many of us dvaita remains the only relevant reality in our daily lives and it is dvaita which continues to drive us emotionally. An important reason why this happens is that we often lose sight of important features and requirements of advaita. Let us review these because without clarity here, we will continue to have unnecessary doubts about advaita.

Advaita is a remedy for a disease

Advaita is not an intellectual exercise to establish some truth for truth's sake but it is a solution to the fundamental human problem of experiencing ourselves as limited beings. In advaita's view, our conclusion that we are small & limited individuals converts our lives into an ongoing struggle to be different than what we think we are now and denies us the permanent peace and fulfilment which is our reality. Advaita holds itself out as a solution to this compulsive & endless striving.

But, for any solution to be effective, it is necessary to first recognise the problem for which the solution is designed. After all, we do not start on a course of antibiotics unless we are suffering from an infection and antibiotics will serve no purpose if disease is not present. And, in advaita's case, it is not enough that we only occasionally experience the problem which advaita is meant to solve. We have to reach a stage where the never-ending search for fulfilment has become a truly serious problem for us on an ongoing basis.

We also have to be convinced that the usual solutions which we have tried so far to obtain fulfilment (pleasures, possessions, people and so on) have not worked except temporarily and will not permanently work in the future as well.

Unless these conditions of discernment and disenchantment with our usual methods are met, we are not quite ready for advaita. Advaita will bring us no real benefits even if we dabble in it when we are not prepared for it; in such a situation, the hold of dvaita over us will remain unabated.

Some of us are not troubled by lack of fulfilment or meaning and by the fleeting nature of our individual lives; we are mostly happy with the results of our usual efforts to remain healthy, comfortable and good. To us, advaita has nothing very special to offer. In fact, we would be much better off in pursuing conventional security & pleasures within the boundaries of ethics and religion and not get too involved with advaita.

Advaita is freedom from the body and mind

Advaita offers freedom *from* the body and mind, not *for* the body and mind. But, if we are unable to discern that our real truth is more than the body-mind (which is one of advaita's early teachings), we will continue to find solutions within dvaita which will have more appeal because they give importance to the body-mind. A certain amount of detachment from our physical and mental adjuncts becomes a requisite if our continued study of advaita is to bear fruit.

Advaita does not change experiences

If we get into advaita on the mistaken assumption that it will alter our experiences or solve the problems which the world places before us, we will be disappointed and tend to retreat to dvaita. Advaita does not bring about any external change, it only reforms our understanding and perspective; this makes a vital difference to the way in which we respond to the world but it does not change our environment or our sensory experiences.

The *mithya jagat* includes us

With some exposure to the teachings of Vedanta, we may faithfully repeat key statements such as '*brahma satyam jagat mithya*' (meaning that brahman is the only reality and the world is not absolutely real). But even as we say this, we tend to gloss over the fact that the *mithya jagat* is not only other people and things but it also includes us—our hopes, ambitions, plans, families, and possessions. And our forgetfulness here is often accentuated when fortunes are kind to us. If we are not able to get over our attachment and identification with our personal world and continue to see it as being absolutely real, we will remain only on the first step of advaita.

Advaita is for an *adhikari*

It is critical to remember that advaita is for a person with some minimum eligibility qualifications, an *adhikari*. Without first diluting our likes, dislikes, attachments, mental reactivity, imbalance and hyper-activity, which is what eligibility for advaita requires, we will not progress in advaita.

Advaita requires proper effort

The study of advaita has to cover the processes of *shravana, manana* and *nidhidhyasana. Shravana* (literally, listening) needs consistent and systematic study of Vedantic texts over a sufficiently long period of time, guided by a qualified teacher. Due to lack of time & commitment and difficulties in accessing a proper teacher, all these conditions are not easy to meet.

Manana (removal of doubts) involves testing whatever we are learning against our personal experiences and mulling over the new ideas given to us, using our own thinking as well as by discussion. But where *shravana* itself is inadequate, the raw material for *manana* remains incomplete.

And *nidhidhyasana* (contemplation) usually gets the shortest shrift because it is a long-drawn and demanding process of unlearning old notions and weaning our emotions & reactions away from comfortable grooves of habit.

Until these processes have been properly used, the fruits of advaita's vision do not become fully available to us and we then vacillate between old & comfortable dvaita and not-yet-settled advaita.

Why Not Both Dvaita and Advaita?

But then, what is the problem if we flit between advaita and dvaita? Aren't these different paths to the truth? Doesn't devotion to god and being a good person lead to the same thing? Why can't we switch between dvaita and advaita, depending upon our mood at the moment?

For those who have properly understood the vision of Vedanta, these questions do not arise any more. They know that there is no need to weigh between dvaita and advaita—they understand that dvaita is just an appearance which occurs in spite of advaita. However, some of us need to take a hard look at these questions because unless we find answers which convince us, we will comfortably coast along without realising that we are trying to move forward using two forces operating in different directions.

But do dvaita and advaita really pull in different directions? And here is real and understandable confusion because both these views run in parallel for a large part of the Vedantic journey. It is only in some critical and advanced aspects that they point to a diametrically opposite vision.

The Confusion

The confusion begins with the basic teaching method of advaita vedanta which is *adhyaropa apvada*. In this method provisional statements, all apparently in line with dvaita, are made and only later are they replaced by other statements which are closer to advaita's vision. Thus, for instance, *brahman* is initially held out to be the cause of the world, seemingly supporting the duality between the world and *brahman*; this is replaced only later, by the statement that *brahman* is neither cause nor effect. Or a student is told that the final freedom promised by advaita *(moksha)* is dependent on the student accumulating adequate qualities which make him eligible for moksha. This statement involves duality and separation—it recognises the student as a real and separate entity who has to reach the distant goal of freedom by effort. It is only at the very end that it dawns on the student that moksha, being our permanent nature, can never be conditional or a future event.

Such statements, seemingly supporting dvaita, are made in the process of teaching only as devices to bring the student to a realisation of the non-dual truth by means of carefully gauged, progressive levels of understanding. But unless this is done skilfully by a good teacher, it has the danger of the student continuing to take dvaita as being absolutely real.

Another important factor which can cause confusion between advaita and dvaita is the use of *karma* yoga and *bhakti* during the process of a student's growth towards advaita. Karma yoga (a certain way of living and attitudes) is necessary to cultivate dispassion and equanimity which are required for the lessons of advaita to go home. Bhakti (devotion to god) not only provides a valuable emotional outlet but also minimises the effects of dvaita for an individual – it does this by taking away his focus from the world of innumerable objects and concentrating it on a single object – *Ishwara*. But both karma yoga and bhakti are entirely in dvaita and they are the means, not ends. And, without proper guidance, there is danger of getting so involved in these dvaita means that the end goal of advaita is lost track of.

Then, a person leading a life of ethics and religion (both of which are in the realm of dvaita) lives as a good human being, with emotional maturity and compassion. A person who has completed the journey of advaita will also display the same qualities and so one may wrongly conclude that these qualities are the goal of both dvaita and advaita; it would then appear that it does not matter which of these two views one follows as long as this goal is achieved. But, in fact, maturity and compassion are only by-products of walking the traditional path of advaita. The real goal of advaita is a radical vision of oneness in which all qualities (including good ones) are only of superficial consequence.

Finally, our bodies, minds and experiences all remain in dvaita, even after we have fully imbibed the vision of advaita. The most evolved swami has to eat &

drink, he responds when he is called, he has preferences and he may run an ashram or teach. He has opinions and falls ill, like the rest of us. He may offer worship in a temple or sing *bhajans*. All these activities are entirely in dvaita.

An evolved person's activities in dvaita continue because that is the nature of his body and mind. Some other activities of choice, like worship and teaching, are also carried out by him because of his past orientation and also to help people at large who benefit from the examples set out by a saint and his life-style.

These activities in dvaita are obviously visible. What is not evident is the change in the understanding and vision of the evolved person. Even as he lives a life within duality he is not affected by it, much as we remain unruffled during a friendly game. He has clear knowledge that his truth is changeless and boundless consciousness to which nothing can be (or needs to be) added or subtracted. Therefore, he has nothing to achieve or fear, not even god. But we are not privy to this inner transformation and get misled by his continuing activities in the dvaita world.

It is because of all these reasons that we mix up the useful tools of dvaita with the end goal of advaita. And the result of this confusion often is that we hang on to dvaita—a bit like choosing to remain on the boat even after reaching the other shore because we have gotten used to the enjoyable boat ride and lost sight of our real goal of exploring the land on the other shore.

The Pros of Dvaita

With this background, as students of advaita, let us play the devil's advocate and assume that advaita is either just a theoretical concept like the perfect point of geometry (which has no length or breadth) or a fancy notion without validity. In the time-honoured Vedantic tradition of starting with the plus-points of the opposing view *(purvapaksha)*, let us begin with the pros of dvaita. What are the features of dvaita which so persistently ensnare us and how valid are they?

Dvaita offers at least six major advantages over the advaita view:

> First, the dvaita thesis tallies with our experiences which are all based on duality. We know that experiences do not always reflect the truth (for instance, based on experience, humanity had believed for centuries that the flat earth was the centre of the universe); but it is always easier to go along with a view supported by our experiences. Dvaita undoubtedly scores high here.

Second, dvaita validates our individualities and egos. Our achievements, plans, responsibilities, emotions, possessions, families and friends all have much more meaning and relevance in the dvaita view. This very persuasively encourages us to not let go of dvaita because our personal world remains dear to us.

Third, once the world and individuals are given the status of reality, this automatically brings in an equally real and supremely powerful creator. A creator with qualities we can relate to gives full scope for devotion (*bhakti*) and provides the comforting refuge of the altar. The idea of such a creator and total reliance on him is all the more appealing to those of us with a larger emotional quotient or when we face significant problems.

Fourth, dvaita treats free will, *karmas* (actions and their results), *janmas* (births) and *punar-janmas* (re-births) as real. This validates our experience of freedom of choice; it also provides comforting explanations, especially for those going through difficult times and brings hope of a second chance, if not now then in the next birth.

Fifth, dvaita provides the comfort and safety of numbers. The majority of people have always taken dvaita to be absolutely real while those who have recognised advaita as the truth have been a small minority. By conforming to the majority view, one does not have to face the problems of opposition from others.

And, finally, learned people like Ramanujacharya and Madhvacharya have pointed out to a number of scriptural passages which apparently support dvaita; even a new student studying the Bhagavad Gita will come across several statements there which seem to support dvaita.

Can Dvaita Stand Up To Scrutiny?

But then what are the implications of dvaita being the final truth? Can it stand the dispassionate scrutiny of our logic? Can the indisputable experiences of dvaita be interpreted in a different light so that they lead us to a conclusion other than the obvious one that dvaita is absolutely real?

The traditional prescription for examining any issue in Vedanta is to use *shruti, yukti* and *anubhava* (scriptures, logic and experience) to establish what is correct. Even though shruti is very important, let us leave aside scriptures for the time being as their interpretation can get very technical. Further, scriptural testimony *(shabda)* and our empirical experiences *(pratyaksha)* are two powerful and independent means of knowledge *(pramana)* which point to opposite conclusions—advaita and dvaita. So, let us focus upon our thinking and a deeper analysis of our experiences to find important issues where the dvaita view does not stand up to examination.

The creator and purpose

If dvaita is the truth, then the world with its myriad objects, living beings and natural laws has to be absolutely real because this is the corner-stone of dvaita. The creation of such a complex and orderly world would need a creator with intelligence, requisite materials and a purpose. After all, when we see a watch, we know that it has been made by a knowledgeable watchmaker, using appropriate materials, for the purpose of showing time. In the case of the world also, we should be able to find its intelligent creator, the source of his materials and the purpose of his creation.

As no one has ever seen this creator, religions come in to present their version of god as the creator. The idea of god is very valuable for a variety of reasons but does it withstand the light of logic? If, as religions say, god created everything, then nothing at all would have existed before his creation. In which case, where did he get the raw materials for creation? If the answer is faith in god's miraculous ability to create something from nothing, this is well beyond any experience or logic and is not capable of meaningful discussion. If the answer is that god created the world by using material from within himself, was he first a great god and is now a lesser god because he has expended himself?

Moving to another aspect, what is the purpose of this creation? We may find purpose for ourselves in our individual lives but we have not found any purpose for creation as a whole. Some religions talk about *lila* or play as the reason for creation. In this scenario, are we ready to go along with the idea of a god who gets bored like us and needs to play a game? And a game which involves massacres, calamities, disease, wars and painful deaths?

And such a god who created and runs everything should be all-powerful and all-knowing; he should also be compassionate as he is the father-mother of all. How does this reconcile with the evil and defects in the world? Why is there pain and suffering? Why are there tyrants and psychopaths? Why did he design eyes which develop cataracts? Why did he create floods & droughts? An all-knowing god should be able to see these problems. An all-powerful god should be able to stop these problems. And an all-compassionate god should want to put an end to these problems. But evil and defects continue in this world.

Some religions again step in to say that god gave us free will and the evils and defects are not god's doing but the consequences of our misuse of this free will. But then why did god give us this free will? So that he can watch us make a mess of things? So that the painful death of a young child from a disease can be explained by some wrong he must have done in his previous birth? And as we are all created by this god, is he not responsible for whatever that is within us which makes us misuse our free will?

There are no satisfactory answers to these questions other than faith, which is not an answer based upon thinking. And even faith is not a universal answer: as different religions have different ideas about god, opposing faiths effectively cancel out each other.

Further, when it comes to explanations for the creation of the world, dvaita schools are divided under two broad categories: one proposes a sentient god as the cause of creation, and the other proposes natural evolution. We have already looked at the problems which arise if there is a real god who is the creator of a real world. The different view of the evolutionists (*prakriti vadins*), that inert nature gradually evolved into the world without any god, also suffers from fundamental problems. How can insentient nature create such a complex and orderly world? Order needs intelligence which has to be associated with a sentient being and this is not compatible with inertness. If biological evolution is the answer brought out to explain the complexity of living organisms, then what is the source of the order which is in-built into the process of evolution itself? And what about the order in non-biological aspects of the world, ranging from planetary movements to the behaviour of atoms? Also, what is the source of all the material for the objects in the world, even if it was all compressed into a tiny speck before the 'big bang'? There are no satisfactory answers to these questions.

Independent and permanent existence

Leaving aside the world's creator and its purpose, let us now look at how justified we are in treating objects in the world as being absolutely real, which is what dvaita does. Let us remind ourselves about what constitutes reality. There are at least two important factors which are needed for something to be called real, based upon our own experiences. These factors are independence and permanence. Let us look at some examples.

We do not consider a reflection to be as real as the original because the reflection has no independent substance—it is entirely dependent on the reflecting medium, the mirror. So, we take the image of our face in the mirror to be unreal while we take our actual face to be real. And we prove this by our very different reactions, depending on whether somebody slaps our face or its reflection!

And we know that water is not really hot while fire is really hot. Hot water becomes cold because heat is not its permanent nature but only a temporary property borrowed from fire. On the other hand, fire is always hot because heat is its intrinsic property.

Now let us extend this thinking to the world which we see as being real.

For something to really exist, its existence should be independent (not like the reflection which has to depend on the mirror) and permanent (not like hot water which becomes cold). Now, what do we know in the world which has an independent and permanent existence? Let us take a simple example of an everyday object, like a spoon. We see the spoon, use it regularly and consider it to be absolutely real. Why do we take this spoon to be real? Does its existence meet the criteria of independence and permanence?

The fact is that the spoon's existence is entirely dependent on the silver from which it is made. (I had first thought of a steel spoon until I remembered Swami Dayananda saying, with a twinkle in his eyes, that never be frugal when giving examples!) There is no actual substance called spoon; the weight, the hardness and the shine of the spoon belong entirely to the silver. We cannot say that the silver and the spoon are two different things because we cannot take away the silver and yet keep the spoon, which is what we should be able to do if they were two different things. And we cannot ignore the silver which is more fundamental than the spoon: while the spoon is entirely dependent on the silver for its existence, the silver can exist even when it is not in the form of a spoon.

And the spoon's existence is not permanent. Before the silver was given its current form, this spoon did not exist and, at some point in the future, the spoon will again cease to exist.

Thus, upon enquiry, we come across fundamental problems about the spoon's reality, by our own standards: we find that the spoon is only a name given to a form of silver. The spoon is undoubtedly experienced and is useful but experience and utility are not tests of reality: the image in the mirror is also seen and used but we do not consider it to be as real as our actual face. The spoon lacks absolute reality because its existence is dependent and temporary while we had earlier concluded that reality requires both independence and permanence.

And this is true of all objects we consider to be real in the world. The table temporarily exists only as a form of wood and the shirt depends on fabric during the period of its existence. And it is not that the wood and fabric have independent and permanent existence; they, in turn, are dependent on cellulose and yarn and these things, in turn, are dependent on the next level of more basic materials and so on. Much as science tries, we cannot find anything which exists independently & permanently because everything is found to be dependent on something else and has only temporary existence. Even abstract things are dependent. Our concepts, such as beauty or justice, cannot exist without dependence on their polar opposites of ugliness or injustice—you cannot have one without the other.

Further, all things also have another, and more subtle, kind of dependence: they depend upon a knower. It is meaningless to talk about the existence of a thing which nobody has known or will know. Therefore, the existence of anything can never be independent of the consciousness of some knower.

Advaita goes on to say that you cannot have an endless series of dependencies (on other substances or on their opposites and on a knower) because this would lead to the logical problem of infinite regression. The series of dependent existences has to come to an end by resting on an ultimate reality which exists independently.

But, then, what about the objects in the world which we see and use? Are they unreal? Advaita places all experienced objects (like our spoon, table and shirt) in a unique category called *mithya*, which is neither absolutely real nor absolutely unreal. But that is not our topic here. Our objective at present is to see the limitations of the dvaita view of the world as being absolutely real, which (as we have just seen) suffers from logical problems.

The end goal

Another major problem with dvaita is its end goal. Most dvaita schools propound that a properly led life will ultimately take one to some sort of heaven, to be in god's presence. But by leading an ethical and religious life, the problem of individuals seeing themselves as small and finite beings does not end—one will remain small and finite, even in god's presence. So what fundamental problem has dvaita solved?

Another problem with devotion or bhakti (beautiful as it is) is that it has a very large emotional basis. Unlike knowledge, emotions can be volatile and changeable. So our knowledge that 2+2=4 does not change whether we are peaceful or angry. But, for many people, their faith in and devotion towards god can evaporate when battered by a series of unfortunate events.

Also, finding a place in god's presence after death, is a promise of a reward in the future which is unverifiable. And even if one gets this reward, what is the point of an infinitely long stay in god's presence?

On the other hand, there are pure materialists who have no faith in god or an after-life (either in heaven or hell). They say that the purpose of life is to find as much fulfilment as one can before life comes to its inevitable and final end. But this 'solution' does not address our never-ending needs for longer lives, more knowledge and greater fulfilment. And accepting that these needs can never be fully met is accepting that nature has given us hunger without the means of satisfying it. This does not tally with our experience of nature where there is no need without a way of catering to it.

Need for the upanishads

Our original scriptures, the Vedas, contain the vision of oneness in their last portions, known as the upanishads or Vedanta. The previous portions of the same scriptures contain prayers, rituals and meditations. These earlier (and much more voluminous) portions already cover what is required to lead a good and religious life. If the end portions did not deal with a completely different topic – a radical vision of oneness underlying all appearances – there is no real need for these portions. Therefore, the dvaita view would make the upanishads redundant.

These are some important reasons which render dvaita untenable on deeper examination.

The Mystical and Supranormal

There are some who say that these arguments against dvaita do not apply to the extraordinary powers and a sense of universal expansion which may be obtained from the use of yogic and tantric practices as well as by the use of mind-altering substances. Popping pills for psychedelic experiences, apart from providing only temporary results, is likely to become addictive and can lead to disastrous physical and psychological consequences. Yoga and, to some extent tantra, can produce beneficial results if properly used. But, by themselves, they again lead to an altered state of mind which is only temporary. And if they produce extraordinary powers, there is danger in getting so smitten by them that one can lose sight of the fundamental human problem of lack of abiding fulfilment which can never be addressed by our finite efforts, no matter how exotic and mystical.

Pros and Cons of Advaita

We have so far taken a look at some of the pros and cons of dvaita. We now need to look at the pros & cons of advaita. Many of these have been indirectly covered when we looked at the pros & cons of dvaita—the appealing aspects of dvaita are problem areas for new students of advaita and dvaita's negative features become advaita's benefits. Thus, we have already seen that dvaita scores high because:

- It tallies with most of our experiences
- Validates our individualities & free will
- Provides full scope for reliance on a creator, and
- Keeps us in line with the majority view.

These are the very same areas where advaita poses challenges for its students. But if one properly pursues advaita for a sufficient period of time, these apparent problems dissipate. This happens as a result of the growing understanding that both we and our world (which we take to be absolutely real before our study of advaita) are actually nebulous and temporary appearances. Our new insights free our minds from ceaseless striving to consume, accumulate, protect and change; in our more settled minds, many of our original questions are now seen as being irrelevant or invalid.

While we are on this topic, mention must be made of the logical problems with the advaita view which were documented by advaita's ardent opponent, Ramanujacharya. Ramanujacharya, in his commentary on the Brahma Sutras (known as the Shri Bhashya), attacked the concept of maya/avidya which Shankaracharya used to explain the appearance of the world from a non-dual and attributeless brahman.

In his objections Ramanujacharya set out seven major flaws which, according to him, make Shankaracharya's advaita Vedanta untenable (*sapta vidha anuplabdhi*). His objections are rather technical and may not interest everyone. However, they are doctrinal so let us take a very brief look at some of them.

To give a flavour of his objections, one of the questions he asked is where is this maya/avidya located? It can only be either in brahman or in the jiva. Because maya/avidya is completely opposed to the pure consciousness of brahman, to say that it is located in brahman would be as ridiculous as saying that darkness is located in light. If maya/avidya is located in the jiva then we have a problem of mutual self-dependence: maya/avidya is the cause of jiva so it must precede jiva and so cannot be dependent upon the jiva. He also pointed out that advaita Vedanta's statement that maya/avidya is not real but also that it is not unreal, is completely illogical. Relying upon the law of logic which we now know as the law of the excluded middle, he argued that things can be only either real or unreal and it is meaningless to say that a thing is neither real nor unreal. In a similar vein he goes on to list his seven major objections.

There are detailed and elaborate refutations to each of the issues raised by Ramanujacharya but we will not get into those arguments. However, what we need to note is that Shankaracharya's emphasis is actually on a singular brahman; avidya-maya is brought in by him only to explain the appearance of a world which has no reality to begin with.

Bringing in something to solve a problem founded on incorrect grounds is humorously illustrated by a story. A wealthy man willed one half of his elephants to his eldest son, one third to his middle son and one ninth to his youngest son. But the number of elephants he left behind was seventeen and an obvious problem began with the share of the eldest son. How could he get half of seventeen elephants without the result being a fractional elephant? This led to a heated argument between the three sons as no one was ready to take less than his full share.

A passing wise man, riding his own elephant, overheard this dispute and kindly offered to add his elephant to the kitty to solve the problem. His generous offer was, of course, accepted. Now, with eighteen available elephants, the division became simple: half (nine elephants) for the eldest son, one third (six elephants) for the middle son and one ninth (two elephants) for the youngest son. The total number of elephants thus distributed, to every one's satisfaction, was seventeen and the wise man walked off with the eighteenth, his own! Thus, the eighteenth elephant was introduced to solve a flawed problem and was removed after the problem was solved, without actually doing anything. (In this story, the flaw lies in the fact that one half plus one third plus one ninth totals up to less than one.) Shankaracharya introduces avidya-maya not as the foundation stone of his vision but as a temporary device (Swami Tadatmananda humorously refers to this as the 'fudge factor'!) to explain the appearance of the world which every one experiences. However, what is ultimately important is not the cause of the world but the realisation that the world lacks absolute reality, because nothing in it is substantial and permanent and also because everything in it is dependent on something else.

Once the world is clearly understood as just a projection, discussion about its cause loses relevance. The cause of the unreal world is then as important as the parents of the unreal snake of Vedanta, which has been mistakenly seen in place of the rope. We then also realise that some of the classic laws of thought which Ramanujacharya used in his arguments (such as the excluded middle and non-contradiction) work only within the rules of the world and cannot be applied outside that ambit which is where brahman is; this is similar to the classical laws of physics which do not operate at the level of quantum objects. Further, we realise the futility of trying to understand everything about the world while we ourselves are an integral part of that same world; an analogy would be a piece of a jigsaw puzzle wanting to view the whole puzzle while remaining a part of the puzzle. Advaita Vedanta's (and Shankaracharya's) focus is not a grand explanation answering every single question because it is primarily a solution to the fundamental human problem of limitation and suffering.

Now, let us get away from this debate between the views of Ramanujacharya and Shankaracharya and go to our final topic in this discussion: the pros of advaita which are found in the fundamental matters where advaita provides consistent explanations. In this context let us consider some important questions which occur to all of us, at one time or the other. These are:

- How do I remain fulfilled?
- Who created the world?
- What happens after death?
- What is the purpose of my existence?
- Am I governed by destiny or do I have free will?
- With what value system should I live?

Advaita provides remarkably novel but satisfactory answers here, which the dvaita thesis cannot.

In the vision of advaita, the world has empirical reality but that reality is not absolute because objects in the world lack independence and permanence. We have already seen the reasons for this in some detail earlier. But while advaita does not grant total reality to the world, it recognises our worldly experiences and labels them as *vyavaharika*. As nothing can appear without being supported by a real substratum, advaita goes on to show that this substratum, behind everything we see as the world, is non-dual consciousness. This absolute level of reality, which is the basis for all that appears and is experienced by us, is termed *parmarthika*. With this background, let us look at the questions we had raised.

All our questions arise only at the vyavaharika level and advaita provides initial answers which are practical but provisional—they are only valid at the level of dvaita. But none of those answers will be completely real because the questions themselves are based on an individual (who is not absolutely real) having issues with the world (which too is not absolutely real). And, at the parmarthika level, these same questions are seen to be invalid or irrelevant. Let us now go to each of those questions raised earlier.

How do I remain fulfilled?

At the level of dvaita, answers to this question would include solutions like moderating our desires, using only ethical means to fulfil them, cultivating qualities of hard work & determination and praying for divine help. These answers are relevant at the vyavaharika level and advaita goes along with them in its preliminary stages. But at the parmarthika level, which is advaita's real goal, we learn that the real problem does not lie in what we want but in the very idea that we are wanting. The idea that we are wanting is rooted in our identification with a limited body-mind, where there is a natural pressure to overcome limitations. Once we come to the settled conclusion that what we truly are is unlimited consciousness, the efforts of the body-mind to overcome limitations lose their seriousness. We can then let these efforts continue by treating them as a friendly game whose results do not really matter because what we really are is naturally and always fulfilled.

Who created the world?

If the world is seen as being absolutely real, as it is seen in the dvaita view, then questions necessarily arise about its creator. These are usually answered by postulating an all-powerful, all-knowing and all-merciful God as the creator; some other views say that natural evolution created our world. We have already seen the problems which exist with reference to both these explanations. Advaita takes a completely different tack by showing us that there is no real world which has been created; what we experience is a projection or a superimposition on the reality of non-dual consciousness which is all that exists. When a snake is seen in half-light in place of a rope, its parents are necessarily implied. But once the rope is seen in full light, the snake disappears, and along with it also its parents. A projection which has no reality does not need raw materials or a creator.

What happens after death?

One interesting thing about this question is that those who do not pay much attention to living their current lives fully & intelligently, pay inordinate attention to death and what happens thereafter! But advaita does not get into all this. It asks a fundamental question: who dies?

When a clay pot is broken or a gold ring is melted, one could call it the death of the pot or the ring. But when a pot is created, is it the 'birth' of a new substance or is it just a name given to a form of an already existing substance? And is the 'death' of a ring just the loss of a temporary form or is it the annihilation of the underlying gold? Do not the clay and the gold remain intact while their various products come into existence, while they remain in existence and even after they cease to exist? In the vision of advaita, consciousness which is our reality never undergoes any change and is beyond birth & death. Individual bodies and minds temporarily appear and disappear but, being insubstantial projections, their birth & death are as real as the birth & death of the characters in our dreams. So, instead of paying too much attention to a question based on giving wrong importance to something which is not absolutely real, we should focus on shifting our habitual identification away from our bodies & minds, to our birthless & deathless reality.

What is the purpose of my existence?

Based on the dvaita view of an absolutely real individual living an absolutely real life, this question assumes a lot of gravity because our minds need meaning and purpose. And there are a variety of answers within the realm of dvaita; these answers include seeking self-fulfilment, contributing to society, helping the distressed, leaving a legacy for history, carrying out one's duties, behaving in accordance with the rules of ethics & religion and earning god's grace for a good life in the hereinafter.

Advaita, of course, has a completely different take on this. In its ultimate vision, the question is irrelevant because there is no real 'me' who is asking the question. This question arises only in a mind with an ego. Other living things such as animals and plants do not have this question because they do not have an ego. And our minds and egos which raise this question are themselves insubstantial, appearing temporarily on the substratum of universal consciousness.

However, to appease minds which have yet to accept their own unreality, advaita initially gives watered-down answers which will help our minds to reach advaita's final vision. These answers range over three main themes: our purpose is to find total fulfilment, or our purpose is to grow up to our full potential, or our purpose is to live in touch with reality. All these three themes lead us to the study and assimilation of advaita's core vision. And this can be the only meaningful goal for us, the individuals, to achieve in our lives. It must be emphasised that this 'goal' is as unreal as the individual who needs a goal; at the level of universal consciousness, which is the truth behind all individuals, there are no goals at all because nothing can be added to or subtracted from the unchanging and the boundless.

Am I governed by destiny or do I have free will?

Is the character in our dream governed by destiny or free will? Within the dream, this may seem a valid question but outside of the dream, in our waking state, the question does not subsist because the dream character is understood to be unreal. However, in our daily lives, we have to operate at the practical level where the effects of both destiny and free will are experienced. Advaita provides mechanisms to deal with these experiences; it does this not in order to grant reality to them but in recognition of the fact that unless these experiences are properly processed, our minds may remain disturbed and be unfit for receiving advaita's wisdom. With this in view, the early teachings of advaita say that both destiny and free will have roles in our lives.

Some matters, such as our parentage, are governed entirely by our destiny. For those who need explanations for the differing destinies of different individuals, the karma theory (where effects of our past actions – including actions of our past lives – result in our current situation) is brought out. But we have free will in choosing the actions which we now take. So, our lives are like a boat in a river where destiny is the river's flow but the boat's direction and speed can be affected by our strength on the oars, our free will.

Our actions can lead to results which may or may not be in keeping with our expectations. Results which are equal to or in excess of our expectations may lead to a surge of pride while negative results may lead to guilt, regret, anger and enmity. In order to modulate these emotional yo-yos, advaita brings in *karma* yoga as part of its preparatory teachings. Karma yoga is a large, separate topic by itself. All that can be said about it here is that it is a combination of behaviour and attitudes designed to make us less self-centred and emotionally more stable, with the goal of making us more receptive to advaita's wisdom. Thus, advaita uses our experiences of destiny and free will to lead us to a higher perspective, even though both these experiences themselves lack absolute reality.

With what value system should I live?

Both dvaita and advaita emphasise the values of dharma and the need to progress from *tamas* to *rajas* to *sattva*. The difference is that while dvaita stops here, advaita goes on to the level of *triguna atita* or the level beyond all qualities, even good qualities.

Values are vital because unless our lives are lived in accordance with dharma or natural order, we will remain in conflict with both our internal make-up and our external surroundings. Actions and attitudes which are contrary to dharma may produce short-term gains but their long-term results are minds in conflict with themselves and agitated by greed, pride, anger, dejection, regrets, fear and enmity. On this emotional roller-coaster, where the lows alternate with the highs, our minds are unlikely to wake up to something of higher value. It is for this purpose that advaita advocates an ethical and religious life, not because ethics and religion are ends in themselves but because they are vital means to achieve mental equilibrium and gain the highest end: the knowledge of reality. In the vision of advaita, all the actions and attitudes which help us to obtain self-knowledge are to be adopted and all those that keep us away from this end are to be avoided. Ultimately, values are tools for achieving the higher goal of self-knowledge.

One interesting thing about religious and ethical values is that in the initial stages of our journey of self-discovery, we have to make an effort and be watchful to comply; however, as we progress in our understanding of the truth, the pressures which propel us away from dharma evaporate and appropriate actions and attitudes come effortlessly because that is in keeping with our very nature.

To Conclude

The dvaita view, that we are real individuals operating in a real world, is supported by our experiences and provides valuable guidance for conducting our daily lives. However, it does not provide full answers to subtler and more fundamental questions. We have just seen some of these questions where only advaita provides explanations from a higher perspective. The vision of advaita is vital not only for resolving intellectual conundrums but also for finding personal fulfilment, which is the common and paramount pursuit in all our lives.

But advaita never denies the experience of dvaita and nor does it ask us to shun dvaita. Once our knowledge of the truth is complete and steady, dvaita can be enjoyed even more, minus its stings and with the serenity that it can be dropped at will, effortlessly and instantly.

Only Advaita Leads to True Fulfilment

Our endless search for fulfilment is usually based on the dvaita view of happiness being a goal to be reached by adding something or removing something from our lives. But this conventional view does not explain many things. If a scoop of ice-cream contains happiness, why do ten scoops make us feel sick instead of making us feel ten times happier? If loud music has happiness within it, why do we ever switch it off? Why does our happiness from a new car diminish when our unfriendly neighbour gets a fancier model? Why do we feel a sense of deep contentment when looking at a beautiful night sky even when all our agendas remain unfinished? And despite a lifetime of clever and ceaseless efforts to obtain happiness, why are we still wanting?

Advaita gives us completely new understanding here by showing us that our reality is unlimited and unchanging. We therefore need nothing to become more complete; we are already fulfilled by our very nature. This natural fullness and the resulting peace is experienced by us every time our mind is temporarily stilled and stops creating the turbulence of demands. This happens in deep sleep or when a demand is met or when the mind is fully occupied by the awe and mystery of a phenomenon such as the splendour of a starry sky. However, these periods of fulfilment do not last because identification with our limited bodies and minds returns all too soon.

Unfortunately, the unlimited can never be reached by our bodies & minds because their abilities and time-spans are finite; therefore, as long as we remain identified with our physical and mental adjuncts, we will always feel limited despite all our efforts and successes. The only solution is to absorb advaita's wisdom which makes our minds realise that we are already whole and complete. This 'solution' is not really a solution in the sense that it does not involve us reaching something away from us or changing ourselves to something we are not at present; it is only a settled recognition of our reality as it is, here and now.

Advaita is Difficult to Accept

But the full recognition of our reality poses problems. Despite studying Vedanta, there can be doubts about the actual message of the upanishads (*pramana shanka*). On the face of it, the upanishads contain many statements which are in line with the dvaita view. Also, there are several respected teachers who teach only dvaita.

Even If we are able to accept advaita as a concept, there is difficulty in applying this in our daily lives by truly accepting our reality to be universal and impersonal consciousness (*prameya shanka*). Most of us find it very difficult to abandon the idea that we are unique and separate. We remain committed to the identification with our individual bodies and minds (termed as *dehaatma buddhi*). Accepting that our bodies and minds are not our truth means accepting that there is no personal me, no personal other, and therefore no personal relationships. This challenges the entire structure of personal relationships which is the area in which the illusion of a separate self clings most tenaciously and insidiously.

We also are not able to accept the fundamental unreality of the world which we experience so vividly and with which we transact continuously. So while we may recite *jagat mithya*, the world continues its hold over us and *jagat* remains *satyam*.

All this leads to emotions and behaviour which are contrary to the real message of Vedanta (*viparita bhava*) and overcoming these problems is a difficult task.

Is Advaita Just A Mind Game?

A question which is sometimes asked about advaita Vedanta is whether the enlightenment it promises is *just* a mind game? This question implies putting the physical world above the mind and consciousness even lower, as a product of the mind. In this context, we need to remind ourselves that we never ever actually confront the physical world because it never enters us. Our impression of the world is only as mediated by the senses and mind. It is affected by the limitations of our senses and by the absence or presence of the mind. The world and our bodies themselves are available only as presented by the mind. To take the example of something seen, an object enters our eyes as light which forms two, tiny and upside-down images on our retinas. These two images are then converted into electrical impulses which our mind presents to us, through an incredible process, of an upright single vision of colours, form and size. It also gives the sight a first person intimacy—*I* see. And there is no world at all in deep sleep where the mind is inactive. So '*just* a mind game' is a misunderstanding because the mind is more important and more fundamental than the physical world. But the mind exists only in consciousness so consciousness is even more fundamental. Understanding consciousness and seeing it as the truth of everything, including our bodies and minds, is far from a mind game; it is the discovery of the ultimate truth.

Advaita Is Not An Answer To All Questions

One other thing that needs to be said here is that advaita is a solution to the problem of an individual endlessly seeking happiness; this does not imply that advaita has answers to all possible questions which may occur to us. Advaita tells us that a single reality is all that exists but it will not answer questions about how that reality came into being or why it supports the appearance of plurality. Questions about cause & effect and justifications belong to the realm of unreal creation while advaita talks about the very substratum of creation, where these questions have no relevance. After all, how much effort should we make in figuring out how it was possible for us to be talking to a long-dead relative or to be both in New York and Tokyo within a span of a few minutes, once we wake up from our dream?

The reality of existence itself cannot be doubted because we ourselves exist. The existence of a single reality is logically more tenable than the existence of multiple realities because more than one reality would lead to problems about the source of raw materials, the purpose of creation and the nature of the creator. Advaita is able to provide good reasons as well as useful examples from our own experiences (such as our dreams) to support its vision of a single reality. And this is validated not only by numerous scriptural statements but also by the testimony of several evolved individuals in our own era, who have completed the journey of advaita.

And, finally, advaita Vedanta is not a philosophy which makes assertions which have to be defended and explained. It deals more with 'what is' rather than 'why is'. In this it is a bit like science which can explain what makes a rose red but cannot explain why it was made red instead of green. Vedanta's value does not lie in winning all arguments but in the efficacy of its methods in removing our unnecessary suffering and opening our eyes to our natural state of fulfilment.

The superiority of reason in advaita Vedanta has been accepted by most. And Vedanta unequivocally declares *jnanam eva moksha*—knowledge is the only means of liberation. But this does not mean that it is the best path for each and every one. It is also universally accepted that the dualistic path of *bhakti* is far more easy and it does resolve many of our issues. In fact, for the present Kali Yuga, the most often recommended path is that of bhakti which is in dvaita.

Further, the ananda brought about by Vedanta is like the impersonal vastness and peace of a tranquil ocean; it is different from the very personalised and individualised upsurge of emotion generated by bhakti. For many who need the joy from bhakti, dvaita can be the only path.

But for those who seek the ultimate goal and need to obtain the culmination of their spiritual journey through the path of reason and logic, advaita Vedanta will always stand out as the highest path. However, even a person who has successfully completed Vedanta's journey can enjoy bhakti, just as he or she can enjoy a well-cooked meal or a good night's sleep. But in the case of such a person, the dvaita involved in bhakti is only imagined *(kalpitam)* and does not displace the basic knowledge of oneness or lead to dependence, not even on god.

So, with determination & enthusiasm, with the guidance of a good teacher, with the companionship of fellow students and with the continuing grace of whichever power that introduced us to this ultimate wisdom, let us continue our journey of liberation from the bounds of dvaita (silken as they may be) to the freedom of advaita.

APPENDICES

It is useful to see the place Vedanta occupies
in the landscape of Indian thought
as well as some of its important differences
when compared to Western approaches to philosophy.

INDIAN PHILOSOPHICAL SYSTEMS

'*Darshan*' is the word used in Sanskrit for referring to what we, in English, call philosophy. Darshan means getting a view. This choice of term is significant because it indicates a certain non-dogmatic attitude in philosophical matters. After all, if what I believe to be true is only a view then I automatically accept that there can be other views which may be equally valid, from a different view-point or from a different perspective. This liberal nature of our traditions, where people were willing to let their convictions be called a darshan or a view and not claim monopoly of the truth, is unique and refreshing.

Tradition places darshans under two categories: *astika* and *nastika*. In popular usage, astika means someone who believes in god and nastika refers to atheists. However, the original meaning of these words is related to the acceptance of the Vedas as being authoritative. Astikas are those who accept the authority of the Vedas (*Veda pramanam asti*) and nastikas are those who do not accept the Vedas as the final authority (*Veda pramanam nasti*).

The six astika darshans are:

- Nyaya
- Vaisheshika
- Sankhya
- Yoga
- Mimamsa
- Vedanta

The main schools of nastika philosophy are:

- Jainism
- Buddhism
- Carvaka
- Ajivika
- Ajnana

(Another listing mentions six nastika schools as Carvaka, Jainism and four different schools of Buddhism but leaves out Ajivika and Ajnana.)

As students of Vedanta, why should we bother about other philosophical systems? There are good reasons why an overview is relevant. Knowing where Vedanta fits in within the scheme of Indian thought gives us some context as we study Vedanta. And many of us find it difficult to operate without putting whatever we are dealing with in context. Further, as we become committed to Vedanta, we need to be aware of the other options in philosophical thought which we are giving up. In fact, even within Vedanta, there are three different streams with very different conclusions so we need to be clear about which one of these three streams of Vedanta will be espoused by us. Finally, when faced with our own doubts or with arguments from others, it is useful to have in our minds a broad picture of the whole philosophical landscape.

Let us now take a very brief look at the astika and nastika darshans and then look at the three interpretations of the Vedanta darshan itself. We will begin with the astika darshans.

Nyaya is ascribed to a sage called Gautama and focuses on logic, analytics and what Western philosophy would call epistemology—a study of how you know things or what is valid knowledge. It holds that your five senses are the only way to obtain knowledge leading you to liberation. In Vedanta we call Nyaya *tarka shastra* (scripture of logic) and use many of its logical processes such as inference, arguments and counter-arguments but do not agree with its other conclusions.

Vaisheshika is associated with Kannada and is a theory which holds that atoms are the primary basis of creation.

Sankhya is ascribed to Kapila and is a dualistic view based on two primary elements: *purusha* and *prakriti*. It is dualistic and atheistic. The Bhagavad Gita contains some terms drawn from sankhya.

Yoga originates from Patanjali; it includes many techniques and emphasises meditation. In many ways its philosophy is similar to sankhya but, unlike sankhya, yoga accepts Ishwara.

Mimamsa is associated with Jaimini; it is an interpretation of the contents of the entire Vedas and is heavily bent on the proper performance of rituals.

Vedanta, on the other hand, was encapsulated by Badrayana and it focuses only on the contents of the upanishads portion of the Vedas.

Out of these six astika darshans the only views which continue to remain current for a significant number of people are Vedanta and Yoga. But while Yoga is widely practised in terms of its techniques, it does not have the development and rigour of Vedanta's philosophy.

Apart from these six astika darshans there are, as we have seen, a number of nastika darshans propounded by those who did not accept the Vedas as the final authority. The main ones are:

> Jainism—A very old and dualistic view propounded by Mahavir. It accepts multiple atmas and says that each atma needs to be purified by karmas—avoid bad ones and accumulate good ones. It emphasises both *ahimsa* and asceticism and rejects Ishwara.
>
> Buddhism—It is, of course, based on the teachings of Gautam Buddha and emphasises balance, moderation and ethical living. Because Buddha did not leave behind any authoritative scripture of his own, his followers came up with widely varying interpretations of his teachings. Two main schools of Buddhism are Mahayana and Theravada and there are many sub-schools within each. The philosophy of one important sub-school, ascribed to Nagarjuna, is very close to Vedantic thought but diverges at the very end where it propounds *shunyata* (nothingness) as the ultimate truth. (However, there are views that

the nothingness referred to here is not a complete void but a fullness without any attributes and beyond description; this, then, would not be different from the ultimate truth as set out by Vedanta.)

Carvaka—The word itself means 'pleasant speech'. It is based on what is popularly known as the "eat, drink and make merry" approach to living. It rejects Ishwara, atma and re-birth. It is pure materialism and hedonism.

Ajivika—It is somewhat similar to carvaka but it is based on total determinism. Here, there is no free-will, everything is predetermined and whatever is to happen will happen.

Ajnana—It is what Western philosophy would call scepticism. The view here is that it is not possible for anyone to know any ultimate truth.

Going back to Vedanta which is one of the six astika darshans, we saw that it is based on the upanishads and encapsulated by Badrayana in the Brahma Sutras. However, the upanishads contain statements which are cryptic, confusing and, at times, apparently contradictory. This has resulted in a number of widely varying interpretations. The three main interpretations here are based on the views of Shankaracharya (*advaita* or non-dualism), Ramanujacharya (*vishisht advaita* or qualified non-dualism) and Madhvacharya (*dvaita* or dualism). While Advaita, Vishisht Advaita and Dvaita are all classified under the common title of Vedanta, Shankaracharya's Advaita establishes that there is only one fundamental reality while the other two hold the view that there is more than one reality.

In Shankaracharya's view, the world and its individuals have no permanent and substantial existence—there is only one underlying reality and the multiplicity we experience is only an appearance on and of this reality, like the snake which appears in place of the rope. In this view, just as the world has no independent reality, the creator of such a world – Ishwara – also has no fundamental reality. We will not get into the details or the rationale for this startling view but just note that it has huge implications for us personally.

Ramanujacharya went with the idea of 'differences within non-difference': a fire and the sparks flying from it where the sparks are nothing but fire and yet enjoy a temporary but real and separate existence. In this example, the fire is like Ishwara and the sparks are like the people and objects in the world.

Madhvacharya gave total reality to everything we experience: there is a real Ishwara who created a real world with a variety of real objects and populated by individuals with separate and real bodies, minds and souls.

The two non-Shankara views, based on duality and acceptance of Ishwara as our ultimate refuge, are the more commonly accepted views. This is because views which accept the reality of all that we experience naturally tally with what our senses tell us and also validate our emotions. Vishisht Advaita and Dvaita-based views are, therefore, the more widely accepted views by people at large, with Dvaita being the most popular. After Madhvacharya, dvaita has been further championed and propagated by well-known people like Nimbarka, Chaitanya and Vallabha. Popular movements like the *pushti marg* and Iskcon are founded on dvaita views.

Advaita, on the other hand, is more abstract; it is difficult to relate to, it requires a lot of preparatory work (for modulating behaviour, emotions and egos) and shifts the ultimate responsibility for our salvation to our own selves instead of reliance on Ishwara to do the job. It is therefore seriously pursued by relatively few.

Post-Shankara, some well-known teachers after him came up with slightly different interpretations of advaita Vedanta itself. These differences are technical in nature, based on different understanding of subtle points. This has led to two main schools of advaita Vedanta. These are known as the Bhamati School and the Vivarana School. Teachers of both these schools teach Vedanta in the traditional way and the minor distinctions between these two schools of advaita Vedanta are not relevant for most of us.

Much later, some people in the late 1800's and then going on to more recent personalities like Ramana Maharishi, Atmananda Krishna Menon, Nisargadatta Maharaj and Poonjaji developed different methods of teaching. These methods, especially the more recent ones, are far removed from the traditional teaching process and do not use traditional terminology. These methods vary amongst themselves and are known by names like neo-Vedanta, Direct Path Advaita and Satsang Advaita. Some of these methods have been adopted and propagated by well-known foreign teachers of advaita Vedanta. While a few students have benefited greatly from these new methods, a majority of seekers run into significant difficulties, sooner or later, in trying to follow the paths shown by such methods.

Now let us move on to one last note on this subject of Indian systems of thought: *tantra*. Tantra doesn't clearly fit into either astika or nastika darshans. The word 'tantra' has various meanings including a 'weaving loom' and 'something which liberates energy while expanding consciousness'. Tantra refers to esoteric and occult practises in both Hindu and Buddhist traditions.Tantra scriptures such as the *agamas* and *Shaiva* & *Shakta* tantras of Hinduism deal with the creation the world, functions of a great variety of deities, different types of ritual worship (especially of goddesses), the mapping of the subtle or psychic body (like the *chakras*), the awakening of a mysterious coiled power (*kundalini-shakti*) and even sacred sexuality (part of the so-called 'left-handed' tantra). Incidentally, almost all the *pujas* that we do today, the architecture of our temples and our iconography are mainly based on tantra, not the Vedas. One notable branch of tantra is called Kashmir Shaivism, propounded by Abhinav Gupta, and it talks about non-duality but in a different way than Vedanta.

We should now take a brief look at philosophical views outside our culture. Away from India, there are philosophical views associated with different religions. One large and important set of views comes from the three Abrahamic religions: Judaism, Christianity and Islam. They have many dissimilarities amongst themselves but they all commonly have belief in a single creator-God who sits in judgement in heaven and whose law is found in one authoritative book of that particular religion (such as the Bible or the Koran) which has to be accepted without questions.(That is why followers of these three religions are also called People of the Book.) But, interestingly, even in these religions, there are small side-streams away from their main flow which speak in a language similar to Vedanta. Examples here are Sufism in Islam and mystical streams of Christianity. Taoism from China also expresses thoughts and uses language which are startlingly similar to Vedanta.

Apart from philosophies embedded in religions which have developed outside of India, mainly in the Middle East and the Far East, there is a wide ocean of philosophy originating in Europe. Western philosophy started with the ancient Greeks and its development continues till date in Europe and America. There is great richness of thought in Western philosophy and a lot of its content has to be respected. But, as students of Vedanta, we must be aware of the important differences between Vedanta and Western philosophy.

First, Western philosophy concentrates on what is observed and does not turn its gaze backwards and inwards, towards the observer. (Though, now, study of consciousness itself is gaining importance amongst thinkers in the

West.) Vedanta, on the other hand, is more concerned with understanding the real nature of the observer. So Western philosophy is most concerned with cosmology, theology, epistemology, ethics, aesthetics and so on; while Vedanta does cover these topics, its real interest is 'I', the observer, the atma. Its final objective is not to understand and improve our bodies and minds but to find the truth which goes beyond bodies and minds. This is why, in Vedanta, theism, cosmology, ethics and similar topics do not form part of its core teachings.

Further, Western philosophy is a search of truth for truth's sake or knowledge for knowledge's sake. Vedanta on the other hand is not some abstract research but a remedy to the disease of lack of total and permanent fulfilment faced by individuals. Vedanta is meant to be a personal solution which becomes truly relevant only to those who discern the nature of the fundamental problem they face and who have also determined that the usual solutions do not work except temporarily. For someone who has not understood the real nature of our basic problem or believes that other solutions (such as pleasures, possessions, fame, ethics or religion) will solve the problem, Vedanta is not very relevant.

As an extension of the above, Vedanta does not offer answers to all possible questions which can occur to a human mind. What it does is to expand our perspective and raises it to such a high level that many questions which seem so important now, lose their importance. In this context, Alan Watt's example of the difference between the natural view of a landscape and the problems in a picture of the same landscape, taken through the narrow lens of a camera, is very interesting. In his example, a natural vista seen by our eyes has no problems but as soon as we try to capture the same view through the limitations of a camera lens, problems suddenly appear: an small twig, barely noticed by our eyes, suddenly becomes a blurred central feature in the photograph and the sky which was perfectly in place for our eyes now appears too wide or too narrow, depending on the way the camera was angled. Our mind is like the camera lens which can restrict and distort our world-view, causing us problems; Vedanta's wisdom expands our perspective to its natural, no-problems state.

While Vedanta is ancient and continues to be immensely useful to those who use it properly, it does not claim any monopoly for its vision of advaita or the oneness of the ultimate truth. As we saw earlier, some other traditions (such as Sufism and Taoism) also have similar views. Where Vedanta scores and is special is in its highly developed scriptures and commentaries, rigorous logic and a superb and time-tested teaching methodology carried forward by a long and unbroken chain of teachers. All these permit a competent teacher to transfer the wisdom and subtle insights of traditional Vedanta to a qualified student. In this, there is no other tradition which comes even close to Vedanta. Unfortunately, the great teachings of Vedanta can be distorted or diluted by some people who are not proper teachers and then many students, especially those who do possess the required emotional and intellectual qualities, are mis-led.

And, finally, admirers of Western philosophy say that it is logical and rational while Eastern views like Vedanta are mystical and not supported by logical thought. This is a topic which needs to be re-visited only after having a good background of Vedanta. For the time being, it is enough to note that while portions of Vedanta are trans-logical (with sensible explanations about why some matters have to be beyond logic), it does not contain anything which is illogical or anything which contradicts our valid experiences; further, Vedanta does not ask us to take any of its teachings on just faith but invites us to test its conclusions with both our thinking and with our experiences.

Vedanta has earned the following and respect of seekers from India and abroad because of its logical structure, because of the great truths it contains and because of its efficacy in dealing with age-old and fundamental problems of human beings. It is a blessing that its ancient wisdom, which remains immensely relevant to us even today, is yet available to us in its pristine form thanks to an unbroken line of great teachers.

A brief overview of the general scheme of Vedanta to put the various elements of its plan into perspective.

SCHEME OF VEDANTA

Four Human Goals

Our scriptures list four *purusharthas* (human goals) as *dharma*, *artha*, *kama* and *moksha*. Artha covers all that we do for acquiring wealth and security. Kama is our pursuit of pleasures at both the body and mind levels. Dharma is adoption of a way of life based on ethics, morality and religion. Moksha is seeking freedom from all limitations. The traditional order puts dharma first in this list of four to show its importance and emphasises that all that we do in any pursuit must remain within the ambit of dharma. Seeking wealth, security and pleasures comes quite naturally to us. Dharma poses problems for many of us because some of its tenets may put restrictions on our unbridled desires and inappropriate actions; dharma, therefore, needs cultivation, awareness and appreciation of its long-term benefits. We finally come to moksha when we realise the limitations of artha, kama and even of dharma. This realisation comes when we see that all our efforts and activities have not succeeded in bringing complete and lasting fulfilment or in providing deeper meaning to our existence which remains an insignificant flicker between our births and deaths despite all our achievements. We then stop hoping that endless repetition of our usual activities will somehow bring a solution to our stubborn sense of limitation and continuing lack of peace and happiness. This propels us towards moksha which focuses not on meeting our specific wants but on questioning the very conclusion that we are lacking and wanting. Vedanta is moksha shastra, wisdom based on our scriptures which shows us a way to find total and lasting fulfilment and gain freedom from fear, sorrow and inadequacy.

Vedanta Is Like a Mother

We are all on an unending search for fulfilment because no matter what we do or achieve, we continue to feel a sense of lack or want. We, of course, experience fulfilment from time to time but it is neither complete nor lasting. Lack of a sense of fulfilment makes us strive endlessly, causes fear & anxiety, compromises our peace and, ultimately, our happiness. These, in turn, can lead to anger, guilt, regrets and hostility. While the issues which cause us unhappiness appear to be many, they can be reduced to three basic factors which apply to all of us. First is our inevitable mortality while the need to remain alive is hard-wired into us, as it is in all living beings. Next, we have an insatiable hunger to know more and more but we can never know beyond a small limit; further, we need to find the cause and meaning of our lives but we do not find convincing answers. Finally, we want to experience full and abiding fulfilment at all times, in all places and in every situation but we never succeed in achieving this utopian end. These limitations constitute our fundamental problem and Vedanta says that it has a solution which will resolve our on-going struggles here. But, despite this, either we do not perceive our fundamental problem to be serious enough to warrant our time & effort or, even if we do, we do not turn to Vedanta for a solution.

Even in the face of our reluctance to turn to Vedanta, our traditions and Vedanta itself try to help us. In this, Vedanta can be compared with a mother trying to feed a distracted and disinterested child. Like this mother, Vedanta too uses a combination of persuasion and temptation to bring us the nourishment which we need to cater to our hunger for a solution to our basic problem. If our endless search for happiness and answers is a real problem and if Vedanta actually has a solution, why would we be disinterested? As intelligent people we should be hammering on Vedanta's door to be let in to grab this solution. But, as we know, there is no great clamour for Vedanta. This is because of a number of powerful reasons.

The first is that we all have regular experiences of happiness, whether from relationships, possessions, music, food, vacations, money, social recognition or from a host of other things. These experiences are temporary and are regularly replaced by opposing experiences of hurt, fear, disappointment, anger, guilt and the like. However, the expectation of a repeat of happy experiences keeps us going and we do not pause to discern that this see-saw between happiness and unhappiness is never-ending. Or, to put it differently, we let our hopes keep on conquering our own experiences.

The second powerful reason is our milieu. Most people we are surrounded by seem to find it normal to work endlessly for the goal of total happiness without ever reaching there; they readily accept lives in which happiness and unhappiness continuously interchange. We do not want to be the oddballs who question this and rock the boat of convention.

Finally, Vedanta's solution requires considerable time and effort but our tendency is to settle for quick and easy fixes. This is what transient pleasures provide. So, we continue with our game-plan of acquiring superficial happiness by conventional methods and make continuous efforts in the same direction. While doing this we forget what Einstein had once pointed out: it is insane to expect that the endless repetition of the same actions will somehow produce a different result the next time!

Religion and Mysticism

Some of us, who stop relying only on pleasures to deal with our fundamental disquietude, often turn to devotion or to the mystical for a solution. Devotion to god, though beautiful and beneficial, is based on emotions which are inherently unstable. Devotion alone also leaves unanswered questions about the nature and purpose of god's creation of the universe. Mystical paths, such as *samadhi* meditation or awakening the *kundalini*, tend to focus on achieving temporary states of mind and acquiring abnormal powers. These paths once again do not provide answers to fundamental questions about the nature and purpose of the entire creation. Further, they do not address our basic issues of mortality, ignorance and an ongoing sense of less than perfect happiness.

Greater Difficulties Now

In addition to all these age-old factors, our inclination to turn towards Vedanta faces extra problems today. The accelerating pace of our lives, the pressure of ever-growing consumerism and the snapping of ties with many values that religion and tradition support, all create impediments. We now devote our attention almost entirely to our physical and intellectual nourishment with much less regard to our emotional health and with hardly any concern for our spiritual needs to bring deeper meaning to our lives and to find a connection with something greater than our mortal bodies and wayward minds. In the past, a religious way of life, exposure to scriptures at a young age, reverence towards patriarchs and gurus, a less competitive society and value for inner growth all encouraged a turn towards the spiritual wisdom of Vedanta. These factors are getting progressively less prominent in our lives now. Further, difficulties in finding suitable teachers at a time and place convenient for us and the hope that innovations in science and technology will bring us solutions to our fundamental problem, all conspire to keep us away from Vedanta's wisdom.

Both effort and good fortune are required for us to turn to Vedanta, while being in a milieu which may not be supportive. But, despite these issues, for some people Vedanta yet becomes compelling.

Road Map

For those of us who start on a serious exploration of Vedanta, we should have an overall view of its journey. The two major elements of this journey are the preparation (*karma* & *upasana* yogas) and the actual learning (*jnana* yoga).

Vedanta's basic premise is that what we truly are is already full and complete, here and now. It therefore holds that proper knowledge of our own selves is the only final solution to our fundamental problems. But we continue to suffer from a false sense of incompleteness because three different obstacles stop us from recognising our own reality. These three obstacles are termed *mala* (impurities or dirt), *vikshepa* (distractions & divisions) and *avarana* (covering or veil). The ways in which these obstacles impede us in obtaining self-knowledge are compared with the problems we may face while capturing a reflection of the sun in a pot of water. In this illustration, the sun is like our reality whose knowledge we seek; the pot is like our body and the water in the pot is like our mind where the knowledge we need can occur. Vedanta holds out *karma yoga*, *upasana yoga* and *jnana yoga* as solutions to these obstacles.

Karma Yoga

If the water in the pot is dirty (mala), it will be opaque and will not catch the sun's reflection. Similarly, if our minds are polluted with strong likes & dislikes and negative emotions such as anger, jealousy and fear, the result will be minds incapable of receiving Vedanta's insights. The solution here is karma yoga which is a way of life centred on right action backed by right attitude, designed to reduce our mental impurities. Karma yoga is a mixture of religious and secular elements which leads to a mental state that is introspective, relatively free of conflicts, emotionally stable, less self-centred and ready to learn. To achieve this state, karma yoga tells us to avoid doing certain things, focus on doing more of some other things and cultivate supportive attitudes as we act and confront the results of our actions. Let us briefly look at each of these.

Reduce Wrong Actions

The first step in karma yoga is to initially reduce and, ultimately, refrain from activities which go against universal values. In practical terms this means not doing to others what we would not want them to do to us. Avoidance of *adharmic* activities, such as needlessly injuring others or being untruthful, is the preliminary step in our journey of internal growth.

Increase Nurturing Activities

From here, we have to progress to doing things which are for the larger good of both ourselves and of our society. Apart from encouraging activities like social service and pilgrimages, our tradition facilitates our inner growth by prescribing five compulsory areas of daily action (termed *pancha maha yagna*). Each of these has a ritualistic and a secular aspect. Very briefly, these five acts which are traditionally required to be done every day, are:

> *Dev Yagna*: Worship of chosen deities and moderated use of the god-given elements of the earth, water, fire, air and space.
>
> *Bhuta Yagna*: Showing consideration towards other living things such as trees, plants and animals.
>
> *Manushya Yagna*: Acknowledging fellow humans to be valuable, treating all with a certain amount of respect and consideration irrespective of their status and offering food & shelter to the needy.
>
> *Brahma Yagna*: Worshipping of the scriptures, rishis & gurus as well as studying & propagating our scriptures.
>
> *Pitru Yagna*: Acknowledging our lineage by showing respect and care for elders in general and parents in particular every day and performing periodic *shraddha* ceremonies for ancestors who are no longer with us.

The pancha maha yagnas are a small attempt to repay our debts to the various aspects of creation which make our lives possible. The real point here is not empty ritualism but an opportunity to reflect daily on our connections with the entire universe. Acknowledging, with gratitude, our dependence on these factors helps in keeping our egos in check.

Attitudes are Critical

Apart from avoiding wrong actions and focusing on doing the right things, karma yoga places a lot of emphasis on our attitudes as we go through our lives. In respect of any action we take, karma yoga encourages us to cultivate the attitude of treating each action as our offering to god, *Ishwara arpana bhavana*. This imbues whatever we do with a certain sanctity and ensures that we give our best, without carelessness or complaints. After all, an offering to god is something that we do with reverence and joy. Further, this attitude also keeps alive our connection with a larger whole and moderates our egos.

Actions obviously produce results and karma yoga asks us to have *prasada bhavana* here (grateful acceptance of all results as return gifts of god). We accept the most meagre of prasada with reverence and gratitude. If we are able to view all the results of our actions with the same feeling, this would equip us to handle any outcome without violent swings of emotions—no excessive pride and exultation if the results are positive and no great depression or anger if results are contrary to expectations.

When religion is a natural part of our lives, these attitudes (of Ishwara arpana and prasada) are not difficult to cultivate. However, those of us who do not have enough connection with religion and god, have to find ways of deriving the benefits of these religious attitudes by relying on our experiences and thinking.

If we can't have Ishwara arpana bhavana, we can use our experience of past efforts to realise that nothing that we have done so far has succeeded in bringing us total and permanent fulfilment. We can then turn to internal growth as a solution and make that our primary goal. Instead of being dedicated to Ishwara, all our activities can now become subservient and dedicated to growth in our maturity & understanding, in the expectation that this will bring us the contentment which has eluded us so far.

Similarly, if we can't look upon all results at prasada, we can again use our own experiences to see that our actions are only one of the several inputs which contribute towards producing a given result. This understanding discourages us from claiming sole personal responsibility for good and bad results and tempers our emotional reactions.

Concentrating on appropriate action instead of focusing on a desired result is a vital part of karma yoga. It is encapsulated in one of the most commonly quoted verses – verse 47 from the second chapter – of the Bhagavad Gita.

Vedanta explains that this attitude is in keeping with reality. And the reality is that while we do have control over the actions we choose, we have no control over results. This is because all results are a product of a number of factors of which our contribution is only one element. The other elements are out of our control and, often, even beyond our knowledge: we know of businesses which succeeded beyond the most optimistic plans because of a favourable change in government policy or the fortuitous closure of a major competitor; we know of children who went astray despite the endless efforts of loving and sensible parents.

Vedanta, therefore, encourages us to put in our best effort in whatever we do but yet learn not to claim total authorship of results which may turn out to be good or bad. This does not mean that we should not plan for favourable results. But it does mean that once we have done whatever we thought was appropriate in a situation, there is no reason for great personal pride if the result is favourable and no reason for self-recrimination or undue disappointment if things do not go our way. This attitude makes our daily lives less of an emotional roller-coaster and teaches us to derive satisfaction from appropriate action instead of basing all our fulfilment on uncontrollable and unpredictable results.

Upasana Yoga

What we have seen of karma yoga so far leads to the reduction of negative patterns in our lives and the increase of positive qualities. This is termed *chitta shuddhi* or mind purification which is like removing the dirt from the water in the pot. But even clean water, if agitated and covered with ripples (*vikshepa*), will not capture the sun's reflection faithfully. Similarly, even a pure mind can remain hyper-active and agitated in trying to accomplish many tasks, even though all these tasks may be legitimate and within dharma. However, Vedanta requires an undivided and a relatively still mind which can hold its focus on new and subtle insights.

For this purpose regular meditation is prescribed and this is called upasana yoga. The object of meditation here is god but even if one chooses to use some other thought or object for meditation, the goal should remain the toning down of excessive mental activity and cultivating the ability to hold one's mind on a subject for a length of time (*chitta ekagrata*).

Incidentally, even though upasana yoga has been given its separate name, upasana or meditation is an activity or karma, and so this meditation is actually a part of karma yoga in a larger sense.

Karma Yoga is Necessary for Jnana Yoga

Karma yoga (which includes upasana yoga) makes us eligible for acquiring the knowledge that Vedanta has to impart (*jnana yogyata*). Whether we are religiously inclined or not, we ultimately have to adopt a life of actions and attitudes envisaged by karma yoga, if we are to grow spiritually. It is a life in keeping with karma yoga which reduces our self-centredness and makes us aware of our connections with a larger whole. This toning down of our egos and concern for the welfare of others gives us a larger and more refined sense of purpose; it also creates a more harmonious family and societal environment. Further, our attitudes towards actions and results help us to process and modulate our emotional swings. There is reduction of pressures which we usually face from our personal likes & dislikes; this becomes apparent in the lesser frequency and intensity of our mental disturbances as well as reduction in the time taken to regain normalcy, after some unavoidable disturbances. (Swami Paramarthananda uses the acronym FIR here where F is for Frequency, I is for Intensity and R is time taken for Regaining equilibrium from mental upheaval—all need to reduce as our eligibility for Vedanta increases.) In addition to this, the upasana or the meditative aspect of karma yoga gives us a single-pointedness of mind which is needed.

With the resulting calmness and confidence, our minds become more objective, pointed and introspective; such minds can make us realise that no amount of our efforts and achievements is going to bring total and permanent fulfilment which we continuously strive for. This realisation equips us with a certain amount of discrimination, dispassion and a strong urge to find the inner freedom promised by Vedanta.

Such willingness to look at our lives afresh is crucial but does not happen to all. Some of us single-mindedly continue to chase conventional success, not realising that how successful you feel is more to do with reducing your unfulfilled wants rather than endlessly adding to your fulfilled wants. Actually, endless growth in anything, without any higher purpose, is no different than the strategy of a cancer cell! And to single-mindedly chase money and fame with the same intensity at 25 years and at 75 years of age only speaks of internal stagnation. However, unfortunately, this is what some do. As Ogden Nash once pointed out, "*You are young only once, but you can remain immature indefinitely*"!

Of course, when confronted with a tragedy many of us do become disenchanted with our usual goals and turn introspective (an apt term for this is *smashan vairagya* or disenchantment in the presence of a funeral pyre); but such dispassion usually does not last long and our original conditioning regains its supremacy. For some other people, it is not the shock of a major upheaval but the surfeit of success and pleasures which makes them ask fundamental questions because they yet do not experience lasting contentment. Whatever may be the trigger, for some of us (blessed by god, karmas, luck, chance, intelligence, good teachers, wise friends—take your pick) this turn occurs and lasts, giving us an opportunity to re-shape our conditioning.

Vedanta is meant for such a prepared person who is now willing to earnestly look at a different approach to his search for happiness and is equipped with qualities and discipline to stay the course. This eligible person is called an *adhikari* in Sanskrit and the full benefits of Vedanta's teachings become available only to a proper adhikari. In fact, the scriptures set out a list of the critical qualities and disciplines which are prerequisites for the meaningful study of Vedanta.

Jnana Yoga

The actual learning aspect, jnana yoga, covers both the acquisition of clear knowledge (*jnana prapti*) as well as a vital process for internalising the learnt knowledge so that it remains available to us at all times, without conscious effort or delay (*jnana nishtha*). This leads to a complete transformation in our understanding of the nature of our own selves, of the world and of Ishwara. The new understanding that Vedanta provides is that individuals and objects in the world are not real, separate entities which they appear to be. They are all temporary appearances in and of single, boundless and changeless consciousness which is termed as brahman or atma.This, of course, initially seems beyond credible because it goes against our personal experiences and against common belief. After all, if the single truth behind us and the world is brahman or atma, why is it not apparent in our own selves or anywhere in the world? Vedanta tells with, with good reasons, why this single reality is not apparent. It then exposes us to the contents of ancient scriptures, using a tested teaching methodology evolved over several centuries, as well as logic and a deeper analysis of our own experiences, to support its assertions.

Once Vedanta convinces us that all that actually exists is a single reality, this cuts at the very root of all our problems. This is because all our fears and sense of limitations arise only because of the existence of others. It is the other people who we want to get closer to or away from, it is the wealth, fame and the objects we want to acquire, it is the power over others that we want to exercise which causes us problems. If we are able to see that everything which appears is, in fact, only a single reality then it follows that our own truth is also not other than this reality. After this realisation, the question of us feeling lacking in one aspect or the other does not arise. And, with this realisation, the need to get something from outside of us also loses its pressure. These insights of Vedanta, if properly imbibed, lead us to total peace and fulfilment.

How do we get these insights? The upanishads list *shravana* (listening), *manana* (removal of doubts) and *nidhidhyasana* (contemplation) as the three steps for obtaining and internalising the wisdom of Vedanta. This is jnana yoga.

To put this in practical terms, jnana yoga is the systematic and consistent study of the scriptures over a sufficient length of time by an eligible student, under the guidance of a competent and live teacher. Each of these factors is relevant and to short-circuit any of them will mar our chances of success.

Vedanta is designed to be taught by a qualified teacher in live inter-action with a prepared student. The proper teacher has to be both well-versed with the scriptures & their traditional teaching techniques (*shrotriya)* as well as personally reflecting the spirit of the teachings in his life-style, behaviour and attitudes (*brahma-nishta*). The prepared student is expected to have followed a life of karma yoga for a sufficient length of time and should be equipped with four main qualities. These qualities, termed *sadhana chatushtaya*, cover discrimination, dispassion, a set of certain helpful attitudes & disciplines and, most important, a strong need to find the final solution to the perpetual problem of finding oneself to be wanting.

All these traditional requirements are difficult to meet now but, while some concessions have to be made to current times, none of these requirements can be totally circumvented. If a student is not pre-qualified, he undoubtedly needs to work on cultivating these required qualities during the process of learning. And if it is not possible for him to have live interaction with a teacher on an ongoing basis, it is necessary for at least occasional exposure to live teaching where there is an opportunity to personally meet the teacher and fellow-students.

Guru

The role of a guru can never be overemphasised in Vedanta's journey. It is the guru who has the entire vision of Vedanta and the methodology to transfer it to us; it is the guru who understands our individual conditioning and finds ways to deal with our wrong notions and prejudices. The guru helps us to resolve our doubts; he provides reassurance and hope when we are going through rough patches. The guru's personal life provides us with a live role-model and exhorts us to grow to our fullest potential. To have such a guru in our lives is truly a great blessing, without which the Vedantic journey becomes extremely difficult.

As we have seen earlier, the teaching tradition of Vedanta is rooted in live interaction with an appropriate teacher who should combine adequate knowledge of Vedanta along with a personal value-system which is in consonance with Vedanta's message. However, it may be difficult at the outset to hit upon the perfect teacher who is both shrotriya and brahma nishta. But there is a lot to be learned from a teacher who is familiar with the scriptures and their teaching techniques even if he leads a life which is not fully in keeping with the spirit of what he is teaching.

Apart from associating with a guru, in the process of learning we also benefit from interaction with fellow-seekers. In fact, there is an old verse which shows the value of inter-action with fellow-students by saying: a quarter of learning is from the guru, a quarter from our own efforts, a quarter from fellow-students and a quarter by the passage of time (or incubation). This suggests that fellow-students are as important a source for our learning as any other factor.

We can also supplement formal teaching by reading a variety of books and by listening to available audio and video material. But we need to exercise care, at least initially, in choosing the material we follow as we study Vedanta. This is because the landscape of Indian philosophy contains many divergent streams of thoughts. There are six recognised, orthodox schools of thought (*darshans* as they are called in Sanskrit) which accept the Vedas as authoritative scriptures; there are other important views (like Buddhism and Jainism) which are termed unorthodox because they are not based on the Vedas. Vedanta is just one of the six orthodox schools and even within Vedanta there several significant variations; the three most important interpretations of Vedanta are advaita, *vishist advaita* and *dvaita*, championed by Adi Shankaracharya, Ramanujacharya and Madhvacharya, respectively.

Being aware of the basics of other schools and being convinced of the validity of Vedanta's views in the face of contrary ideas is very much part of Vedanta's teaching tradition. However, during our self-study where we are not being guided by a teacher, it is helpful to initially restrict ourselves to the basics of Vedanta as expounded by Shankaracharya and his followers. This is not to support any personality-based cult or to restrict our thinking but it is to have a firm grounding in the school with which we have started, before taking off to explore other schools.

The Teaching Process

The actual teaching involves the teacher carefully and systematically taking the student through a detailed study of some upanishads, the Bhagavad Gita, some important *prakarana* texts and, perhaps, limited portions of the Brahma Sutras. Apart from the formal study of texts, the traditional teaching process also includes sessions of guided meditations as well as *satsangs* which are Q&A opportunities.

The goal of traditional teaching is to equip the student with doubt-free and steady knowledge covering the nature of *jiva* (the individual), *jagat* (the world confronting the individual), *Ishwara* (the creator), *bandha* (the bondage experienced by the individual), *moksha* (liberation from bondage) and *moksha sadhana* (the means for liberation). In fact, our traditions do not consider any *darshan* (philosophy) to be complete unless it covers all these six aspects.

In the teaching process, apart from the unfoldment of scriptural material, the teacher relies upon well-tried methods and examples to make the teachings come alive for the student. The *prakriyas* (methods) used in teaching include *drik drishya viveka* (seer and seen discrimination), *avastha traya* (analysis of the three states of wakefulness, dream and deep sleep), *pancha kosha* (analysis of the five layers which constitute our body and mind) and *dashamas tvam asmi* (the tenth man story). Analogies which are also very effectively used include the rope-snake, the ocean & its waves, the sun's reflection in several water containers and our personal dreams.

Quite apart from this, the teacher helps the student by giving meaningful answers to his questions, with the answers being calibrated to the student's stage of progress. The teacher also encourages him to work on improving his eligibility qualities, where the teacher finds a lack.

Finally, the teacher's presence and company of fellow students provides an environment which is nurturing and conducive to this unusual study, as well as providing support and encouragement when student's understanding or enthusiasm is at an ebb.

The Basis of the Teaching Method

In the process of learning, it is important to be aware of the basic method which underlies all the teachings of Vedanta: *adhyaropa* (stating something which is not entirely true) and *apvada* (negating that statement and replacing it with something closer to the truth). Let us look at an example of this method in a non-Vedantic situation.

Imagine that we are on a game-drive in a jungle when our naturalist suddenly stops, points and whispers "*Leopard*". We, of course, cannot spot anything which even faintly looks like a leopard and so our guide helps us to see what he has already seen:

> *"See those two big, dark trees in front of us ?"*
> *"Now, look between their trunks—about 10 metres behind, there is a round, black rock."*
> *"To the right of the rock, there is a tree with yellow bark."*
> *"Look up its trunk till you get to the two branches forking out on the left."*
> *"Follow the lower branch and about midway is the leopard—he is lying with his head towards us."*

And with all this help we finally spot that beautiful cat. But did the leopard have any connection with the two big trees which were pointed out to us first? Was the leopard on the black rock? Was he to be found climbing the yellow trunk? All these objects were unrelated to what we wanted to see and, yet, they were useful stepping-stones towards our objective.

Vedanta uses a similar technique to guide us towards its actual objective. Many statements made in the course of teaching Vedanta are provisional, to be replaced later by other statements closer to the truth. It is important for us to keep in mind that these twists and turns are with a purpose and we should not get confused or start doubting Vedanta's validity before we reach the culmination of its teachings.

Why does Vedanta use this rather convoluted method? Such a method has to be used because Vedanta wants to give us knowledge of our own selves. To know anything we need consciousness but the self we need to know is consciousness itself so trying to know ourselves, in the way in which we know usual things, would be like the eye trying to see itself! This then raises the obvious question that if Vedanta cannot show what it wants to show then why waste our time in a fruitless pursuit? There are good answers to this question but it is only after we embark upon a detailed study of Vedanta that we understand that Vedanta's scheme does bear fruit but in an unusual manner. Let us just note that similar to a mirror with which we can see our own eyes, the teachings of Vedanta are a mirror which makes self-knowledge possible.

Teaching in Steps

One important aspect of the teaching method of Vedanta is that it leads a seeker to the understanding of the truth in three distinct steps. First, it helps him in extricating consciousness from all that is objectively known to him by using techniques like the seer-seen discrimination. In the second step, the student is made to see that this consciousness is unchanging, ever-present and without any attributes or limitations. Finally, he is led to discover that consciousness is not simply a witnessing presence within him but it is the only reality in which and of which *all* objects (including the student's body-mind) and experiences appear, without any reality of their own.

This process has to be skilfully used because, otherwise, it can lead to serious misunderstanding. When a student is told that consciousness is the fundamental reality behind the entire universe, he may end up taking the universe to be a real creation, giving it a reality which it does not possess. On the other hand, when he is told that *jagat* is *mithya*, he may wrongly understand that the world is non-existent. The student has to be made to see that an illusion is always based on the support of reality; it is only that what appears is not what it seems to be. It is in this context that the Zen master Huang Po observed that people neglect the reality of the illusory world!

All this has to be properly unfolded by the teacher, in stages, so that the seeker finally realises Vedanta's true vision.

Renunciation

Some people remain averse to Vedanta based on the idea that cutting off worldly activities and ties is a prerequisite. To be a jnana yogi or a serious student of Vedanta, it is not necessary to formally renounce the world and become a *sanyasi*. However, it is necessary to cultivate many qualities of a sanyasi (such as dispassion, humility, compassion and focus on finding the ultimate truth) without disengaging from the world.

An important part of this process is to reduce the sense of being the controllers of our own bodies and minds as well as of other people and of possessions associated with us; apart from being false, this idea of being in total charge causes unnecessary anxiety which is detrimental to our commitment to learning and growth. Another required aspect here is the reduction of our possessions, obligations and activities; only a simple and relaxed life can provide us with time, energy and an uncluttered mind required for the study and absorption of subtle truths.

All this does not mean that one becomes indifferent to one's responsibilities and relationships; but it does mean not letting our own desires, as well as the desires of others towards whom we owe special care and responsibility, guzzle the bulk of our time and rob us of energy and tranquillity. This can only happen if freedom by knowledge remains our real goal and everything else becomes secondary. With this in mind, we should fulfil our reasonable commitments to others without neglecting our own growth. However, in trying to maintain a balanced approach, we should not carelessly slide back to a desire-driven and ego-led life. Some of us may believe that we can continue to lead lives based on past values and priorities. We keep on adding to our possessions and continue with hyper-active minds and yet hope to make spiritual progress by meditating for 15 minutes every day and attending a Vedanta class once a week. This approach is as useful as trying to fill a bucket with a big hole in its bottom, it does not produce meaningful and lasting results.

Internalising

Obtaining Vedanta's insights and clearing our doubts will arm us with valuable new understanding in vital areas of our lives. This is *jnana prapti* achieved by sharavanam and mananam. But just understanding does not always help us where it matters the most. We all know people who ignore their health or remain shopaholics despite knowing that remaining unfit or living beyond their means is harmful to their own selves. This is because just understanding does not necessarily lead to the discontinuation of damaging habits.

With Vedanta too, our old habits and conditioned reactions can continue despite the overlay of the new understanding. We can even write learned books on Vedanta without real inner transformation which is needed for the fruits of Vedanta to be personally available to us. So, there has to be *jnana nishtha* without which *jnana prapti* is of limited use. This necessary transformation has to be achieved by a long process of internalising what we have learnt so that this knowledge does not remain superficial but becomes fully integrated with our personality and over-writes grooves of old habits. This is called *nidhidhyasana* and is done by a variety of methods including repeatedly going over the teachings, sharing what we have learnt with others, contemplating/ meditating on what we have learnt and remaining aware of the contradictions between our new knowledge and our actual behaviour. Ultimately, our feelings and emotions have to fall in line with our understanding which, however deep, will otherwise remain sterile and not deliver personal benefit.

In the context of nidhidhyasana we must keep in mind that brahman or atma, which Vedanta tells us about in great detail, is not something to be memorised and recalled. It is our truth which is ever present and the basis of all or any experience. We have to understand that the contemplation and practices of nidhidhyasana are not to memorise something but to reinforce full and proper recognition of our ever-present reality.

Age and Sequence

Traditionally, human life was divided into four quarters with the first quarter devoted to studying, the second to career & family, the third to gradual withdrawal from social responsibilities and the last quarter to a life of total renunciation, with the sole focus being spiritual growth. But this generalised model need not and should not apply to everyone. Both our scriptures and even recent history are replete with examples of people who have reached the pinnacle of inner growth, irrespective of their age, gender or status.

And an important aspect of learning Vedanta is time. The traditional time period for the study of Vedanta was considered to be twelve years. Depending upon the qualities of the student and the teacher, an individual can complete his learning much earlier or much later. Be that as it may, a certain minimum amount of time is required for the extraordinary vision of Vedanta to be properly understood, accepted and internalised; an attempt to speed this up will be as effective as an attempt to get a flower to bloom before its due time.

Finally, karma yoga and jnana yoga are not sequential—we can and should expose ourselves to Vedanta's teachings even as we continue to re-format our actions and attitudes to increase our eligibility for this wisdom.

The Result

What is the result of successfully undertaking this journey of Vedanta? One verse in the Mundaka Upanishad summarises the results as:

> *When that brahman, which is in the form of cause and effect is recognised, the knot of ignorance in the heart resolves, all doubts go away and all his karmas get exhausted.*

It is the ignorance of our own reality which gives us a sense of separation from the rest of the world and makes us feel restricted to the confines of a single body and mind. With the knowledge imparted by Vedanta we realise that our reality is *sat chit ananda atma* and the reality behind the world is *satyam jnanam anantam brahman*; we further realise that *atma* and *brahman* are just different terms for the one and the same reality which is unchanging and boundless consciousness. This releases us from the spectres of a mortal life, of inadequate knowledge and of limited fulfilment.

While the limitations of our bodies and minds continue even after imbibing Vedanta's vision, we can now relax in the knowledge that what we actually are remains unaffected by successes and failures at the body-mind level. None of our experiences can actually touch us, the very basis of all experience, just as light without which no seeing is possible, remains unaffected by all that is seen. While we continue to play whatever role we are destined to play, we stop taking our individuality—our achievements, shortcomings, hopes, plans, relationships, possessions, experiences, reputations—so seriously.

We now understand that all the usual happiness we experience is just a reflection of our own, true nature. Experienced happiness needs a mind and is affected by the mind just as a reflection is affected by the condition of the mirror; unhappiness is obstruction of that reflection due to the mind's movements or vrittis. Our real ananda is never an experience; it is a natural fullness where there is no real 'other', no limitation and no lack. Once we are clear about our truth, there is no compulsion to seek experiences of joy just as we don't constantly need a mirror to re-assure us that our face is still there.

It is not that our minds become free of pleasant and unpleasant experiences after Vedanta. But the mind which until now told us we are bound now shows us that actually we were and are free. Life with its pleasurable and challenging moments now becomes like a game which never affects our inner peace and contentment.

Prayer

And finally, as we walk along this great path, we should remember that apart from our own effort there are more powerful forces outside our control and even outside our knowledge, which affect our journey. The only thing we can do to minimise bad luck and to maximise serendipity is to pray:

> *asatoma sadgamaya*—From the false lead me to the true
> *tamasoma jyotirgamaya*—From darkness lead me to light
> *mrityorma amritamgamaya*—From death lead me to deathlessness
> *om shanti shanti shanti*—May there be peace in all aspects of life.

GLOSSARY

A

Abhaya mudra: gesture or stance in an idol of god depicting protection, thus removing fear from the devotee's mind

Abhyasa: repetition, regular and constant practice

Adharma, adharmic: opposed to natural order and righteousness

Adhikari: an eligible or suitably qualified person; a student with qualities necessary to benefit from Vedanta's teachings

Adhikari bheda: differences between qualified students

Adhikaritvam: preparedness or eligibility for the study of Vedanta

Adhyaropa apvada: superimposition and subsequent negation; refers to Vedanta's teaching method of initially stating some things which are not entirely or finally true and then gradually replacing such statements with truer statements in calibrated steps

Adrishtam: invisible; depending on the context, it refers to results of actions where there is no apparent connection between the action and its results

Advaita: not two; non-dualism, non-duality

Advaita vedanta: the non-dual interpretation of Vedanta whose most well-known exponent is Adi Shankaracharya

Advitiyam: without a second; non-dual

Agni: fire

Ahimsa: non-violence, non-injury

Aikyam: oneness

Ajata vada: non-origination; the view that there is never any real creation

Akasha: space

Anadi: without a beginning

Ananda: joy or bliss

Ananda tandav: joyous dance of Shiva in his form as the Nataraja

Anantam: unending, limitless

Anirvachaniya: not capable of being expressed or explained

Anubhava: experience

Apa: water

Apara vidya: lower knowledge; secular knowledge

Aparoksha: immediate, direct and personal

Apoorvata: uniqueness; referring to something not seen before

Aroopa: formless

Artha: security; wealth

Arthavada: praise or eulogy

Asat: non-being; unreal

Ashram: a halting place; hermitage

Asi: are (in the context of the mahavakya tat tvam asi – that you are)

Astika: orthodox, accepting the Vedas as being authoritative

Atma: inner self; the reality which is the substrate of the individual and is identical with brahman, the reality of the entire universe

Avarana: covering, veil (in Vedanta used to refer to ignorance which covers or veils our true nature)

Avastha traya: three states; refers to the three states of waking, dreaming and deep sleep

B

Badha: negation or elimination

Bandha: bondage

Bhajans: devotional singing

Bhakti: loving or worshipful devotion to god

Bhashya, bhashyas: commentaries on original texts

Bhashyakara: commentator writing commentaries on original texts

Brahma nishta: one who is established in brahman; one whose life is lived in keeping with spirit of the teachings of Vedanta

Brahma satyam jagat mithya: brahman is real and the world is a temporary and dependent appearance (an often-quoted statement of Adi Shankaracharya)

Brahma Sutras: "threads of the absolute"; brief aphorisms written by Badrayana, summarising and harmonising the teachings of the upanishads

Brahman: the great or the big; the ultimate reality, the ground of the universe

Brahmin: highest of the four traditional castes in Hindu culture

Bubhuksha: basic hunger to consume, to experience fulfilment

C

Caravaka: agreeable or pleasant speech; the Indian school of materialism

Chaitanyam: consciousness, awareness

Chakra: wheel or circle; energy centres or nerve complexes in the body

Chandala: the lowest caste or an outcaste in the traditional Hindu caste system

Chatushtaya: four-fold

Chidabhasa: reflection of original and universal consciousness in an individual mind

Chit: original and universal consciousness

Chitta ekagrata: unifying and focusing the mind

Chitta shuddhi: mind purification

Citta vritti nirodha: stopping all modifications of the mind, leading to a thought-free mind

D

Dama: control over senses and physical reactions

Darshan: sight or view; refers to different schools of Indian philosophical thought

Dashamas tvam asmi: you are the tenth (referring to the apparently missing tenth man story used in the teaching of Vedanta)

Dehaatma buddhi: taking the body to be the real self

Dharma: natural order, righteousness

Drik drishya viveka: discrimination between the seer and the seen (more generally, between the knower and the known)

Dvaita: duality

E

Eka roopa: single form

Ekam: single

G

Guna: quality

Guru: remover of darkness, teacher; in the tradition of Vedanta, a teacher who both knows the scriptures and traditional teaching techniques as well as personally embodies and lives the wisdom he teaches

I

Ishta devata: personally cherished or preferred deity

Ishwara: god as the combined material and intelligent cause of the universe

Ishwara arpana bhavana: attitude of treating each action as an offering to god

Ishwara anugraha: grace of god

Ishwara srishti: god's creation

J

Jadam: inert

Jagat: the world, entire creation

Jagat nimitta upadana karanam: single cause of the universe, combining both the intelligence and material required for creation

Janma: birth

Jati: birth, class at birth

Jignasa: basic hunger to know more

Jijivisha: basic hunger to remain alive

Jiva: an individual person

Jiva srishti: an individual's personal creation

Jivan mukti: liberation in the current life itself

Jnana: knowledge

Jnana nishtha: full assimilation of knowledge which is then always available without doubts, delays or conscious effort

Jnana phala: fruits or benefits of knowledge

Jnana prapti: acquisition of knowledge

Jnana yogyata: eligibility or fitness for acquiring knowledge

K

Kalpitam: imagined

Kama: pleasure, desire

Karika, karikas: independent expositions based on original texts

Karma, karmas: depending upon the context it can mean actions or the result of actions

Karma phala data: giver of the fruits of our actions (refers to Ishwara)

Karma yoga: set of religious and secular mechanisms to govern our actions and attitudes in order refine our minds and make them amenable to spiritual growth

Kevala: in Jainism it refers to complete understanding or supreme wisdom

Kripa: benevolence or grace

Kundalini: coiled divine energy said to be located at the base of the spine

L

Lila: play or sport (usually of god)

M

Madhurya bhava: feeling or emotion of love for one's beloved

Maha purusha samshraya: shelter or protection from a great person; finding a guru

Mahavakya: literally, great sentence; refers to four different sentences, picked out of four different upanishads, which encapsulate Vedanta's core message

Mala: impurity, dirt

Manana: thinking, questioning and discussion for removal of doubts

Mandir: Hindu temple

Manolaya: temporary dissolution or absorption of the mind

Manonasha: destruction of the mind

Manushyatvam: humanness; being born as a human being

Medha: incisive intellect

Mithya: lacking permanent and independent reality

Mithyatvam: being mithya (see mithya)

Moksha: complete freedom or liberation from all limitations

Mukti: liberation, release

Mumukshutvam: the urge for liberation from all limitations

N

Na: no, not

Nama rupa: name and form

Namaste: a respectful greeting (literally, I bow to you)

Nastika: unorthodox, not accepting the authority of the Vedas

Neti neti: not this, not this

Nidhidhyasana: repeated contemplation of the teachings to make them fully assimilated, real and first-hand knowledge

Nimitta upadana karanam: intelligent and material cause

Nirguna: without any distinguishing attributes or qualities

Nirvana: literally 'blowing out'; freedom from all bondage, goal of life in Buddhism

Nirvikalpa: unchanging, immutable

Nishtha: steadiness, adherence

Nivrutti: getting rid of, being free of

Nyaya prasthana: scripture based on logic

O

Om: primordial sound of creation, symbolic sound-form representing the highest divinity

P

Pancha kosha: five sheaths or coverings

Pancha mahabhutas: five basic elements according to Indic cosmology

Pancha mahayagnas: five great sacrifices; refers to five activities ordained to be carried out daily to acknowledge and repay an individual's debt to various aspects of creation

Papa: sin, demerit

Paramarthika: highest, absolute

Paroksha: second-hand and indirect

Phalam: fruit or result

Prakarana: dissertation on a chosen topic

Prakriti: primal nature

Prakriti vadins: those who hold that natural evolution created this world

Prakriya: mechanism or technique

Pralaya: dissolution

Pramana: valid means of knowledge

Pramana shanka: doubt about what a means of knowledge is actually telling us

Prameya shanka: doubt about the conclusion that a means of knowledge has led us to

Prarabdha: destiny; the results of past actions

Prasada: (literally, favour or grace); food, water and other offerings to a deity who is believed to partake of it and then return the offering, thereby consecrating it.

Prasada bhavana: attitude of gracefully accepting each outcome as return gifts from god

Prasthana trayi: three gateways

Pratibhasika: subjective or projected reality, existing only in appearance

Pratyaksha: evident to the senses

Preyas: pleasurable in the short run

Prithvi: earth

Puja: ritual, ceremonial worship

Punar janma: re-birth

Punya: merit, meritorious acts

Purusha: spirit, indwelling form of god

Purushartha: four basic human goals of righteousness (dharma), security (artha), pleasures (kama) and freedom from all limitations (moksha); wilful effort towards achieving these goals

Purva mimamsa: one of the six main orthodox schools of Indian philosophical thought

Purvapaksha: opposing view

R

Rajas: quality of energetic desires and actions

Rajoguna pradhanam: dominated by rajas

Rishis: ancient sages

S

Sadhana: necessary means or tools; practice or process

Sadhana chatushtaya: four means; a set of four-fold qualities to be acquired by a proper student of Vedanta

Sadhana chatushtaya sampanna: having the four-fold qualities necessary to benefit from Vedanta; an adhikari

Sadhana prasthana: scripture emphasising the means of liberation

Sadhya vastu: a goal yet to be achieved

Saguna: with attributes and qualities

Sajatiya bheda: a different object within the same type of things

Sakshi chaitanya: witnessing consciousness

Sakhya bhava: feeling or emotion of friendship

Sama: control over mental reactions

Samadhan: attentiveness, ability to stay focused on a topic

Samadhi: meditative absorption

Samana satta: existing at the same level of reality

Samsara: the flux and flow of the world, the objective universe

Samskaras: tendencies or habits ingrained into an individual

Sankhya: one of the six orthodox schools of Indian philosophy founded by Kapila

Sanyasa: renunciation, monkhood

Sanyasi: a renunciate, monk

Sarvajna: all-knowing, omniscient

Sarva shatiman: all-powerful, omnipotent

Sarva vyapi: all-pervading

Sat: truth, permanent & independent reality

Sat chit ananda: unchanging existence, consciousness, bliss; used to refer to our reality, atma

Satsang: being in the company of evolved people; open-house interaction with the teacher including opportunity to ask questions

Sattva: refined human qualities such as love for learning, harmony and contentment

Sattvaguna pradhanam: dominated by sattva

Sattvic: with sattva

Satyam: truth, permanent & independent reality

Satyam jnanam anantam: changeless existence which is conscious and boundless

Shabda: word, scriptural testimony

Shad lingas: literally, six signs or pointers (originally from Purva Mimamsa darshan but used in Vedanta for determining the real meaning of scriptural content)

Shastra: scriptures

Shraddha (shraddhaa): faith

Shraddha (shraaddha): after-death rituals

Shravana: listening; acquiring knowledge from a qualified teacher

Shreyas: good for the long term

Shrishti: creation

Shrotriya: one who has heard; one who has received knowledge of the scriptures and can handle traditional teaching methods

Shruti: scriptures

Shruti prasthana: upanishads

Shruti tatparyam: the highest or core message of scriptures

Shunyata: nothingness, void

Siddha vastu: a goal already achieved

Smashan vairagya: disenchantment with

usual goals when at a funeral; temporary dispassion

Smriti: that which is remembered

Smriti prasthana: scripture based on that which is remembered

Stithi: continuation in a steady state

Svagata bheda: different within itself

Swarupa lakshana: intrinsic, essential qualities

T

Tamas: baser human qualities including dullness, inertia and ignorance.

Tamoguna pradhanam: dominated by tamas

Tantra: weave or compose; refers to esoteric practices in Hinduism and Buddhism for invoking powerful deities to acquire supernatural powers and lead to spiritual growth

Tat: that

Tat tvam asi: you are that (literally, that you are)

Tilak: a dot or other mark, usually applied to the forehead, in veneration or to show one's affiliation

Titiksha: forebearance, ability to put up with difficulties

Triguna atita: beyond the three basic qualities of tamas, rajas and sattva

Trikala abadhit: not bound by the three modes of time; timeless

Tuccham: unreal (see asat)

Tulsi: holy basil

Tvam: you

U

Upadesha prasthana: scripture emphasising instructions for the aspirant

Upakrama upsamahara: beginning and conclusion

Upapatti: reasoning, argument, fitness, propriety

Uparati: liking

Upasana: devotion and meditation

V

Vada: theory or view

Varna ashrama dharma: mandate to follow a life-style and duties appropriate to one's caste and stage in life

Vatsalya bhava: feeling or emotion of parental love

Vayu: air

Videha mukti: liberation in a subsequent life

Vijatiya bheda: different from other type of things

Vikshepa: division, fragmentation, projection

Viparita bhava: contrary thoughts, emotions and reactions

Vishisht advaita: qualified nondualism; a theistic school of Vedanta expounded by Ramanujacharya

Vishwa roopa: universal form

Vivarta vada: the view that all creation is only an apparent or illusory transformation of the underlying reality, brahman

Vyavaharika: objective or transactional reality

Y

Yagna: sacrificial ceremony

Yoga: (literally means 'union') one of the six traditional schools of Hindu philosophy propounded by the sage Patanjali, where meditation has a key role

Yukti: logical thinking

Yukti prasthana: scripture emphasising logical thinking

ABOUT THE AUTHOR

Dhruv S Kaji has been a career finance professional with a leading business group in India. He has been studying Vedanta over many years with Swamis, professors and other teachers, both traditional and non-traditional.

While Vedanta is his core pursuit, he is also a certified pilot and an experienced scuba diver. His other interests include sailing, wild-life and gastronomy.

He lives in Mumbai, travels extensively and sits on the Boards of some well-known listed companies in India. He is reachable at dhruvskaji@gmail.com